The Kings of Casino Park

The Kings of Casino Park

*Black Baseball in the Lost
Season of 1932*

THOMAS AIELLO

THE UNIVERSITY OF ALABAMA PRESS
Tuscaloosa

Copyright © 2011
The University of Alabama Press
Tuscaloosa, Alabama 35487-0380
All rights reserved
Manufactured in the United States of America

Typeface: Granjon

∞

The paper on which this book is printed meets the minimum requirements of American National Standard for Information Sciences—Permanence of Paper for Printed Library Materials, ANSI Z39.48-1984.

Library of Congress Cataloging-in-Publication Data

Aiello, Thomas, 1977-
The kings of Casino Park : Black baseball in the lost season of 1932 / Thomas Aiello.
p. cm.
Includes bibliographical references and index.
ISBN 978-0-8173-1742-3 (cloth : alk. paper) — ISBN 978-0-8173-8568-2 (electronic)
1. Monroe Monarchs (Baseball team)—History. 2. Negro leagues—Monroe—Louisiana—History. 3. African American baseball players—Monroe—Louisiana.
4. Racism in sports—Monroe—Louisiana—History. 5. Discrimination in sports—Monroe—Louisiana—History. 6. Baseball—United States—History. I. Title.
GV875.M59A44 2011
796.357′640973—dc22

2010051458

Cover: The Monroe Monarchs were the pride of the city, black and (eventually) white, in 1932. Still, after their success, the status of black Monroe allowed their memory to fade. For example, the Monarchs didn't technically win a Southern League pennant in 1932, and the Crawfords didn't win a pennant in the National League, because there was no National League in 1932. Courtesy of the Ouachita Parish Public Library Special Collections.

For my mother

There is no "depression" on when a baseball fan desires to see a good team play.

> —Cole's American Giants press release, *Kansas City Call,*
> April 15, 1932

Northern Negroes may ordain it indecent to read a Negro newspaper more than once a week—but the Southern Negro is more consolidated. Necessity has occasioned this condition. Most Southern white newspapers exclude Negro items except where they are infamous or of a marked ridiculous trend. . . . While his northern brother is busily engaged in "getting white" and ruining racial consciousness, the Southerner has become more closely knit.

> —Southern Newspaper Syndicate advertisement, *Atlanta
> World,* February 28, 1932

A few years back, along in 1928, if one would ask an easterner, northerner, or a gentleman from the far west, of the town of Monroe, Louisiana, pertaining to its geographical location, the answer would probably bring about some mean words—words that you probably wouldn't take from dear old dad— but now, the name of MONROE stands out in letters twenty times the point of the ones printed in this article. Every baseball fan in these United States will tell you today that Monroe is the home of the nationally famous Monroe Monarchs.

> —*Shreveport Sun,* September 10, 1932

Contents

Acknowledgments

My friend and advisor Dr. David L. Chappell provided invaluable advice and editing, without which this book would be a rambling epic that probably confused more than it clarified. Dr. Neil Lanctot and Dr. Robert McMath also provided criticism and commentary that vastly improved the work.

Even more helpful were four others. Carol Fuller and David Flickinger were integral to the early development of this project. They drove me around Monroe and convincingly feigned interest. Pete Aiello met me in Nashville and made hunting for the remnants of long-dead Negro Leagues officials far more fun than any reasonable assumption would allow. Throughout the bulk of this project, Katherine Winsett acted as a chauffeur and de facto research assistant. Without her these pages would probably be blank.

Paul J. Letlow, former sports editor of the *Monroe News-Star* and fellow Monarchs historian, provided valuable research help and contact information. Much of what follows stems from his interviews and research. Jeff Newman and Scott Greer of the Monroe Monarchs Historical Association also provided research and interested, critical ears.

Ollie Burns, Tracy C. DeWitt, Vivian Hester, Carolyn Kennedy, Jean Stovall Lee, Margaret Newman, Clara Poe, DeMorris Smith, and Roosevelt Wright were all very generous with their time. So too were Bijan C. Bayne, Philip Lowery, Deborah Tuggle, Mary Quaid of the House Legislative Services Department of the Louisiana House of Representatives, Debbie Pendleton of the Alabama Department of Archives and History, Sharon Hull Smith of the Tennessee State University archives, Tom Kanon of the Tennessee State Library and Archives, Benetta Waller and Barbara Grissom of Meharry Medical College, Angela Clark of Campbell University, Blake Wintory of the Mosaic Templars Research Center, Rhonda Stewart of the Butler Center of the Little Rock Public Library, Clara

Freeland of the Ouachita County Historical Society, and Ty Blackburn and Sheila Lewis of Morris Brown College.

The Special Collections Department and Reference Desk of the Ouachita Parish Public Library, Larry Foreman in particular, the microfilm librarians and Cyndy Robertson and Glenn Jordan of the Special Collections Department of the University of Louisiana at Monroe, the interlibrary loan department of the Mullins Library at the University of Arkansas, the Sheriff's Department of Ouachita Parish, the Ouachita Parish Clerk of Court, the librarians of the multimedia collection of the Earl K. Long Library at the University of New Orleans, the librarians of the multimedia department of the Noel Memorial Library at Louisiana State University at Shreveport, the special collections librarians of the Hill Memorial Library at Louisiana State University in Baton Rouge, the athletic departments of Southern University and Grambling State University, the Negro Leagues Baseball Museum in Kansas City, Missouri, the librarians of the A. Bartlett Giamatti Research Center at the National Baseball Hall of Fame in Cooperstown, New York, the librarians of the Kenneth Spencer Research Library at the University of Kansas, and the librarians of the Division of Rare and Manuscript Collections in Kroch Library at Cornell University were each very kind and helpful.

I would also like to thank the editors and peer reviewers of *NINE: A Journal of Baseball History and Culture,* the *Baseball Research Journal,* The Hall Institute of Public Policy, the *Arkansas Historical Quarterly,* the *Ozark Historical Review,* the *Journal of the Illinois State Historical Society, North Louisiana History,* and *Louisiana History,* all of whom provided valuable editorial advice. Portions of this book (in vastly modified forms) can be found in each of these publications. Similarly, the commentators and questioners at the various conferences where I discussed this work all contributed to the final project and are greatly appreciated. In the final stages of this project, Lady Vowell Smith proved a conscientious and dedicated editor. This book would be far more muddled and confused without her.

Much of the research that constitutes the appendices of this book was made possible by a generous Yoseloff Baseball Research Grant from the Society for American Baseball Research (SABR). Their support, combined with the interest of SABR's membership, made this project far easier than it should have been.

There were myriad others who made this project possible. Larry Lester, Robert Weems, Leslie Heaphy, Ray Doswell, and John Crowley all helped with photographs, as did Pat Kelly at the National Baseball Hall of Fame, and Gil Pietrzak at the Carnegie Library of Pittsburgh. The graduate students and faculty of the

Department of History at the University of Arkansas provided immeasurable support and kindness during this process, in particular Brent Riffel, Chet Cornell, Krista Jones, Geoff Jensen, Scott Cashion, David Kirsch, and Kim Johnson, as well as Dr. Patrick Williams, Dr. Randall Woods, Dr. Jeannie Whayne, Dr. Rick Sonn, and Dr. Elliot West. So too did my colleagues at the University of Louisiana at Lafayette. Finally, Melissa and Madison French have made the final leg of this race infinitely enjoyable simply by being around. They are the circumference of all my world will ever be, and as such, they are the walking personification of perspective.

Many others I have surely forgotten, but I thank them nonetheless, wherever they are.

The Kings of Casino Park

Introduction

The 1932 Negro Southern League: Depression Baseball, Black Monroe, and the Meaning of Sport

Fred Stovall stayed long hours at the drilling company in 1932, as he had the year before and the year before that. Such was the nature of hard work, the same hard work he had been taught from his earliest days, before the oil fields of Texas had given way to the gas fields of north Louisiana, and before those had given way to the wealth that so many found bubbling underneath the earth. But with wealth came responsibility, and the pressures of the job were already adding gray around his wrinkling, white temples and pounds around his increasingly fleshy waist. He was relying on his glasses more than he used to. The offices of his Stovall Drilling Company were on the 1000 block of Desiard Street in Monroe, Louisiana. When the work was done, he would drive the block to North Eleventh Street. He would take a left, through Adams, and see the J. M. Supply Company, another of his businesses, on the corner. After crossing Washington, he would come to Breard, take a right, and find Monroe Colored High School just past St. Matthew's Catholic Cemetery. He would drive from Breard back to Desiard, then down Desiard, to the tired road's 2900 block, just outside the city limits.[1]

There, Fred Stovall found another source of money and responsibility. But Casino Park was different. There he would see his Monroe Monarchs warming up for another game in their Negro Southern League season, with swells of black and white fans waiting for their segregated grandstand seats to see the players who would become the only World Series team Louisiana would ever generate and the first from the American South.

Of course, the Negro Southern League was new for the team. In the interregnum between the 1931 and 1932 seasons, the formerly vaunted Negro National League foundered under the hard weight of the Depression, giving way to two new leagues to compete for "major" status: Cumberland Posey's hastily constituted East–West Colored League and the perennially minor Negro Southern League. The East–West folded prior to the season's halfway point, but the Southern survived the summer, giving the outfit its first and only season of "major" league status.

If the Negro Southern League was perennially minor until 1932, the Texas–Louisiana League was hopelessly obscure. But the Monarchs won the Texas–Louisiana championship in 1931, and their success (combined with a series of backroom negotiations) earned them a spot in the newly constituted major league. It wasn't a popular decision among all the team owners. Monroe was a town of twenty-six thousand in the northeast corner of Louisiana, the hub of a poor cotton-farming region in the Mississippi Delta approximately seventy miles from the river and forty from the Arkansas border. In the late 1910s, the *New Orleans Item* declared the area to be the "lynch law center of Louisiana," and the exigencies of the Depression served as no salve for racial tension, as demonstrated by a consistent and devastating history of racial violence in the area.[2]

Perhaps more significantly, the Southern League had its eye on large-market non-southern teams such as the Chicago American Giants, the Indianapolis ABCs, and the Cleveland Cubs, all of whom joined the ostensibly "southern" group. Chicago was the prize—a team founded by Rube Foster, the staple of the original Negro National League—and officers hoped the team's prestige would keep everyone else afloat during the troubled summer of 1932 and cement the Southern's status as the nation's premier black league. With the aggregation set, the Louisville Black Caps hosted a series of meetings for the league in early March. Schedules were organized and prepared for publication. Salary caps, team rules, and umpiring policies were established. April 22 would open the season, and July 4 would close the first half. The group elected Reuben Bartholomew Jackson as league president, Robert Cole, new owner of the Chicago American Giants, as vice president, and Thomas T. Wilson, owner of the Nashville Elite Giants, as treasurer. The three officers would prove a daunting triumvirate for the Monarchs. Their opposition to Monroe's membership would ultimately lead them to collude to steal a pennant from the team. In the process, they would forge a bond that would transform black baseball for the duration of its existence. Cole and Wilson would join forces with William A. Greenlee, owner of the Pittsburgh Crawfords, the following year, shaping the new Negro National League and its staple East–West All Star game, which would become the core of the new league.[3]

When Jackson settled a dispute between the Monarchs and Cole's American Giants in Chicago's favor, the press queued up to take sides. Black newspapers in the South rallied to Monroe's cause, railing against the league and the bias of black newspapers in the North. Jackson's decision (discussed in chapter 7) was unfair at best, corrupt at worst, but it was clearly the most responsible decision for a league president attempting to maintain a black baseball league in the midst of the Great Depression. Chicago was bigger. It was more prominent. It had money. Either way, at the conclusion of the second half of the season, black newspapers from the South declared Monroe the Southern champion, newspapers from the North touted Chicago. The American Giants played the Nashville Elite Giants for the championship of the Negro Southern League, and the Monarchs played the Pittsburgh Crawfords in what was touted as the "World Series." The resulting confusion has hindered historical understanding of the 1932 season.

The Negro Leagues Baseball Museum describes 1933 as the beginning of the "Golden Years" of Negro League baseball. The previous period on its timeline ends in 1931.[4] Disillusionment with the National League collapse, apprehension about the ability of the leagues to complete a season, and the complications of player trade disputes and low attendance figures led to a muddled portrait of black baseball in 1932. The black press only fed the disillusionment and apprehension of its readers, aiding what would become a historiographical lapse in coverage of the season. The papers' initial bias and eventual apathy only added further confusion. Of course, the principal reason for that disillusionment and apprehension was the sorry state of an economy not fit for baseball. Black weeklies weren't in cahoots, weren't scheming to raze the edifice of black baseball so that a stronger version could be built in its place. Columnists and reporters wrote what they saw. The muddled portrait of the season was, in all likelihood, an accurate rendering.

And so, the team and its successes have drifted from black baseball's historiography, as has its integral role in the creation of the new, more successful Negro National League the following year, and thus the Negro Leagues as they exist in historical memory. Along with an argument for Monroe's importance to black baseball's historiography, however, this book also makes an argument with a very different trajectory. Monroe was the hub of the cotton-farming parishes of northeast Louisiana and had all of the racial codes and mores of other small Deep South cities. It was, after all, "the lynch law center of Louisiana." When the baseball season started in 1932, interracial contact and black community development seemed unlikely. But sports mattered. In the face of losses to economic, environmental, and racial opponents, winning mattered. Black Monroe valued sport so much that crime rates fell with the Monarchs' success in 1932.

The team's success contributed to the birth and high sales of a local black newspaper. And social contact between black and white citizens increased as more and more people of both races attended the ballpark (half of the grandstand was reserved for whites before the season's midpoint, and racial overflows led occasionally to integrated crowds). The Monarchs thus gave the black population a sort of cultural currency that is hard to measure but demonstrable in the team's success throughout the second half of 1932. They also gave the white community a new definition of civic pride, one that included the triumphs of its black counterpart.[5]

Of course, the team didn't create some sort of utopia for blacks in an otherwise Depression-era Jim Crow state. They weren't exceptions to the entire realm of Jim Crow. They created, for the duration of one remarkably successful season, an exception to Monroe's race relations. The representation of the black population in Monroe's mainstream white dailies improved. Those same white dailies published accounts of the Monarchs' games, printed their advertising, and aimed that advertising at white readers. Those same white newspapers began referring to the "Negro Monarchs" as "Monroe," and, even more tellingly, "we." As the team continued to win, as many as half of the grandstand seats at Casino Park were reserved for white patrons. Winning baseball created a willingness on the part of whites to interact with the black community in ways they hadn't before.

This culture-changing power of a baseball team demonstrates the importance of sport in cultural and social history. That importance comes not from community pride or other clichés into which references to sport (and particularly references to black baseball) often fall. Black southerners cared about sports very deeply, and white southerners, at times, cared about black sports, too. This was one of those times. The positive self-identity associated with winning trumped (in part) white Monroe's positive self-identity associated with being white. The intersection of white and black in 1932 Monroe, Louisiana, demonstrates that success in sport—even in the Deep South—could alter the power of race.

And so, the Monarchs served as two significant, simultaneous bridges: one linking the frayed edges of the two Negro National Leagues, the other linking the fraying self-conceptions of white and black citizens in violent, troubled Monroe, Louisiana.

Accordingly, chapter 1 is only tangentially about baseball. This chapter describes the 1919 lynching of George Bolden and the legacy it left for the white and black residents of the "lynch law center of Louisiana." Chapter 2 describes the development of both Monroe and the fledgling state of black baseball from the troubled reaches of 1919 to the early onset of 1932, a year that would prove to be fraught with its own troubles, for northeast Louisiana and baseball alike. For Monroe, the most devastating flood in the city's history dominated the first three months of that year. The catastrophe even outstripped the water levels of the famed 1927 Mississippi River flood. Chapter 3 uses that disaster to frame the obstacles facing both the city and its black baseball team as preparations for the season got under way, while chapter 4 evaluates the ragged state of national black baseball and the segregated state of baseball in Monroe in 1932. White and black promoters continued to radiate confidence and form new leagues, even as fans lost their jobs, savings, and homes. The teams, however, did begin playing, and chapter 5 carries the Monarchs, the Crawfords, and the rest of black baseball through their spring paces. Chapter 6 describes the first half of the 1932 season. Chapter 7 evaluates the championship controversy in early July, arguing that league collusion took a rightful pennant from Monroe. Chapter 8 describes the fragmented, staccato progression of the season's second half from July to August, and chapter 9 details the World Series that followed, when Pittsburgh and Monroe played for the title of season champion. Of course, not everyone thought the contest would decide a legitimate champion. Through an analysis of the black press in 1932, interspersed throughout the narrative, the book also evaluates the confusion the season engendered and compares Monroe's white dailies with the nation's only black daily, the *Atlanta Daily World*. It also examines a Monroe daily's coverage of the local black community to draw conclusions about the relationship of that community to its baseball team. Chapter 10 describes the season's legacy, the teams' fate, and Monroe's memory of its championship team. That memory faded in the decades that followed Monroe's major league season, but surged in the late twentieth and early twenty-first centuries. One of the goals of this book is to contribute to that memory. It has something to say about the relationship between race and baseball, the press and sport, and sport and memory. But above all, this is a baseball story. It is a reclamation project, an effort to restore the Monroe Monarchs to the broader stories of baseball, race, and depression.

History is not written by winners. It's written about them. And if the quality of victory is measured by the volume of such writing, southern black baseball in the first half of the twentieth century was a compendium of loss. But it wasn't in 1932. That season is largely seen as an interregnum between the two incarnations of the Negro National League. For most of the black baseball world, that analysis is fair. Organization was tenuous, money was scarce, and the starved and sated alike had other things on their minds. But the tumult of that season helped create the new National League and its massive success that followed. In a small

Jim Crow cotton hub in northeast Louisiana, it helped create a black social prosperity not previously present.

The 1932 season unified the two disparate timelines of Negro League baseball, and it unified, however briefly, Monroe, Louisiana.

Every move the Monroe Monarchs made in early 1932 indicated that despite racism, natural disaster, and crushing poverty—and despite all the national signs warning against baseball success—the team was going in the right direction. That largely unknown, largely unsuccessful 1932 season spurred efforts to create the new, more successful National League the following year, and thus the "Golden Years" of the Negro Leagues. The collusion to prevent Monroe from winning the pennant formed the bond between Robert Cole, Thomas T. Wilson, and William A. Greenlee. Though Monroe was a cause celebre during the summer of 1932, it was not included in the new league, owing largely to its small market, its stifling segregation, and the absence of a legitimate pennant. Its presence, however, was integral to the development of black baseball in the 1930s. At the same time, the team managed to last from 1930 to 1936 within a segregated, economically depressed society. In so doing, it dramatically affected civic participation and pride in its hometown—in both the black and white communities. It even reduced crime.

Of course, Fred Stovall wasn't particularly worried about such things. The white businessman was, to the extent that it helped him, a champion of the black community, but he was no egalitarian. He was the owner of a baseball team, and what had begun as an extracurricular activity for the black employees of his various businesses had turned into a hobby, an enthusiasm, a passion. When Stovall finally made it to the 2900 block of Desiard, he wasn't concerned about racial harmony, and he wasn't concerned about the long-term health of black baseball. Rather, Stovall had the same thing in mind as did all of his paying customers—as did all of Monroe. Stovall wanted to win.

I

The Horror

Race Culture in the "Lynch Law
Center of Louisiana"

At 2:30 on Tuesday afternoon, April 30, 1919, George Bolden lay on a cot in a baggage car of the Vicksburg, Shreveport, and Pacific Railroad, on his way to Shreveport, Louisiana. The wounds that had taken off his right leg were new, as were the memories of three attempts on his life in fewer than forty hours. His wife accompanied him among the "Negro baggage" as both hoped the slow train would help them escape to Shreveport faster, faster, faster. But at 2:34, only eight miles outside of Monroe, Louisiana, near the small community of Che-niere, someone pulled the bell cord for an immediate stop. A group of white men boarded the car, threw Bolden to the ground outside, and riddled him with bullets. The train began moving again almost immediately, and Bolden's wife, prevented by the mob from disembarking, continued a lonely journey west. Her mind was probably racing with memories of the previous night, when a mob had entered the Negro ward of the St. Francis Sanitarium, Monroe's only hospital, and tried forcibly to remove her husband—and how the nurses and nuns of the hospital bore the mob back.[1]

The fight against lynching trudged through another tumultuous year in 1919. Editorials throughout Louisiana and the South decried the practice, accompany-ing broader calls for cessation in the national media. The NAACP held a widely publicized national conference on lynching, the hallmark of the organization's decades-long crusade against white southern "justice." The United States' to-tal of eighty-three lynchings in 1919 was never matched in subsequent years. But through these seeming successes, no federal anti-lynch law was ever passed, a significant drop in yearly lynching totals did not happen until 1923, and the Red Summer of 1919—a series of riots and other forms of racial violence in the North as well as the South—did not end until October. Lynchings continued, as did the crusade against them.[2]

Bolden's murder would serve as a public emblem of north Louisiana's intransigent racism and reputation for violence. A New Orleans editorialist would brand the event "the Monroe Horror."[3] Bolden's story began on March 11, 1918, with the shooting of Charles L. Thomas, a white railroad agent for a Missouri Pacific station just south of Monroe. Clyde Williams, an African American, was indicted for the crime by the Ouachita Parish Grand Jury. But sheriff's deputies kept Williams in neighboring Caldwell Parish, fearing mob reprisals. On April 22, their fear was realized. A mob dragged Williams from a train bound for Monroe and killed him. The wounds to Thomas had left him blind, and the charitable donations of his friends and family built a new cottage for him and his wife on Lee Avenue.[4] Just over a year after the lynching of Thomas's alleged attacker, on Saturday, April 27, 1919, a lewd note appeared on the door of the Lee Avenue cottage. With her husband incapacitated, Thomas's wife gave the note to family friends. Each saw that the note was signed "George Bolden."[5]

George Bolden worked as a paperhanger, painter, and carpenter. He endorsed his paychecks for those jobs with an X. Like more than a quarter of Monroe's black population, he could neither read nor write.[6] Nevertheless, friends of the Thomas family arrived at Bolden's house en masse around 11 p.m. Sunday night. They fired five shots at Bolden, and though four missed their mark, one bullet shattered his right shin. After the crowd dispersed, Bolden's wife managed to get her husband to the sanitarium, where doctors amputated his leg.[7]

Bolden recuperated in the "colored ward" of St. Francis Sanitarium through the following Monday, until a group of white men came calling for him around nine o'clock that night. The two nurses on duty told the men that Bolden was gone, but the mob attacked a man they assumed to be Bolden, driving him into a state of shock that persisted until his death the following morning. The group dispersed after the police arrived. A local officer gave the nurses a pistol to ensure their safety. When the mob returned in an hour with reinforcements, the nurses and nuns held them off, one wielding the gun and daring the group to enter the ward. She fired a warning shot into the air, dispersing the crowd. The nurses even caught one of the throng, held him, and turned him over to the police upon their second visit. The police, however, waited half an hour before responding to the nurses' call and allowed the prisoner to escape after removing him from the sanitarium.[8]

Immediately following the incident, Mayor H. D. Apgar ordered the sheriff's office to take charge of Bolden. At two o'clock early Tuesday morning, sheriffs took him to the city jail for the rest of the night. When day broke, Bolden's wife took custody of him. Fearing reprisals from yet another mob, the two boarded the 2:10 passenger train to Shreveport, but never made it past Cheniere.[9]

Bolden's lynching was part of a broader "Red Summer" of racial violence. Americans were just settling into their mistrust and vilification of Soviet Russia. (Monroe's Lyceum Theatre, in fact, presented *A Midnight Romance* on the day of Bolden's death, an Anita Stewart silent film depicting a sordid love affair between a wealthy man from an established family and a deceitful woman, played by Stewart. Her trickery is finally forgiven when the mysterious woman explains that she is a princess who is ever-threatened by Bolshevism.)[10] But Red Summer was named for the blood it produced.[11] While the majority of American eyes were focused firmly on Paris and the peace conference that ended the Great War, violence at home kept them glancing back to their own domestic trouble. Beginning in Charleston, South Carolina, a series of twenty-six race riots from May to October shook the optimism brought by peace. Washington, D.C., Baltimore, Omaha, and Chicago, among other cities, would all soon follow. Over eighty-three were killed.[12] Still, while the racial violence was incredibly troubling for a nation emerging from a war "to make the world safe for democracy," the riots demonstrated something fundamentally different from the violence in Monroe. Those northern cities—Chicago, Baltimore, Washington—had thriving black communities, willing to fight against racial unfairness in whatever form it took.

Baseball was both a representation of black social and economic strength and a constituent part of its existence in such northern urban areas. While the Bolden case dragged on through the summer of 1919, and race riots consumed the cities, black baseball remained a staple in the metropolitan North. African Americans had played baseball since the game's inception in the 1850s, and the game continued to grow throughout Reconstruction, particularly in the East Coast hubs of New York, Philadelphia, and Washington. But such growth wasn't limited to the Northeast. New Orleans, for example—the nation's fifth largest city in the 1860s—was a hotbed for baseball in the Civil War era, and black teams thrived, often playing teams of area whites. Still, New Orleans was an exception to the general southern rule, as the progression of baseball—black and white—lagged behind that of the industrialized North. And with the onset of Jim Crow in the early 1890s, even the interracial contests of the South's largest city disappeared.[13]

Meanwhile, the teams of the North soldiered on, and as the nineteenth century became the twentieth, the profusion of independent baseball clubs led to fledgling attempts to organize them into a league. But the International League of Colored Baseball Clubs in America and Cuba, founded in 1906, wouldn't last. Nor would the National Association of Colored Baseball Clubs of the United States and Cuba. Teams developed in every major northern urban area, however, and various barnstorming aggregations emerged to ensure that intercity rivalries would continue to pay dividends. The 1919 season would prove decisive. While the Boldens suffered in northeast Louisiana, Harlem's Lincoln Giants, Atlantic City's Bacharach Giants, and Chicago's American Giants all played to sellout crowds. The Royal Giants of Brooklyn, the Hilldale club of Philadelphia—all performed well. All made money. But a New York ownership monopoly kept teams from the Midwest out of the New York market. There were secret negotiations, backbiting, and territorial disputes, and the arguments would lead many owners to push for a league formation that would mitigate such tensions. Still, such bickering would not have been possible without strong owners and successful businesses, each competing for their share of the black baseball market. That kind of infrastructure was simply absent in the South, and its absence was one of the many reasons the hangman's noose was able to dominate the region.[14]

To highlight its 1919 push for anti-lynching legislation, the NAACP held a national conference on lynching at Carnegie Hall in New York. In conjunction with the event, John R. Schillady, the association's national secretary, sent a telegram to Louisiana governor Ruffin G. Pleasant, urging him to "demand legal authorities proceed energetically to apprehend lynchers and bring them to trial." The request, unsurprisingly, would fall on deaf ears. Though Louisiana seemed legitimately frustrated by the continued racial violence in Monroe, the messages of the NAACP's anti-lynching campaign were fundamentally different from those of the state's pundits in the wake of the Bolden lynching.[15]

They were also different from the messages of the broader anti-lynching movement in the South. The year following the Bolden murder, a group of racially moderate southerners created the Commission on Interracial Cooperation (CIC), which assumed the mantle of southern interracial reform for the next two decades. The group attempted to secure better housing and education for the growing black middle class. The CIC also sought to end mob violence, but it specifically argued against a federal lynch law. Segregation was the "Southern Way of Life"—as was racial inequality. Any federal legislation directed toward southern race relationships would set a dangerous precedent, as well as infringe upon the solemn right of the states to make such decisions themselves.[16]

Herbert J. Seligmann described the Bolden lynching, among others, as a symptom of a perverted desire to protect southern womanhood. "For the benefit of those unfamiliar with the increasingly popular sport of 'protecting Southern womanhood' it should be noted that the objects of this sport are usually United States citizens of dark skin—Negroes." From Bolden's phantom signature on his note to Mrs. Thomas to his murder outside of Cheniere, Seligmann portrayed the entire debacle as a misapplication of southern notions of chivalry.[17]

The lynching debate in Louisiana, and Monroe in particular, seemed to validate Seligmann's argument. The *News-Star,* Monroe's only newspaper in 1919, took a defensive stance from the outset, titling its coverage of the first attack on Bolden "Insulting Note Costs Negro a Leg." The following day, coverage of the St. Francis attack and the Cheniere train murder was straightforward, without praise for the nurses and nuns or condemnation of the mob. Along with the New Orleans press, newspapers in Little Rock and Memphis ran similar Associated Press wire stories. The failed attempt on Bolden's life at the hospital was secondary to coverage of his murder the following afternoon.[18]

The reporting, however, seemed inadequate to the nurses of St. Francis, and the following day, an unknown number of them published a letter to the editor on the front page of the *News-Star*. "It was with great surprise and indignation that we read the account given in yesterday's *News-Star*," the letter began. It recounted the capture of a member of the mob and the fear and apprehension the events of the evening created among the nurses. "It certainly seems strange," the letter stated, "that the man who was caught could be held by ladies, but made his escape from the officers." They concluded indignantly, "We think it a disgrace to Monroe for a mob to come to the sanitarium to carry out their vengeance, and to scare the nurses and patients, when they easily could have waited until the patient was carried home." The letter was signed, "The Nurses."[19]

During the following two days, letters to the editor appeared in the *News-Star* denouncing the violence at the hospital. "The whole thing savours of what we considered was peculiar to our Teuton foes," said the first. The letters decried the practice of mob action, but only mentioned "this mob action of last Monday night"—the mob's entry into the sanitarium. "Even the 'Unspeakable Turk' spares from attack the hospitals of his enemy," noted the second letter. The pastor and congregation of Monroe's First Baptist Church also registered their indignation with a formal resolution passed at a Victory Liberty Loan rally on Sunday, May 4. Again, the nurses' situation was the principal focus of ire, as the congregation "emphatically register our protest and disapproval of the unwarranted and cowardly actions of the mob which unlawfully entered our good sanitarium recently and tried to intimidate its nurses into submitting to their unlawful purposes. This and subsequent actions of the mob stand as a blot on the fair name of our city." Bolden's murder was never mentioned.[20]

At the time, the *New Orleans Item* chided Monroe as the "lynch law center of Louisiana" and told of its "several lynchings" in recent months. That was an understatement. From the turn of the century to the close of 1918, the region found thirty of its black citizens lynched. Between 1889 and 1922, Monroe's Ouachita Parish witnessed more lynchings than any other county in the nation. It was, per capita, the most racially violent place in America.[21] The *Item* reminded readers that hospitals are "filled with sick people, people recovering from operations; not negroes alone, but white people of high standing." It wondered "what Monroe will do now. Will it stand for the forcible invasion of a hospital full of sick white people, conducted by white nurses, by a masked mob bent upon murder?" The indignation now turned to the reputation of Monroe, and the *News-Star* was quick to fire back. It correctly described its role as news hub for a large rural coverage area in northeast Louisiana and southeast Arkansas, explaining that lynching news from within that broad swath carried Monroe datelines, thus marring the city's name by default. It also correctly explained that the colored ward of St. Francis was a separate building that held no white patients.[22]

The *News-Star*'s defense of Monroe's general white population (and its subsequent denial of the local culture's role in supporting mob violence) then drifted further from anger at the mob murder. "Whenever a negro violates the sanctity of the home of any white man, or insults any white woman, he may as well send a hurry call for the undertaker," it explained. "The great majority of the people abhor and detest the resort to mob law, but they recognize the fact that it is infinitely preferable to deal quickly and summarily with the negro who steps over the forbidden bounds." The editorial argued that the mob should not have entered the sanitarium looking for a man whose guilt was far from certain. The *News-Star* blamed law enforcement. If officials had enforced the laws and swiftly meted out justice, then the white populace would never have been put in such an unfortunate position. And did not law enforcement officials lose the nurses' prisoner? "So, after all, the officials, from the highest to the lowest, are in a large measure, directly responsible for the contempt in which many people hold the courts and the officials."[23]

On May 13, new city leaders took an oath of office at Monroe's city hall. A board of commissioners replaced the former aldermanic administrative system. There were high hopes for new mayor Arnold Bernstein and his fellow commissioners. "These men," reported the *News-Star,* "will lessen and somewhat relieve the City of Monroe of the odium and unenviable notoriety which has come upon it." Bernstein would serve for the next twenty years, presiding over the city throughout the Monarchs' run as a professional baseball team. He was perhaps the most successful mayor in Monroe's history. He oversaw the construction of parks and schools, an electric plant, and a natatorium. Along with other city leaders, Bernstein proved instrumental in the creation and promotion of Northeast Junior College, Monroe's first endeavor into higher education. But success did not seem so obvious in 1919. "There is much to be done," reported the *News-Star,* "before Monroe will take her proper place in the procession of progressive municipalities."[24]

Two days after the commission government took office, Judge Fred Odom called a special session of the Ouachita Parish Grand Jury, to meet on May 19. He did not specifically mention the Bolden lynching or the sanitarium invasion. He didn't need to. The grand jury summoned three St. Francis nurses, two of the African American patients of the colored ward, and the crew of the Vicksburg, Shreveport, and Pacific Railroad on duty at the time of Bolden's murder. They made their official report to Odom the following afternoon, indicting no one for the crime. The grand jury only indicted one man, R. R. McCord, for carrying a concealed weapon and for trespassing on sanitarium grounds. He paid a $100 bond the same afternoon.[25]

The editor of the *Item* remained suspicious. "This grand jury showed about as much energy in investigating this lynching as southern grand juries usually display in lynching cases." The paper noted that the body's brief report followed only one afternoon of nine interviews. It titled its story "The Usual Result." The *Times-Picayune* accused the grand jury of indulging in suspicions, arguing that the investigation was "barren of results." It was "unsatisfactory and [does] not set that town and Louisiana right before the country." The paper charged the body with dereliction of duty, and concluded that "the anarchy and outlawry of Russia, Germany and other countries of Europe warn us against tolerating such lawless ideas." The *News-Star* responded by accusing the *Times-Picayune* of engaging in hearsay. It again condemned the invasion of the sanitarium as indefensible, but acknowledged the need for mob action in capital cases devoid of swift justice. It defended its "twelve men, good and true" who constituted the grand jury, and concluded, "The taking of human life is repulsive to every sane human being, we believe, and mighty few white men care to participate in a mob that kills a human being."[26]

Again, Bolden's murder was never emphasized. "If Monroe sentiment condemns mob rule it has overlooked several very fine opportunities to prove it," noted the *Shreveport Journal*. The collective outrage at the actions of the Bolden mob centered not on the murder, but on the sanctity of the hospital and the virtue of the nurses. A letter to the editor of the *News-Star* in early June served as the paper's final word on the debacle, and a fitting culmination of the mob rule debate. "Do not understand me to advocate lynching," wrote W. W. Cook, "for I do not. I have never participated in a lynching and never expect to. At the same time, under certain circumstances, I cannot say just what I might do." He lauded the fairness of Monroe citizens and professed to "appreciate a law-abiding, obedient negro." There was obviously a simple way to remove the injustice from the southern landscape: "First do something to stop the negro from committing crimes that justifies his neck being broke." Cook closed with a wish of success and prosperity for "honorable negroes."[27]

Though denunciations of mob murder were loud and frequent in 1919, regional opinion was more skewed. Monroe, Louisiana, was angry that mob rule had brought infamy to its doorstep, but the focus of its ire never touched on black male murder. The town was excoriated throughout the state, from New Orleans to Shreveport, for further weakening Louisiana's reputation, but that opprobrium was only tangentially related to lynching itself. Instead, it focused on white female sanctity. Fittingly, Monroe's actual lynch mob also focused on white female sanctity. The white press defended the nurses, the mob defended Mrs. Thomas, and the 1919 consensus against lynching never coalesced into a force for change. With such a variety of approximate denunciations, there was never really a consensus at all. This might not seem surprising. Such failures were the norm in the Jim Crow South, as white newspapers manned the barricades in the fight to protect the "Southern Way of Life." Still, in just over a decade, that same white press would man a very different barricade, touting the city's black baseball team and defending it against challenges from Negro Leagues officials and the cities they represented. That kind of turnaround would have seemed beyond comprehension during the hot summer of 1919.

The day after George Bolden's lynching, Monroe's Lyceum Theatre presented John S. Robertson's *The Test of Honor,* starring John Barrymore. The film depicted the relationships of wealthy white southerner Martin Wingrave and his ruthless attempt to preserve his honor at any cost, even through attempted murder. Barrymore's character was only one in a long line of spokesmen for the devotion to honor paraded in front of Monroe audiences.[28]

The day of Barrymore's Monroe debut, Paris bureau chief Wilbur Forrest contributed an editorial to his *New York Tribune,* titled "Baseball Won the War." He credited American sports and the values they instilled as cornerstones of Allied victory in the Great War. He quoted E. W. Dickerson, president of the white minor Western League, who described American soldiers' "agility and ability for quick determination, ability to withstand hardships and nerve wracking fire—it all developed from our national aptitude for sports." For Dickerson and Forrest, baseball was far more important than racism. It was the elusive Fifteenth Point that could bring Wilsonian democracy to the world. "That is why," wrote Forrest, describing Dickerson, "he sees the world series being played in London or Paris within the next decade or two."[29]

Dickerson's sentiment was perhaps overly optimistic, but it was representative of a new American attitude. Why couldn't baseball change the world? As the riots of Red Summer coalesced into a frustrating stalemate, the 1919 Negro National League season came to a close with similar frustrations. The teams provided an outlet for the fans of individual cities and demonstrated the power of black economic institutions. They were a haven for northern urban communities in the final, halting throes of the Industrial Revolution. But ownership disputes and internecine squabbles left black baseball's leadership aching for a haven of their own. While the actions of postwar Monroe would establish a precedent for justifying racial violence and cement attitudes about the region's racial propensities, the actions of black baseball teams of the urban North—free, in many respects, from the harsher dictates of the racial climate of places like Monroe— would establish the need for reform, for organization, for a league. They would get it early the following year. Though the status of black citizenship was tenuous in every part of the country, grounding institutions such as professional baseball in the urban North provided a kind of institutional stability that alleviated, if only temporarily, racial pressures.

But the criticism and sniping of the New Orleans and Monroe dailies in the aftermath of the Bolden murder suggested that the racism of the city was different from that of the small town. Monroe was far less reticent than most about showing the blood on its hands, and statistics demonstrated that it had more blood on its hands than anywhere else in the nation. In the interregnum between 1919 and 1932, overt violence would decrease, but there was little indication that the town would be ready to share the national stage with its urban counterparts.

2

The Jazz Age and the Depression

The Different Trajectories of Monroe
and Black Baseball in the 1920s

In the decade spanning Bolden's murder and the 1932 successes of the Monroe Monarchs, American sports reached new heights of popularity. On September 23, 1926, 130,000 people watched Jack Dempsey fight Gene Tunney for the world's heavyweight championship at Sesquicentennial Stadium in Philadelphia—the largest civic gathering in United States history to that point. Though Dempsey lost the fight, he had unprecedented celebrity in a sports-mad nation. College football had already reached previously unimagined levels of popularity, but in the 1920s, it spread west and south from its home in the Northeast, becoming a fixture of state identity, particularly in areas (such as the South) that didn't have much else going for them. In 1926, the University of Alabama traveled to the Rose Bowl, where they defeated the Washington Huskies, firmly establishing the South's passion for and appropriation of the game. Baseball also experienced an unprecedented rise in popularity, fueled by the end of the dead-ball era and the rise of the slugger. Jimmie Foxx, Hack Wilson, and, above all, Babe Ruth took advantage of new hitter-friendly rules following the 1919 Chicago Black Sox scandal. On August 5, 1921, the first baseball game was broadcast on radio. The Philadelphia Phillies–Pittsburgh Pirates contest left a lasting legacy for network broadcasting, a legacy that would spread the participatory power of fandom throughout the decade to tens of thousands who couldn't afford a ticket to see Jimmie Foxx, or Babe Ruth, or Jack Dempsey, or the Crimson Tide.[1]

These sports would combine with film, flight, depression, and prohibition to create a nation in 1932 far different from that of 1919. But in 1932 Monroe, much looked the same. There was no Jack Dempsey, no major league baseball. And the boundaries of racial identity were still defined by the Booker T. Washington district running along the edge of town. "If you happen to be a customer of the B.W. Willis Dairy, you have probably noticed the colored youth who brings the milk to your doorstep," reported the West Monroe weekly, the *Ouachita Citizen*. "You probably have not realized that you are being served by a youth with a Bachelor of Science degree."[2] This anomaly could have been reported in any number of newspapers throughout the South in 1932. The spate of lynchings that dominated the early century diminished in the years following the Bolden incident. In 1920, southern whites lynched fifty-three Negroes. In 1921, the number was fifty-one; in 1922, fifty-nine. 1923's total of twenty-nine African American lynchings represented a decline that would only continue, aided by the continued work of groups such as the NAACP and CIC.[3] Still, consistent racism and the legacy of that violence kept tensions high in Monroe.

Meanwhile, black baseball rode the wave of the new Jazz Age infatuation with sports. In February 1920, club owners from midwestern cities met in Kansas City and founded the Negro National League (NNL), voting Andrew "Rube" Foster president. In the early century Foster was a player and manager of Chicago's Leland Giants, but in 1911 he left the team to create his own, the Chicago American Giants. He was the undisputed driving force behind his new Negro National League, and in the first half of the 1920s, it grew exponentially under his watch. The Giants won the first three Negro National League championships from 1920 to 1922. Teams from the Northeast, however, were left out, and in late 1922, they responded to the National's success by founding the Eastern Colored League. In 1924, the two began playing a World Series. In 1926 and 1927, Foster's American Giants won back-to-back championships, but by 1926 Foster had retired as manager of the team, preferring instead to act solely as owner and booking agent. Both of the American Giants' World Series victories, then, came under the team leadership of Dave Malarcher.[4]

In 1928, the Eastern Colored League folded, and the National's success was wavering as well. Foster's retirement both from the team and league operations in 1926 was the result of a diagnosis of mental illness. He was ultimately institutionalized in Kankakee, Illinois, where he died four years later in 1930.[5] St. Louis Stars co-owner George B. Keys had served as vice president of the league under Foster, and briefly assumed the presidency after Foster stepped down.[6]

Judge William C. Hueston, from Gary, Indiana, succeeded Keys as president of the NNL in 1927. His election was influenced by the hiring of Kenesaw Mountain Landis to a similar post in Major League Baseball in 1920, following the disastrous Black Sox World Series scandal the previous season. Hueston had worked successfully as both a lawyer and investment banker before taking on his new position, but his attempt to revive the Negro National League faltered after the collapse of the economy late in the decade. The league could not sustain itself with depression-ridden gate receipts, and Hueston was powerless to address the problem. "Failure and final dissolution of the Negro National Baseball League," the *California Eagle* concluded, "may be laid directly at the doors of Old Man Depression."[7]

Of course, the whole of black business suffered under the newfound weight of depression. Particularly in northern urban areas, a burgeoning black population (fed largely by southern migrants) helped fuel the development of a black middle class of business owners catering specifically to the needs of African American patrons in the 1920s. It wasn't just baseball. Service industries such as barbershops, restaurants, and funeral homes flourished, as did the broader real estate market. The number of black dentists, doctors, and lawyers also rose during the decade—as did the number of those in the artistic community: actors, authors, and musicians—but the rise was far from evenly matched between North and South. Louisiana, for example, recognized only eight black lawyers in 1930. And everywhere in the South the vast number of black professionals were clergymen and teachers. By the early 1930s, however, African American businesses in both North and South would feel the same harsh realities that black baseball experienced. Many black-owned institutions collapsed, and black professionals scurried to find employment with local white businesses.[8]

But white ownership had always been there. In metropolitan areas from Kansas City to New York, the hubs of black entertainment were often owned by whites. Whites, in fact, owned every dance hall in Kansas City. They owned Harlem's Cotton Club, and it was that kind of white patronage that fed and facilitated the artistic movement known as the Harlem Renaissance, concerned as it was with the creation of a new black identity. Similarly, Fred Stovall wasn't the only white owner in Negro League baseball. J. L. Wilkinson owned the Kansas City Monarchs. The Baltimore Black Sox went through a series of white ownership groups. Many black teams in the Northeast also used white booking agents to secure parks and dates with white semiprofessional teams when northeastern leagues foundered or collapsed. White baseball owners and booking agents dealing directly with black teams, however, were few and far between below the Maryland border.[9]

"Is Judge Hueston trying to kid the gentle baseball public or is he trying to kid himself?" asked *Chicago Defender* sports editor and syndicated columnist Frank "Fay" Young, responding directly to black baseball's seemingly tenuous state in the face of broader economic collapse. He noted that the 1931 season witnessed drastic declines in both attendance and baseball quality. The year 1932, he reasoned, would be no better. "When [Rube] Foster died, Negro baseball as a league died."[10]

But this statement did not apply in the South. Though it always held minor status in the pantheon of black baseball, the Negro Southern League (NSL) was founded in March 1920, just two weeks after the Negro National. Original teams represented Chattanooga, Knoxville, Nashville, Atlanta, Montgomery, Birmingham, Pensacola, and New Orleans. By 1931, that number had faltered under the hard weight of the Depression. The league included six teams that year: Nashville, Memphis, Birmingham, and Montgomery, along with the Chattanooga Black Lookouts and the Knoxville Giants. But it grew as the second half of the season began, adding Atlanta and Little Rock to its roster. Nashville edged out Memphis for the league championship. Reuben Bartholomew Jackson was elected president of the NSL in October 1931, after the close of the season, and in early January he issued a press release announcing a meeting of possible franchises for a newly reorganized league at Birmingham's Rush Hotel. He expected representatives from Knoxville, Chattanooga, and Nashville, Tennessee; Montgomery and Birmingham, Alabama; New Orleans, Monroe, and Shreveport, Louisiana; Louisville and Lexington, Kentucky; Atlanta, Georgia; and Little Rock, Arkansas. All would be vying for limited spaces in next year's newly formed group. "One of the most interesting features of this meeting," Jackson's press release noted, "will be to organize and formulate plans with the Negro National Baseball league if there is one this year."[11]

But there would be no Negro National League that year. In late March, Young's prophecy came to fruition. Hueston issued a statement declaring that the league would abandon play for 1932, the first time it had done so since its organization. Still, the Southern League press release demonstrates that the group was already thinking about taking a larger national role even before the National League's collapse. They would jump at the opportunity.

Monroe was listed in the Southern League press release as being an applicant for membership, but its chances to gain admittance were slim. It was a small town, far from any of the main thoroughfares, with a long history of racial violence. And its reputation hadn't improved in the intervening years between the Bolden lynching and 1931.

Monroe was founded in 1820 through the efforts of Jean-Baptiste Filhiol, a Frenchman who arrived in 1783 on behalf of Spain, which then owned the territory. A Louisiana State Senate act that year designated Monroe a town, and the area's prosperity grew throughout the antebellum period, driven almost exclusively by a plantation cotton economy. Its twentieth-century prosperity, however, would explode from the earth, just north of the city.[12] "Natural gas and carbon black are two of the principal factors in the lives of practically all of the people who reside in and about Monroe," boasted a publication of Monroe's Natural Gas Company in late 1931. Twenty-three years prior, in 1908, Mayor Andrew Forsythe proposed drilling a test well for natural gas, and a series of fits and starts by various entrepreneurs finally led in 1916 to profitable wells.[13] Thirteen more wells came in 1917, creating far more supply than local demand could ever absorb. Into the breech came the budding carbon black industry. The Southern Carbon Company, from Charleston, West Virginia, was the first to enter the area, but many soon followed. By 1924, Monroe would be the largest carbon black producer in the world. That year, the Monroe gas pool held between 4 and 6.5 trillion cubic feet of gas over almost five hundred square miles. It was the largest gas field in the country.[14]

The boom had dramatic effects. In 1917, Monroe had a population of 10,500. By 1931, it had 29,750. In that same time, the population of West Monroe—just across the Ouachita River—quadrupled from 1,500 to 6,000. Monroe's 1917 assessed value of $6.5 million grew to over $30 million by 1931. The city's prosperity was unequal between white and black residents, but everyone felt its effects.[15]

"The most impressive thing about Monroe is Desiard Street," wrote John L. Clark, press agent for the Pittsburgh Crawfords, "which is a continuation of the highway, and runs straight through town to the bridge across the Ouachita river. On the upper end is the Negro section, which ends (or begins) at Sixth street." Black neighborhoods and schools were consistently placed next to railroad tracks and cemeteries. "Yet, with all these disadvantages the best equipped drug store we have ever seen is operated by a Negro at the corner of Tenth and Desiard. Although a visitor to Monroe might say that no compliment should be passed on the way Negroes are huddled together, they seem to get along alright, and enjoy themselves." And according to Clark, they weren't abused by the authorities like the black population of Pittsburgh. "Police make raids only on complaint and the fines are graduated for each offense. Incidentally, the policemen all seem to be over 6 feet high and weigh over 225 pounds."[16]

Still, though the 1920s had roared sufficiently for Monroe, that success would make the town increasingly vulnerable to the vagaries of the market. "Times are hard," said a *Louisiana Weekly* advertisement, "but you can't improve conditions by making the world more conscious of its ills. The period of hardship has about worn itself out. Now it is our turn. [Business theorist] Roger Babson says that a man can only run halfway into the woods, the other half finds him running out of it." But others were not so optimistic. Norman Thomas, commenting on the Depression in 1934, argued that "the tragedy of these years has made Thomas Carlyle's remark a commonplace: 'A man willing to work and unable to find work is perhaps the saddest sight that fortune's inequalities exhibit under the sun.'" The Depression created a cultural as well as an economic problem. "So familiar have we become with this living tragedy that by some instinct of escape we turn away from the plays, novels, or actual records which would bring its poignant meaning home."[17] People neither needed nor wanted tragedies. They wanted the possibility of success, vicarious or otherwise. They wanted simple rules, clear victories, and hope. Many of them would turn to baseball.

Robert and Helen Lynd helped explain that phenomenon when they argued in 1929 that the lives of Americans were inordinately affected by "motion pictures, advertising, and other forms of publicity." People were defining themselves by what they observed, and baseball played a prominent role in this mass culture based on observation. As literary scholar Rita Barnard (among others) has more recently observed, the financial difficulties of the Depression "did not immunize Americans against dreams of abundance or modest luxuries." Finding identity in movies, products, or teams allowed the unemployed and struggling their own sort of success.[18] That identity was easier to find at some times than at others. Just over two hundred miles from Monroe, in Destrehan, Louisiana, the local black semipro team seemingly answered Roger Babson's call and validated the Lynds' argument when it named itself the Depression Stars.[19]

"The Negro was born in depression," said Clifford Burke, a community volunteer who described his Depression experience for Studs Terkel. "It only became official when it hit the white man." African American urban unemployment rose to 50 percent by 1932, making the maintenance of black business—baseball or otherwise—a tenuous prospect at best. In the North, approximately half of all black families were receiving some form of depression relief. It was even worse in the South. For example, 65 percent of Atlanta's black families needed aid. But the Depression affected everyone. In 1929, the estimated national income was $83 billion. In 1932, it was $39 billion. In 1929, average per capita income was $1,475. In 1932, it was $1,119. In 1929, 1.6 million people—3 percent of the labor force—were unemployed. By 1933, that number had grown to 12.8 million, a full 25 percent of workers. Throughout the first decade of the Depression, one-fourth of all southerners were tenants or sharecroppers, as were half of all southern farmers, and by June 1932, farm prices had dropped to 52 percent of the 1909–1914 average. At the same time, farmers paid taxes 166 percent higher than in 1914.[20]

Monroe was far from immune. Between 1930 and 1935, total assessed property value in Ouachita Parish plummeted from almost $65 million to just over $43 million. Its agricultural income fell by almost 65 percent. Similar drops in total payroll and retail sales stood as testaments to the economic devastation in the region. Thirty-five percent of the fifty-five thousand Ouachita Parish residents were black, and more than 19 percent of that group was illiterate. The illiteracy rate dropped slightly to 17 percent within Monroe, Ouachita's parish seat. In 1930, 48 percent of the Ouachita African American population was unemployed, a number that surely rose in the lean years between the census and the 1932 baseball season. The city population did not fare much better; 43 percent were unemployed.[21]

Hoover's programs to solve such problems were not only ineffective, but they also included virtually no black representation.[22] Black Republicans had been integral to Hoover's election, and they saw the lack of African American appointments as a betrayal of a de facto 1928 quid pro quo. The incumbent, furthermore, sought to sanitize his party's image by removing an anti-lynching pledge from the party platform. Even worse for Hoover, he remained silent when black leaders pressed him on his southern policy or his seeming abandonment of his black constituents.[23]

That betrayal, combined with Hoover's general lack of success, ensured that the 1932 presidential election would be particularly contentious, and Hoover was at a decided disadvantage against Democratic challenger Franklin Roosevelt.[24] On January 30, black Democrats in Shreveport and Bossier Parish voted without incident in the Democratic primary. On February 23, however, in the runoff primary, black voters were refused. Election officials denied the voting credentials they had accepted one month before, stating that a misunderstanding in Shreveport had allowed African Americans to vote in what was supposed to be a white primary. White primaries, however, were not the only safeguard used by white Louisiana. The state required a poll tax, $300 in property, and the ability to read and write for voting privileges.[25]

As in Bossier Parish, the vote in Monroe's Ouachita Parish would be almost entirely white. And it would be almost entirely Democrats. Of the 6,427 people who voted in Ouachita Parish, 5,968 voted for Democrats. The Republicans of Monroe weren't voting because, for the most part, the Republicans of Monroe were black. White Monroe, like much of white Louisiana, kept the black population from the polls, even after the state's repeal of the poll tax in 1934. Charles H. Meyers, a registered Republican and president of Monroe's NAACP branch, complained in 1938 that "the parish officers have refused [over the past years] to let any colored people register."[26] But Monroe's 1932 voting statistics didn't exist in a vacuum. They mirrored the state's figures. 268,804 citizens voted in Louisiana. Of those, 92.8 percent voted for Democrats. By 1940, black citizens in Louisiana made up only 0.16 percent of the voting population.[27]

Things weren't much better nationally for Louisiana's black voters. The Republican National Convention was held in June 1932 in Chicago, and as the Monarchs played to white and black audiences in notoriously racist Monroe, Louisiana's black delegates to the convention bowed to pressure and abrogated in favor of the competing lily-white contingent from the state. B. V. "Buddy" Baranco, Dr. John H. Lowery, and S. W. Green were each prominent and qualified members of the delegation. They had served since 1920. "What next?" asked the Associated Negro Press. The three "had left their interests and professions at a sacrifice to continue the fight for proper recognition of Negro delegates in Louisiana and elsewhere through out the southern states." But the political pressure finally became too great.[28]

In such a racialized climate, even demonstrations of progress proved problematic. In 1930, for example, Monroe officials charged Jack Ross—without any conclusive evidence, as in the Bolden case a decade prior—with sexually assaulting a white woman and shooting her male companion. The NAACP raised money for Ross's defense, hired a successful white lawyer to represent him, and watched as, against all odds, he was acquitted. But the fact of his arrest and the local assumption of his guilt was enough to remind black visitors that northeast Louisiana was still a monumentally unaccommodating place. If, for example, a member of a traveling baseball team was to be falsely accused of a similar crime, would the locals rally to his defense as they had for Ross?[29]

It was a fair question. At the beginning of 1932, southern cities stood at the top of the murder lists, largely, said reports, due to "lynch law and lawlessness." In Birmingham, Alabama, 54.8 murders per 100,000 people led the nation, followed by Memphis, Tennessee, and Atlanta, Georgia.[30] In such a hostile climate, the South's urban black population turned to its Negro Southern League baseball teams as an outlet from the debilitating racism and the debilitating Depression swirling around them. But Monroe seemed to present something even more ominous. It was rural, not urban. It had no history of sustaining professional sports. And in a region with a brutal apartheid system, it had the worst race relations of any county in the South. Since the 1890s, in fact, no other county in the nation had witnessed the level of racial violence in Ouachita Parish. As the Ross case demonstrated, even the trend against overt violence had not stopped the culture of suspicion that plagued the area. Of all the places in the South seeking to take advantage of the Negro Southern League's good fortune following the National's collapse, Monroe was the most unlikely.

But Monroe's litany of disadvantages was about to grow longer. As 1932 began, the worst natural disaster in the city's history fell from the sky.

3
The Flood
Water, Race, and the Monarchs in Early 1932

The first week of January 1932, government forecasts predicted a high water-mark of forty-six feet on the Ouachita River. "It is unfortunate," read an editorial in the *Monroe Morning World,* "that the task of dealing with high water should be added to the general economic difficulties which are common throughout the country. But there is nothing in the situation that should cause us to lose our equilibrium." The editorial worried that undue apprehension could create a panic that might affect relief efforts. "No such situation as that which prevailed in 1927 need be feared at this season of the year, in spite of the fact that the present overflow is in itself unusual."[1]

As January progressed, floodwaters continued to rise. The popular comic strip *Tarzan* portrayed a violent rainstorm throughout early January, an irony not lost on the residents of Monroe. An anonymous article in the *Monroe Morning World* compared the waterlogged West Monroe to Venice. "Of course," it noted, "there are vagaries in any comparison." The local gondolas, for instance, "are somewhat different, architecturally, if compared with those of Venice (Italy or California), and many of them are equipped with outboard motors." During the first weeks of January, women and children played barefoot in the rising water: "An enjoyable time was had by all."[2]

But the curiosity of winter flooding soon gave way to far more serious concerns. "Conditions are becoming increasingly serious," reported W. L. Workman, head of the Monroe branch of the Salvation Army. "We will take anything," said Workman, "groceries, clothing, bedding, and distribute it without cost to the city. . . . We are working eighteen to twenty hours a day, and on insufficient funds and donations, we cannot meet the needs of our requests."[3]

Meeting in special session, the Ouachita Parish Police Jury called on citizens to cooperate with authorities in whatever way necessary. The *Morning World* worried in print about the possibility of mishandled refugee camps and outposts being established by those having a less enjoyable time. "Women and children will suffer from cold and exposure unless proper shelter is provided," it warned. "Above all things, it is essential that the establishment of a refugee camp of tents shall be avoided."[4] Nonetheless, even as the police jury met, the frantic citizens of West Monroe, pushed by the rise of the Black and Toni bayous, moved south of town, establishing a makeshift community of tents and abandoned houses south of the Illinois Central railroad tracks. Black and white citizens crowded the area. They lived side by side in a way that would have been unthinkable when the homes were permanent. Hunger and weather-related illnesses dominated the integrated neighborhood. But in a time when hunger was commonplace, integration was not.[5]

In these circumstances, need often trumped racial division, even when tragedy was unavoidable. At 7:30 in the evening on February 10, twelve miles northeast of the Monroe city limits, J. G. Pate, his wife, and their two children, ages four and two, began paddling a small boat on the backwaters of the Ouachita from Sterlington to Fowler to visit Pate's mother. Violent winds blew freezing water into the boat and blurred Pate's view. As the boat began sinking, one child found her mother's hand, but she lost her father. Mrs. Pate frantically searched for her other child and her husband, but soon floated through the freezing water to a barbed-wire fence. She screamed, and Gus Tarver and three of his friends ran to the sound of the terrified voice. The black Tarver was able to rescue the white Pate, but both her children and husband were drowned, victims of the water that continued to rise around everyone.[6]

The racial cooperation was telling. As mentioned, Monroe was generally understood to be a racist bastion, known as much for its occasional lynchings as it was for its floods. But the urgency of the situation surpassed typical prejudices. When towns in the region sent aid to the city, black workers accompanied the white, and the integrated crews ate sandwiches and drank coffee together in cramped quarters before manning the sandbag lines for shifts lasting between twelve and fourteen hours. "Not merely hundreds, but thousands of white and black workers have been brought into the city to lend their aid in filling sandbags and building up the temporary protecting dykes about the two cities," noted a *Morning World* editorial.[7]

So black and white could come together in times of life-threatening crisis, and could work for the common goal of not dying. As the end of the flood would demonstrate, however, when the threat disappeared—when not dying was once again assumed—inequality returned, and the black population was pushed back to the waterlogged fringes of a broken town. It would be impossible to prove that the racial cooperation demonstrated during the flood crisis made the city's white population more open to recognizing, even appropriating, African American athletic achievement. But the flood did breed racial cooperation, and, a few months later, those same white sandbaggers would be cheering for a black baseball team. The same newspapers that reported the floodwaters' devastation would defend the Monroe Monarchs in their pages. Of course, that would not come until the end of the flood. And the flood wasn't over yet.

The dire situation prompted Mayor Arnold Bernstein to create a central committee to coordinate area relief. The flood, the new committee noted, was not creating a relief burden; it was adding to an already cumbersome financial drought in the region. Relief efforts required money, and relief agencies were operating on fumes.[8] The committee divided the problem of unemployment relief—an ongoing problem in Depression-torn north Louisiana—and flood relief, and concerned itself solely with the economic problems existing before the water began to rise. The group estimated that "an irreducible minimum" of $31,000 would be needed over the next four months to provide a base of adequate care for those in need. The *Morning World* noted, "Experience in the last few weeks seems to prove conclusively that the public either cannot or will not voluntarily contribute any adequate sum for welfare and unemployment relief," and suggested that requests for federal aid might be necessary.[9]

On January 27, with the Ouachita higher than in 1927, over a thousand men, many recruited from relief lines and refugee camps, went to the flood lines to fill sandbags. The state highway department supplied the machinery that carried the sand from the pits to the water.[10] "Like an army trooping into battle," the local newspaper reported, "volunteer workmen from surrounding parishes and cities poured into Ouachita Parish and Monroe yesterday to help city, state, and federal forces battle the rampant Ouachita River." Water had only risen less than a tenth of a foot as of 2:30 that morning, but it placed water levels above 49.3 feet—a record for the area—and water began spilling over the levees in many places. A break in a levee just south of Sterlington (fifteen miles to the northeast of Monroe) caused a growing fear that Monroe's levees would be next. Many young men attending Ouachita Parish Junior College and Ouachita Parish High School donated their services. Neville High School suspended classes to allow its male students to man the levee lines.[11]

Hundreds of women from Monroe and West Monroe also supplied food and clothing to both workers and refugees. "They do it all with a fervor and a grace that are only matched by the cheerful demeanor which belies tired bodies and aching muscles, unaccustomed to long-continued and strenuous labor," the *Morning World* thankfully editorialized. "Monroe will not be likely to forget what its women have done in this crisis."[12]

But there was still more to do. By the end of January, over five thousand levee workers manned water-prevention sandbag brigades. The Red Cross and Salvation Army fed them, and the National Guard mailed their letters home at no cost. By late February, 1,100 families had received aid in Ouachita Parish alone.[13]

On February 3, the federal government took over the task of feeding the volunteers, instituting a ticket system among levee workers for gauging valid requests. Black and white levee workers received a ticket for their shift, which they could redeem at one of a series of feeding centers in various downtown locations. But the new organization came with the same old restrictions. On February 12, a woman entered the Baer Building on St. John Street, where a makeshift cafeteria had been established for levee workers, her head hung low with a man's coat and cap covering her hungry female body. Only a ticket demonstrating that the patron had worked on the levees could garner a hot meal. The woman presented such a ticket, but women were not allowed to work on the levees. "Hey, look here," yelled the Reverend Tom Roberts, state chaplain of the American Legion and manager of the operation. "We've got a girl dressed like a man." Following an encounter with the police, the woman escaped the cafeteria without food.[14]

At the beginning of February, St. Francis Sanitarium established an emergency ward at the downtown hospital and within the week treated 490 men suffering mostly from colds, flat feet, and blisters. One worker, sixteen-year-old Allen Coates, collapsed after working three days and three nights continuously on the levees. Another worker, suffering from pneumonia and attempting to return from Monroe to his home in Arkansas, fell unconscious in an abandoned cotton compress on South Eighth Street on the outer edge of Monroe. He was discovered by a group of children and sent to the hospital, one of hundreds helped by the Ouachita Parish Health Unit, St. Francis, and the Red Cross medical unit.[15]

Disease, too, was increasingly a problem. Dr. John W. Williams, director of the Ouachita Parish Health Unit, administered an area-wide typhoid vaccination project, traveling to various outlying areas and assuring the wary that the medicine was free and that "these vaccinations will incapacitate them in no way." His efforts to stave off an epidemic were ongoing since mid-January. "I cannot stress the importance of these vaccinations too strongly," he announced. "The flood waters are contaminated beyond realization, and while there is no danger in drinking water in the city mains, one is very likely to contract typhoid from

merely wading and working in the flood districts." Williams also began an awareness campaign about the dangers of malaria from a growing mosquito infesta-
tion. The standing water provided a fertile breeding ground for the insects, particularly as the temperatures in late February and early March began to rise, and
Williams reminded parish residents that "there are strict state laws compelling
the people of Louisiana to oil pools of water to kill mosquitoes, and the city or-
dinances also cover such conditions."[16]

As the pools of water rose, both city employees and prisoners continued to fill
sandbags and build temporary levees. To give officials (and reporters) a better
understanding of the scope of difficulties in the area, Delta Air Service treated
them to an aerial view of the city. They estimated that as of January 31, a full
25 percent of the city was submerged. "Looking down from a height of 1,000 to
2,000 feet above the surface of the earth, and glimpsing the vast expanse of water that covers so large a space of that surface, the beholder absorbs some idea of
the magnitude of the pervading flood."[17] A week later an entrepreneurial photographer advertised in the local paper that he could provide flood scenes "with
the usual Jared quality." One phone call would give the customer an opportunity for postcards and photographs. "FREE: One Air View With Each Dozen
Postals!"[18]

Aerial views showed that much of the farmland outside the city limits also
was under water. The winter flood exacerbated the effects of a fluctuating cotton
market that left the one-crop region vulnerable to a volatile depression economy
and only augured more future problems in more traditional flood seasons. In
response, a group of parish farmers formed the Ouachita Valley Truck Growers' Association. Supported by area banks, the group emphasized diversification
through "truck crops"—or crops, like cantaloupes, that could be easily trans-
ported by truck. "By such diversification of crops, with smaller acreage planted
to cotton, farmers of this section will depend less on the cotton for income," directors explained, "with less danger of loss of crops." The farmers brought in agricultural agents, fruit supply companies, and railroad executives to learn about
the transportation and sale of melons. At the initial meeting, 250 acres were devoted to cantaloupes, with more to be added. If California could grow fruit,
north Louisiana could, too.[19]

The floodwaters had long given way to baseball when the plan failed. While
the agricultural agents preached the compatibility of north Louisiana soil with
the nutritional needs of cantaloupe seeds, they neglected the area's humid climate. Cantaloupes are unique among melons in their susceptibility to fungal dis-
eases, making the arid air of places like California, Arizona, or Colorado neces-

sary. Years later, strawberries would grow successfully in Ouachita Parish, but in a year when new pools of water inundated an already overly humid region, the saturated air never created the conditions needed for the Truck Growers' diversification plan.[20]

But as the farmers pursued false hopes, the situation was improving. On February 11, the Missouri Pacific railway line between Monroe and Farmerville resumed. Though water remained on portions of the route, the journey was finally manageable. And then it was March. The cold was breaking, and though the Ouachita would not dip below flood level until April 12, people were hopeful and determined—with a resolve that only comes from drowning for two months—to ensure they were safe from the Ouachita River.[21]

On Monday, March 21, Dr. Joseph Samuel Clark, president of Southern University in Baton Rouge, spoke at Monroe Colored High School, accompanied by the Southern University Quartet, as the African American residents of Monroe looked on, flush with the pride that comes from weathering the worst of nature's disasters. That same day, the Monroe branch of the NAACP held its annual meeting. National representative Dr. Aubrey Maurice Mackel spoke to the crowd on the personal and social benefits of NAACP membership. State representative J. Leo Hardy presented his case to the members in a speech titled "Why Negroes Should Pay Their Poll Tax and Register." The flood was over. And when the immediate danger had abated, it was time again for black Monroe to plan against the pressing long-term dangers that racism placed in front of them.[22]

But through this seeming late-March success, the Monroe black community had a new disaster developing only a few blocks away at the Zion Traveler Baptist Church. Founded in 1871, the church had been a prominent and viable part of the community since its inception, led by pastor William Hamilton. Two years after Hamilton's death in 1902, revivalist minister Warner Washington Hill replaced him. Hill served the church through the first decades of the twentieth century, leading to a dramatic growth in membership. He spearheaded the effort to build a new facility on the corner of Eleventh and Grammont streets when a 1923 trash fire destroyed the church. But in 1932, a dissenting group calling themselves the Harmony Club sought a change of leadership.[23]

In early February, as deacons and other church members were volunteering at the levees, the Harmony Club, led by George Daniels and David Hodge, held a meeting of congregation dissenters and voted Hill out of the pulpit. Hill responded by writing an open letter to Judge Percy Sandel and the Ouachita Parish District Court. He claimed that those seeking his ouster were a small faction of the church population, which still overwhelmingly supported him. The Harmony Club, in turn, went to court in early March seeking an injunction to bar Hill from acting as pastor. Hill then countersued for access to what he believed to be his rightful pulpit. Though he lost the suit, his supporters responded to the Harmony Club by voting to reinstate him. Throughout March and April, the church, on the verge of breaking apart, held sessions to resolve the controversy. But as baseball season began, the controversy was far from resolved. It would continue through the season, as chapter 6 will describe.[24]

There were, in fact, plenty of controversies and problems for the black population as the floodwaters receded and spring training began. Describing its hope for baseball as a potential port in the storm of the continuing Depression, the *Memphis World* had commented at the close of the 1931 season,

The members of the [Memphis] Red Sox [Negro League] club are to be congratulated upon having kept high spirits through our conflicting interests including poor sports, naggers, broken morales, poor salaries, commission, playing dissatisfaction, and what not. It might be interesting to know that very few things are long lived in Memphis where Negroes [*sic*] interests and amusements are concerned. Swimming pools have dwindled down to one. Bakeries have been a failure. Building and Loan companies have lost out, cafes on Beale street in combination with hotels have sung the swan song and are sleeping their last sleep. The Memphians are now doing their banking in dime banks helped upon the shelf, three colored journals have gone the way of the strike out route and teams that were once in prime as the Diamond Stars, the Memphis Black Devils, and other teams are talk of the past.[25]

A similar lament could have been made by the citizens of Monroe. And yet, just as the Memphis black population still had its beloved Red Sox, Monroe still had its Monarchs. And this year, unlike any other, it would be a major league team. "Their interest seems to be centered on their own community and its activities," wrote columnist John L. Clark of Monroe's black population. "They believe the Monroe Monarchs can beat any team in the world—and they bet as they believe."[26]

That they did. But the floodwaters threatened to derail team owner Stovall's plans for the season. Fred Alonzo Stovall was born September 17, 1882, in Dallas, Texas. At the turn of the century, oil was discovered in the Spindletop area around Beaumont, and the area's production made the region an oil hub for decades afterward. In 1901, at nineteen, Stovall left his native Dallas to join one of the new drilling companies springing up in the region. He would remain on various oil fields in Spindletop for sixteen years. While in south Texas, he developed relationships with Louisiana oil and natural gas entrepreneurs. He also met and married Fay Ray Wherry of Rusk, Texas. Ten years after the couple's 1907 wedding, Fred, Fay, and their two sons, Earl and J. C., followed the new natural gas boom to northeast Louisiana.[27]

Fred was lighting out on his own, attempting to start the sort of business that had owned his interest for so many years. But he had no funds. Stovall and his family struggled for their first five years in Monroe, until June 1922, when hard work and saving finally provided the seed money for the Stovall Drilling Company. His knowledge of the Texas and Louisiana oil and natural gas landscape gave the company immediate success, and the following year he invested the company's profits in the new J.M. Supply Company (which acted as a machine shop, explosives dealer, drilling supply retailer, and mineral resource land acquisition agency, among other things). It was the first of several substantial business deals for Stovall in the 1920s; by the Monarchs' 1932 season, he also owned navigation and construction companies.[28]

But baseball was his passion. He built Casino Park—at a cost of approximately $75,000—for the black community because he employed many black workers. "He didn't have to do that," said DeMorris Smith, son of Hilton Smith, the Hall of Fame pitcher who played with the Monarchs before moving on to greater fame with Kansas City. Smith portrayed the park as a donation to the black community, and historian Robert Peterson backs his contention of generosity. Of course, Stovall was a businessman, and the entry fees of twenty-five and fifty cents demonstrated that profit was also a motive.[29]

The date of Casino's opening is unknown. But the J.M. Supply Company bought the Casino Park land in 1927, then sold it to Stovall in 1930. Stovall essentially sold the property to himself. On June 30, 1930, a sixteen-year-old drowned in the swimming pool of "the Negro amusement park two miles east of the city" after being "struck by a chair that fell from the lifeguard's tower in the center of the pool." This is the first mention in the *Monroe Morning World* of what could be Casino Park, which had an adjacent pool, a dance pavilion, and casino attending the ballfield.[30] The Monarchs' first season also came in 1930, as Stovall culled together a club from the most athletic of his black employees. On May 11, 1930, the minor league Monarchs played their first recorded game with the Newtown Braves, winning 5–4 on eighth- and ninth-inning rallies. The team's first manager, Alonzo Longware Jr., pitched Barney Morris in the game. Morris would remain the one surviving link between the 1932 team and the original squad.[31]

Less than two months later, the Monarchs played a three-game series with the Lake Charles Giants at Casino Park, the first contests at Casino described in the local press. Fifteen hundred fans watched as the Monarchs moved the winning run across in the bottom of the fourteenth inning, giving the home team a 4–3 victory.[32]

The ball field was situated at the 2900 block of Desiard Street, just outside the city limits. Its dimensions were modest compared to many parks of the day, when spacious outfields and long fences dominated stadium construction. At 410 feet in center, 337 in left, and a 266-foot short field in right, the park was perhaps ideally suited for left-handed batters. But in the 1930s, larger outfields remained the norm. The dimensions were ideal for hitting, and the stadium's other appointments ensured that it was ideal for spectators, as well. It sat 3,500 people and was often compared to the best white minor league fields of the day.[33] There was no artificial lighting, but for rare night games, the Monarchs also had access to Forsythe Park, home of the white Monroe Twins, members of the 1932 Cotton States League. Four days prior to the 1930 amusement park drowning, the white minor league park had added lights for the first night baseball game in Monroe.[34]

Nighttime sports made an even more dramatic debut in Louisiana a year later in 1931, when on October 3, the LSU Tiger football team played its first game under artificial lights in Tiger Stadium. Thomas Pinckney "Skipper" Heard, a graduate athletic manager and eventual athletic director, first introduced the idea, arguing that night games in Louisiana were only logical. They allowed fans and players to avoid the state's notorious heat and humidity, and they gave working people a better chance to attend games. LSU's football attendance immediately rose.[35]

Stovall never incorporated his team, choosing instead to govern the Monarchs through either his drilling or supply companies. Stovall's records no longer survive, but it is likely that he administered his club through the Stovall Drilling Company. It was his first and largest company, the seedbed for all of his other endeavors. Also, he had no equal partners in the Drilling Company, as he did for J.M. Supply and other ventures. Finally, before Stovall built Casino Park, he officially purchased the land from J.M. Supply, rather than building on company-owned land.[36]

Jean Stovall Lee, Stovall's granddaughter, explained, "He did employ some of [the players], you know, so they could afford to make a living besides just playing baseball."[37] Stovall provided a home for the team on nearby Magnolia Street, a sort of dormitory complete with a cook and house manager. His devotion (or, perhaps, obsession) to his team led him to begin 1932 by purchasing three new Fords for its travel. The cars, however, served as more than simple transportation. "They wouldn't rent us a room at most places," recalled the Monarchs' second baseman Augustus Saunders, "and sometimes we'd just end up sleeping in the car." Such were the vagaries of playing black baseball in the Jim Crow South. In 1992 Saunders revealed that the second baseman received a five-month contract worth $125 per month. Though he never mentioned any other team payments, Saunders portrayed his salary as typical for Stovall's players, but higher than other teams with whom he was familiar. Marlin Carter, briefly a Monarch third baseman in 1932, told *Black Ball News* in a 1993 interview, "Fred Stovall was a very wealthy man. . . . Most importantly, we always got paid." This in a year when black baseball salaries dropped to all-time lows, and some players were not even receiving their paychecks. Many teams just gave players 70 to 75 percent of the gate earnings for the day, allowing them to divide the money. Monroe, by comparison, was a success story.[38]

John L. Clark, syndicated columnist and beat writer for the Pittsburgh Crawfords, gave perhaps the most laudatory of evaluations of the Monarchs' owner. "Although Southern born and bred he shows none of the prejudiced qualities which are usually attached to Southern white men," Clark reported. "To know Fred Stovall makes one forget that one is in the South."[39] Augustus Saunders described a game in which the white seats had not filled and black fans were still hoping to enter the park: "Mr. Stovall came out there and stopped the music and everything. He said, 'God made all of us—why have that rope? Take that rope down and everyone come on and take these seats.' We filled it up after they took the ropes down. Blacks and whites began to sit together."[40]

So water wasn't the only phenomenon that brought the races together in the tense climate of Monroe. Through depression, flood, and controversy of all kinds, there would always be baseball. And Stovall was determined to take advantage of it. He had big plans for his team in 1932, but the flood would prove to be only one of the obstacles in his way.

1. A major flood in January and February 1932 threatened to wash away Monroe's promise as a budding city that would continue to grow in the years to come. Yet, even such vagaries of the weather and the cloister of racism didn't hold it back. Courtesy of the University of Louisiana at Monroe Special Collections.

2. The city was built on the banks of the Ouachita River, making it a business and farming hub for the region. Courtesy of the University of Louisiana at Monroe Special Collections.

3. Desiard Street ran through Monroe's downtown, seen here, but as it continued farther north, it also became the backbone of the "Booker T. Washington" district of the town, eventually running behind the left field fence of Casino Park just outside the city limits. Courtesy of the Ouachita Parish Public Library Special Collections.

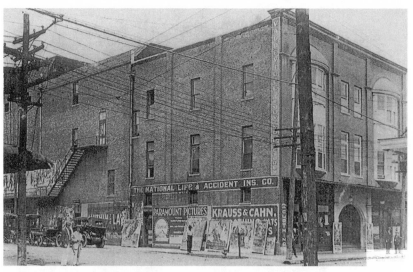

4. The Paramount Theatre was the hub of non-sports-related entertainment in Monroe. By the 1930s, the segregated complex took over the role from the also-segregated Lyceum Theatre that dominated from 1910 to 1920, and then declined in the following decade. Courtesy of the Ouachita Parish Public Library Special Collections.

5. Downtown Monroe sought to sell itself as a burgeoning metropolis in northeast Louisiana, making it uncharacteristically willing to celebrate the Monroe Monarchs as a national phenomenon. Courtesy of the University of Louisiana at Monroe Special Collections.

6. Monroe Colored High School was the sole source of secondary education for black teens in Monroe. The school's football team played its games in Casino Park after the baseball season concluded. Courtesy of the Ouachita Parish Public Library Special Collections.

7. The devastating winter flood of 1932 affected baseball throughout the region. The ballpark in nearby Brownville saw significant damage as floodwaters overtook it. Courtesy of the University of Louisiana at Monroe Special Collections.

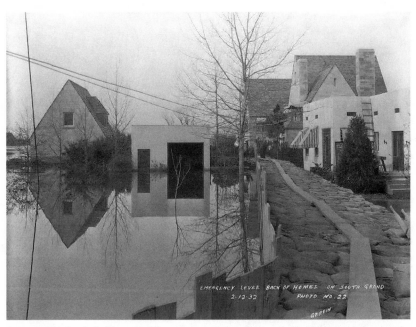

8. During the flood of 1932, artificial emergency sandbag levees protected the homes closest to the river, which also happened to be the homes of the most affluent citizens of Monroe. Courtesy of the University of Louisiana at Monroe Special Collections.

9. Proximity to the river, however, wasn't the only condition that portended danger during a 1932 flood that enveloped the city to its edges. Courtesy of the University of Louisiana at Monroe Special Collections.

Fred A. Stovall

10. Fred Stovall began as a Texas oilman, but his time in Louisiana made him a fixture of the city. The wealthy entrepreneur would found the Monroe Monarchs as a club team for his other businesses, but would soon develop it into a legitimate professional force. Courtesy of the University of Louisiana at Monroe Special Collections.

11. Stovall, with his wife and children, displays his car on the outskirts of Monroe. Courtesy of the University of Louisiana at Monroe Special Collections.

12. In 1932, the Zion Traveler Baptist Church would become the most important story in black Monroe after the Monarchs. The turmoil over a supposed pastorship led to a violent confrontation before baseball season's end. Courtesy of Katherine Winsett.

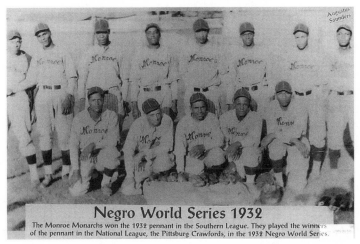

Augustus
Saunders

Negro World Series 1932
The Monroe Monarchs won the 1932 pennant in the Southern League. They played the winners of the pennant in the National League, the Pittsburg Crawfords, in the 1932 Negro World Series.

13. The Monroe Monarchs were the pride of the city, black and (eventually) white, in 1932. Still, after their success that year, the tenuous status of being black in Monroe allowed mainstream whites to let the memory of the team fade. For example, the Monarchs didn't technically win a Southern League pennant in 1932, and the Pittsburgh Crawfords didn't win a pennant in the National League, because there was no National League in 1932. Courtesy of the Ouachita Parish Public Library Special Collections.

14. William A. "Gus" Greenlee owned the Pittsburgh Crawfords. In 1932, one of the worst financial years in American history, he assembled a veritable all-star team of baseball talent and built the premier black baseball park in the country, Greenlee Field. Courtesy of Carnegie Library of Pittsburgh.

15. Cumberland Posey, Greenlee's Pittsburgh rival and owner of the Homestead Grays, founded the East–West Colored League as a replacement for the defunct National League in 1932. Unlike the Negro Southern League, however, Posey's group would collapse before the season's first half came to a close. Courtesy of Carnegie Library of Pittsburgh.

16. Robert A. Cole was a new baseball team owner in 1932, taking over the Chicago American Giants, renovating the team's park, and maneuvering his team into the Negro Southern League. His relationship with Greenlee, Nashville Elite Giants owner Thomas Wilson, and 1932 Negro Southern League president Reuben Jackson would help shape the new Negro National League in 1933. Courtesy of Robert A. Cole Jr. and Robert E. Weems Jr.

17. Thomas Wilson owned the Southern League's Nashville Elite Giants. Along with his business partner Reuben Jackson, he helped organize the group's one major league season. The principal instigator of Southern League opposition to Monroe's entry, Wilson would conspire with Jackson and Cole to steal a pennant from the Monarchs. Courtesy of Larry Lester and NoirTech Research, Inc.

Ever Ready Filling Station on Bass Street and Ridley Boulevard

18. Reuben Bartholomew Jackson, seen here with one of his business partners, H. C. Floyd, in an advertisement for a local Nashville gas station, served as president of the Negro Southern League in 1932. At season's end, he would combine with Tom Wilson, another of his business partners, to also found the Negro Southern Football League.

Office Hours: 11 a. m. to 1:30 p. m,
5:30 p. m. to 7:30 p. m.
Phones—Office: 7-7711. Res, 6-0328
If no answer call 3-0018

Dr. R. B. Jackson

Physician and Surgeon

Medical Examiner Nashville Colored City
Schools
Office 1123 1-2 Cedar Street
Up Stairs

19. Though Reuben Jackson was involved in various businesses, many of them centering on black southern sports, he was a physician by trade, simultaneously serving as medical examiner for black primary and secondary schools in Nashville, as demonstrated by this advertisement for his services.

20. The 1932 Pittsburgh Crawfords, seen here during spring training at Hot Springs, Arkansas, were one of the best baseball teams ever assembled. Among its stars were Ted Page, Jud Wilson, Josh Gibson, Judy Johnson, Oscar Charleston, Sam Streeter, Ted Radcliffe, and Satchel Paige. At the time of this photo, Radcliffe had yet to join the team, and Gibson, seen out of uniform, was nursing an injury. Courtesy of National Baseball Hall of Fame Library, Cooperstown, New York.

21. In the years that followed the Monarchs' success, various incarnations of white Monroe minor league squads would call Casino Park home. Here, the 1938 Monroe White Sox pose in front of Casino's outfield fence. Courtesy of the Ouachita Parish Public Library Special Collections.

22. Today, houses stand on part of the original Casino Park land. Courtesy of Thomas Aiello.

23. The rest of the land remains undeveloped. Courtesy of Thomas Aiello.

4
The Monarchs and the Major Leagues
The State of Black Baseball in 1932

"With the primary election over and spring making its appearance, all eyes are now turning toward America's greatest pastime, baseball," declared a 1932 Chicago American Giants press release. "There is no 'depression' on when a baseball fan desires to see a good team play."[1]

Dick Lundy, manager of the Baltimore Black Sox and columnist for the Baltimore *Afro-American,* appeared similarly optimistic. "In former years," he wrote, "there have been attempts by outlaw club owners to fight organized baseball, but the fans have become more and more conscious each year that only through organization can the proper competitive spirit and interest be injected into the game."[2]

Fred Stovall believed in organization, too, and he wanted to be part of a new league in 1932. His Monarchs had won the championship of the 1931 Texas–Louisiana League. But that league organization was not headquartered in Monroe, nor was it a "major" league, and the success of his team the previous year led the owner to make an attempt for one or the other. It seemed initially that creating a league headquartered in Monroe would be the most feasible endeavor. The presence of any major league, in fact, appeared tenuous at best.

His first move of the 1931–1932 intercession was to hire business manager H. D. "Doug" English from the Shreveport Sports, a fellow Texas-Louisiana League team the previous season, to administer both the team and a possible league. It didn't take long for the new officer to develop a heady reputation. "This young, modest gentleman just about carries Monroe in the palm of his hand when it comes to publicity," wrote John L. Clark. "He has the full cooperation of the white dailies, public utilities and radio. He has three periods on the air, croons and plays requested numbers and makes his own announcements. He is more responsible than any other single individual for the reputation which

Monroe has as a baseball town." The *Shreveport Sun*'s Pitman Nedde called English a "young brainy skipper, full o' pep and rarin' to go," who "will try by the hardest to put over a winner for the boys this season. Your scribe is well acquainted with this bird, 'Doug' English; he knows his onions when it comes to putting pep into a team, together with the gag he carries on with at a piano. English tried hard to put the Black Sports on the map here, last season; he is a fellow who seemingly never tires of keeping up and at 'em."[3] The hire appeared wise.

Stovall then called a meeting of potential owners in Monroe, with representatives from New Orleans, Baton Rouge, Shreveport, and Alexandria from Louisiana; Little Rock, Hot Springs, Pine Bluff, and El Dorado from Arkansas; and Vicksburg, Natchez, and Jackson from Mississippi. The Tri-State League, as the aggregation would be called, met on January 22 with floodwaters rising around them. "There seem[s] to be a change coming up the road," wrote Nedde, "but don't get glad too quick—it's a little too early." He was, at best, cautiously optimistic. The idea of the Tri-State League appeared to be the perfect remedy for depression-ridden north Louisiana, but the effort of Monroe officials seemed almost too good to be true.[4]

Those early meetings didn't ease Nedde's skepticism. Though the Monarch delegation was "courteous in inviting other towns of Louisiana to join this league, there is evidently no chance for another Louisiana team to be able to join a baseball league," reported Nedde. Shreveport's potential Tri-State entry, the Shreveport Black Sports, was led at first by Charlie Jones, a Shreveport native who Nedde touted as having starred with the Homestead Grays, Hilldale Daisies, and Kansas City Monarchs. By the end of January, the Sports planned on being part of the new league.[5]

From that first short meeting came the possibility of recruiting the much more prominent Memphis Red Sox for the new league. "Memphis," reported the *Kansas City Call,* "would find this a better territory and more profitable than the Southern League." And the Tri-State would certainly find itself more profitable with Memphis as a member. With a power vacuum at the top of the black baseball world, the lowly new outfit began setting its sights even higher. The Kansas City Monarchs, Cuban Stars, Pittsburgh Crawfords, Indianapolis ABCs, and Chicago American Giants—all large-market franchises—were considered potential associate members (a sort of honorific that would ensure the teams barnstormed through the new circuit). Monroe, New Orleans, Little Rock, and Jackson, known as the "Big Four," formed the nucleus of the potential league, and each team chose a representative to scout the region surrounding its respective home cities and to investigate the conditions of other applicant towns. But the originally invited smaller-market teams fell to the monetary guarantee and the franchise purchase requirement, leaving only the larger-area cities. Those payments would be made at a two-day meeting in Monroe in early February, to determine the final four members of the new endeavor. Tri-State officials expected delegations from Shreveport, Baton Rouge, Alexandria, and Hammond in Louisiana; Hope, El Dorado, Hot Springs, and Pine Bluff in Arkansas; and Vicksburg in Mississippi. They held out hope for the appearance of Memphis Red Sox officials, as well.[6]

But two weeks later, no news from the meeting had reached the two principal Louisiana black newspapers. Nedde and the *Shreveport Sun* seemed content. The sports editor's familiarity with Doug English, combined with the uncertain status of the Shreveport Sports' application to the league, kept angry editorials from the sports page. The New Orleans–based *Louisiana Weekly,* however, was overtly suspicious of the Monroe dealings. Neither the paper nor Peter Robertson, owner of the New Orleans Black Pelicans (supposed member of the Tri-State League) had made contact with English, nor with anyone else in the Monroe organization.[7]

This wasn't exactly rare. Leagues and teams had a reciprocal relationship with the black press, as Jules Tygiel has noted, and each helped create the success of the other. Baseball provided fodder for the sports pages of the weeklies, which in turn provided the publicity that teams needed to remain relevant in the community. The black papers often did not send beat writers to cover teams, relying instead on the clubs themselves to submit their own statistics and scores. A *Louisiana Weekly* notice urged its contributors who submitted articles about upcoming games to note that such submissions "come under the head of advertisement and must be paid for as such." Only reports of games already played would be printed free of charge. "Write the articles in a legible hand and get them into the 'Den' before 7 o'clock Tuesday evening."[8]

This was an obviously unreliable practice, but necessary for papers that couldn't afford a pool of beat writers. And it certainly did not mean that the black press was a passive medium of sports promoters and booking agents. A frustrated Earl Wright, writing for the *Louisiana Weekly* during football season, explained the fine line reporters walked with their subjects. "Frequently our duty calls us to criticize folk, oftimes they are our friends. When the story breaks, that friend, unless he can 'take it' is lost to us."[9]

And there in the spring of 1932, the *Louisiana Weekly* did its duty. "Since that last session," the paper reported, describing New Orleans's frustration with Monroe, "Robertson has sent letters by special delivery and long distance messages but at this writing has not received a reply." The *Weekly* described the Pelicans' owner as anxious and dubious. "So Pete's theme song these days runs something like, 'Oh, Gee, How I'd Love One Sweet, Sweet Letter From You!' and it is pointed at English up in Monroe." English's silence, however, was not the result of incompetence. His February was consumed with an effort to achieve Stovall's other, more far-reaching goal for his Monarchs—membership in a "major" league.[10]

On January 23, still unsure of the National League's fate, the Negro Southern League met in Birmingham, including representatives from Atlanta, Birmingham, Memphis, Montgomery, Little Rock, and Nashville. At the meeting, league president Reuben Jackson spoke of the need for a moral center in baseball. He argued that capable student athletes should be allowed to play professional baseball, which would, among other things, help lower the average player salary. He noted the exigencies of the Depression and the resulting requirement that the NSL improve its product to remain solvent. The need for greater attendance loomed over the meeting as the most dire of requirements. Thomas Wilson, owner of the Nashville Elite Giants, followed him with another speech on the history of baseball and the prospects for the season. Jackson and league officials hoped for either eight or twelve teams to form the league, depending on viable membership applications. The group made an official declaration of congratulations to the new league forming in Monroe, and offered an invitation to a Tri-State League representative for the NSL's next meeting.[11]

"Baseball in the South is once more on the upward climb," announced William J. Moore, sports editor of the *Birmingham Reporter,* "if the echoes from the recent meeting at Birmingham mean anything. The final touch will be added on [February] 24th when the members of the league get together at Nashville." At that next meeting, concessions were made to allow NSL teams to play larger independent clubs such as the Cuban Stars and House of David. Keeping with Jackson and Wilson's insistence on the necessity of greater attendance, the league courted the large-market but decidedly non-southern Pittsburgh Crawfords, Indianapolis ABCs, and Chicago American Giants, under the new ownership of Robert Cole. Chicago, it was hoped, would be the league's cash cow.[12]

English attended the Nashville meeting along with the large-market teams, but he wasn't acting solely as a representative of the Tri-State League. At the conclusion of league business, the Monarchs' business manager was able to report that he had successfully lobbied for Monroe's inclusion in the NSL (his charisma apparently not limited to local radio). He even managed to win the position of league statistician.[13]

This was a coup of the highest order. The action understandably destroyed the possibility of the Tri-State League, but reaction from the Louisiana black weeklies was begrudgingly congratulatory rather than overly critical. "You can't blame 'em for jumping," wrote *Louisiana Weekly* sports editor Earl M. Wright. "Nevertheless the other clubs that had contemplated joining the proposed league are in a very uncomfortable position." The teams who did contribute and sincerely planned on participating were left out in the cold. Most, however, had not paid, giving them no real claim on league membership in the first place. "If [proposed teams] couldn't or wouldn't come up with the cash demands, then who can blame the Monarchs? No one with brains and an idea towards fairness."[14]

In his column in the *Shreveport Sun*, Pitman Nedde, never very confident in the ability of other Louisiana towns (including his own) to produce consistent baseball organizations, described Monroe's jump to the Southern as a "brave move," a shrewd reaction to the lethargy of local teams. "It's a wise step in the management of the Monroe Monarchs, who seemingly knows how to maneuver out of an approaching baseball upset." Nedde's pessimism about his own town proved prophetic. In early May, in north Louisiana's other corner, Shreveport's Biedenharn Park—home of the Shreveport Sports, but also the part-time home of the city's Black Sports—burned to the ground. "Excepting Monroe," wrote Nedde, "we're sunk for organized baseball here."[15]

When English returned from Nashville, he held an informal press conference along with Frank Johnson, the team's manager. He proudly announced that the Monarchs, along with teams like Chicago, had joined the Negro Southern League. Exhibition tours of all the top teams would make stops in Monroe, and this year the Monarchs would put up an even greater fight. All but three of the players had signed contracts, and those would surely sign in the coming days. Johnson noted that spring training would begin March 5. It did, and the team went through its paces daily throughout the month.[16]

Early in March, the Louisville Black Caps hosted the next meeting of the Negro Southern League. William Scott, John Dixon, and Moses Jackson of the Black Caps presided over a series of substantive meetings where league schedules were reorganized and prepared for publication. Salary caps, team rules, and umpiring policies were put in place. A silver baseball trophy would be given to the team with the highest opening day attendance. April 22 would open the season, and July 4 would close the first half. The group also reelected Reuben Jackson to the league presidency, and named Robert Cole, new owner of the Chicago American Giants, vice president; Thomas T. Wilson, owner of the Nashville Elite Giants, treasurer; and Birmingham's L. S. N. Cobb secretary.[17]

Upon the release of the Southern League schedule, syndicated columnist Fay Young criticized the new Southern League schedule as the "same old 'song and dance' that the baseball fans of this country have had to stand for during the history of Negro baseball leagues in the west and south." He noted that Chicago would leave home only twice during the first half, and those trips were to nearby Indianapolis and Louisville. The deck, it seemed, was stacked in their favor, giving the Giants a competitive advantage over other teams in the league. "We know that Chicago or any other club north will fight going south to Birmingham or Atlanta twice during the playing season." Young cited the high price of rail and bus fare, as well as poor attendance in southern parks. Of course, Giants attendance was also drastically low. "The better class of Negroes long ago deserted the Giants' park for the major league parks. The regular Giants' fan, with his pay cut, came out as long as he could and then had to stop." There were other things in the early 1930s demanding of one's meager paycheck. "With Chicago hard hit by the depression, the road will be rocky for any new owner," Young observed. "The Southern league will have to alter its schedule before the season is two months old."[18]

Jackson remained undaunted. On March 31, he announced that the league had adopted an official ball—the Worth ball—that would have the president's name on it. It would be required for official league games. He named some new managers of new teams in the league, such as John Dixon and his Louisville Black Caps, S. M. Terrell and the Cleveland Cubs, and Jim Taylor and the Indianapolis ABCs. But he saved his greatest praise for Chicago. "Everybody in the baseball category is predicting that David Malarcher will revive the old fire with Robert A. Cole's Chicago American Giants."[19]

The American Giants were a more logical choice for the Southern League than might initially be assumed. Historian Jerry Malloy attributes much of the team's popularity to southern support. Its winter headquarters were in Palm Beach, Florida, which it used as a home base while barnstorming through the South. Southerners also had access to the *Chicago Defender* through a makeshift pipeline established by black porters of the Illinois Central Railroad.[20]

But in 1932, Chicago's championships of the mid-1920s were distant memories, and the team's return was far from assured in the months leading up to its affiliation with the Southern League. "The baseball situation in Chicago— if there be such," wrote *Chicago Defender* editor Al Monroe, "is beginning to worry a number of folks." As of late January, the city assumed that its team would be a new outfit led by Kansas City Monarchs owner J. L. Wilkinson. But negotiations for the use of the original American Giants' Schorling's Park faltered. Sports promoter Abe Saperstein then made his bid, hoping to use the name

"American Giants" for a new team. He did just that in the year's early months, barnstorming throughout the South (see chapter 5), but his team would eventually move to Cleveland. Chicago again revived its hopes in early February, when baseball men in Cleveland, Cincinnati, Louisville, Indianapolis, Chicago, Dayton, Toledo, and Detroit entered discussions to begin a Midwest baseball league. This effort too came to naught.[21]

Finally, on February 15, Robert A. Cole announced his purchase of the American Giants franchise—at a cost of roughly $25,000—complete with manager Dave Malarcher, leader of the famed Chicago teams of the mid-1920s. "We want the best team Malarcher can assemble," Cole announced, "or else we'll stay out of baseball until we get what we want." The following week he announced plans to completely renovate Schorling's Park on Chicago's south side and to purchase some of the best national talent available. "We may not get them all," he said, "but we intend signing all the good ones we can arrange for."[22] Cole, the owner of Chicago's Metropolitan Funeral System, did have the experience to justify such confidence. He had been involved in basketball promotion in the city, and had worked with Clifford O. Starks to bring the Tuskegee-Wilberforce football game to Chicago in 1931.[23]

The new owner renovated the American Giants' Park at Thirty-ninth and Wentworth, and the updated field was ready for the team's April 23 opener against the Indianapolis ABCs. Cole poured thousands into the newly named Cole Field, improving the grandstand seats and dugouts, installing a loudspeaker, and adding a new façade to the structure. He also hired Horace Hall, a former college football promoter, as his business manager.[24]

"It is the intention of the management," said Cole, "not only to give Chicago the very best team possible but also to give the fans a real park. To this end we have been striving during the off months and we believe that they will be satisfied."[25] Cole had taken over the team in late February. Only two weeks later he was named vice president of the Southern League. Though the media put pressure on the new owner to purchase players from Kansas City and St. Louis, he instead spent his money on Chicago players, reasoning that people would be more prone to spend their meager funds on a hometown team composed of hometown boys. He had, to the relief of Al Monroe and the *Chicago Defender,* "come out of the wilderness" to "take the place vacated by the great Rube Foster years ago."[26]

Cumberland Posey, owner of Pittsburgh's Homestead Grays, was skeptical of, if not bitter about, Chicago's inclusion in the Southern League. "Kipling sang about East is East and West is West and never the twain shall meet. Well, mebbeso, but the South and the North have come together in a baseball way." He argued that the Southern's move beyond the South infringed upon his own interests. And Posey's interest was the East–West Negro Baseball League, which he founded.[27]

The death of the National League in March 1932 left room for more than one major circuit that year, and most of the big-league teams in the north chose to take part in Posey's East–West League. But unlike the Southern, which was a traditionally minor league receiving a bump in its usual status, the East–West was attempting to pull a phoenix from the ash of the National—selectively choosing former National League teams to create a new organization. Posey's heavy hand and consistently questioned ethics made the attempt controversial and unstable. That controversy and instability would eventually spill over into the Southern League and would ultimately sway the course of its development.

But that was yet to come. Posey held the first meeting of his East–West League in Cleveland in late January. Representatives of Detroit, Cleveland, Pittsburgh, Baltimore, Newark, Hilldale, and New York appeared, as did Syd Pollock, owner of the Cuban House of David. Kansas City was expected, but when the team's possible move to Chicago was cancelled, its interest in the new league diminished.[28]

One of the new features Posey's East–West League planned to introduce was daily baseball. Traditionally, black teams played league games only on weekends because low wages and long hours for the majority of the black population made weekends the only time Negro League games could draw Negro League fans. In the early 1930s, some leagues played Sunday doubleheaders; others did not. Soon, Sunday baseball would become commonplace, but 1932 was still a year of transition. African American clubs were far more likely to play on Sunday—not because of a lack of religious devotion (bans on Sunday baseball were essentially part of city blue laws for most white minor league teams) but because their clientele was more likely to be available on Sunday. *Shreveport Sun* sports editor Pitman Nedde admired the boldness of Posey's decision, but doubted its efficacy. "Even in former days when baseball in Negro sports was at its highest heights," he wrote, "every day baseball did not pay. Of course a great more attended games [than] do now."[29]

After the meeting, Posey defended his league, anticipating the criticism that his reputation was sure to cause. "There will be many players and players' friends who will look upon this organization as a plan to band owners together to cut players' salaries. This would have been necessary, league or no league, and few teams would have attempted to operate on a salary basis without a league." Posey was probably right, but other criticisms loomed larger. Structural flaws were built into the East–West League policy that conspired to hurt teams' bottom lines. "The most drastic action taken was the agreement that no league team can play any club within 20 miles of the city wherein a league club is located." Designed to counter unscrupulous booking agents who charged high commissions for inferior competition, it actually precluded many teams from scheduling extra games and gave them an incentive to pull out of the league at the first sign of financial loss.[30]

Crawfords press agent John L. Clark argued that Posey's East–West League was designed specifically to harm the Crawfords and the New York Black Yankees. The Crawfords played without an official league affiliation in 1932. Posey wouldn't let them join the East–West, and though the Crawfords would maintain an association with the Southern, they would never officially join. Posey, argued Clark, created the East–West specifically to give his team a competitive leg up against its crosstown rival. It was, Clark claimed, intended to hold a monopoly on talent, keeping players from joining other teams in the East, Midwest, and South. Meanwhile, the Crawfords would face the best southern competition available after being shut out of Posey's group. But Clark assumed they would only be the better for it. "Negroes are no different from any other race, and usually take the path of least resistance. Southern attractions have an almost religious appeal to Southern people. And there is no argument against the fact that Crawfords Park is set up in the midst of Southern Patrons."[31]

Clark was clearly an advocate for the Crawfords, but he had a point. Posey understood the threat posed by the Crawfords and the money that owner Gus Greenlee used to entice players from the rival Homestead Grays. "It seems," wrote *New York Age* columnist Lewis E. Dial, "as though Pittsburgh baseball fans are in for a feud."[32]

Although *Courier* columnist Rollo Wilson saw plenty to criticize in Posey's league, he claimed that Clark's criticism was personal.[33] He argued that the West Penn Service—the news wire for western Pennsylvania that served essentially as the *Pittsburgh Courier*'s syndication agent—"seems to have been created to give publicity to attacks on Cum Posey." Wilson quoted Clark's claim that "the Soviet plan of control is about to be undertaken by Posey and Company," letting the statement stand without comment as a testament to its own hyperbole. The East–West, however, did not escape his criticism either. He, too, questioned the twenty-mile rule, as well as the efficacy of allowing Pollock's Cubans into the league. The Cubans were nominally based in Tarrytown, New York, but had no home park there. They were a barnstorming team, and a fair schedule would be impossible to make when one team played all of its games on the road.[34]

The absence of the Crawfords in the East–West led owner Gus Greenlee to publish a rejoinder to those who argued that he was avoiding participation in the league. "First of all, Posey wanted me to sign a five year contract with the league," he wrote. "In this contract he or his brother was to manage the Craw-fords." Posey courted the team because public relations deemed it necessary. "You probably know that Posey's interest in a league came after the Crawfords had their first successful playing season."[35]

That it did. William A. "Gus" Greenlee served in Europe during World War I before returning to his native North Carolina. In 1919, he moved to Pittsburgh, where he began a numbers racket. He also became a bootlegger and liquor thief. But he maintained a relatively respectable community presence for someone in his line of work, and in 1925, he used a growing fortune to purchase the Craw-ford Grille, which historian Jim Bankes has described as "Pittsburgh's version of Harlem's Cotton Club." The Grille also served as headquarters for Greenlee's numbers-running operation, headed by Teddy Horne.[36]

Greenlee maintained his reputation through supporting local baseball. In 1930, he began financing the semiprofessional Crawford Colored Giants. Formed in 1925 as a Playground League team sponsored by the Pittsburgh Press, the Col-ored Giants represented the city's Crawford Recreation Center. Owners, how-ever, had bigger plans for their team, and in 1930 they convinced Greenlee to back the club. The following season, Greenlee used his fortune to build the team into a black baseball powerhouse. He began buying players—his first major ac-quisition was Satchel Paige in late 1931—and started construction on a new sta-dium, Greenlee Field, which sat 7,500 people. He also developed a black base-ball organization, and his first employee was John L. Clark, who served as team publicist and secretary. Clark was a newsman who had often used his column in the *Pittsburgh American* to denounce numbers men like Greenlee. He had also helped found the team Greenlee ultimately took over. Still, after Greenlee hired him, Clark became a tireless champion of the Crawfords organization. The two established the West Penn Service to disseminate Clark's columns to black news-papers across the country. (And so, in a way, Rollo Wilson had been right. The West Penn Service had been created for publicity, some of it designed to attack Cum Posey.)[37]

Clark noted that Pittsburgh's Forbes Field charged Negro teams 30 percent of the gross as rent. The Crawfords' new stadium, Greenlee Field, would charge less, facilitating easier access to baseball venues and making Homestead's cross-town rival seem like a must for any league including western Pennsylvania in its circuit and hoping to sustain itself for a season. That being the case, Clark's Pittsburgh colleague Sellers McKee Hall also questioned the Crawfords' absence from Posey's new group. They were, by Hall's reckoning, the best Negro team, "and it behooves the League to be friendly with the Pittsburgh Crawfords and get all the money that it is possible to get, if the League is desirous of running a full season." If the league was a vehicle for profit, then excluding Pittsburgh seemed self-destructive. "Any Dummy knows that to play the Crawfords this season means many thousands of extra dollars in their coffers in spite of the financial depression."[38]

And so the Crawfords, shunned in the Northeast, instead attended the meetings of what would become the other major league—the Southern League—and accepted associate membership to bring in new teams to Pittsburgh and to widen the team's base of possible opponents. The inclusion of Indianapolis and Chicago in the new league only bolstered its reputation and made even a minimal relationship with the Southern attractive to Greenlee's squad.[39]

Meanwhile, the East–West's next meeting took place—minus the Crawfords—at the Christian Street YMCA in Philadelphia in February. Teams would be required to pay a $1,000 deposit. A radio contract was pending. Officials decided on salaried umpires compensated by the league, but the race of those umpires was yet to be settled.[40]

Black baseball teams traditionally employed their own umpires, creating a situation in which most officials were connected to certain ballparks. Many of them were white, and there were some clear advantages to using white umpires. They gave games more legitimacy with white fans. They made games with white clubs easier to schedule. But, the counterargument went, they took potential jobs from older or injured black players, the most likely black candidates to enter the umpiring field. Besides, black fans didn't need white umpires to find legitimacy in Negro League games. As the Crawfords prepared for the season, they announced that they would use black umpires when possible, and that "at least one colored umpire will be on duty at Greenlee Park for all home games. If no serious objections are raised, they might employ two." The team also announced its interest in using "race umpires" for road games. "There will be ample work for race umpires," the team announced. "The Crawfords will see to that."[41]

Cumberland Posey, in his "Pointed Paragraphs" column for the *Pittsburgh Courier,* considered the issue of black umpires at length. "We have dumb, square umpires among the white umpires; we have dumb, square umpires among the colored umpires. We have out and out 'homers' among both races. We have mediocre umpires in both races." More than anything else, Posey was generally against umpires of all colors, but he did clearly see black umpires as more problematic than whites. Their calls were worse, but much of that lack of success was caused by in-stadium conditions. Players and fans were far more likely to virulently argue with umpires who looked like them. Black umpires were less intimidating, and most fans shared this opinion. Posey's article, in fact, came at the prompting of a letter from a fan concerned about the phenomenon. "Until the year 1929," wrote Posey, "the writer was very much biased against colored umpires. The year 1932 finds the writer very much in favor of colored umpires." The tide, it seemed, was turning. Players and fans were more and more willing to hate any umpire, regardless of color.[42]

Pennsylvania sportswriter Lloyd P. Thompson also voiced an opinion on the "umpire problem," arguing that integrated crews would suit the East–West. "Many white umpires who have been out in class A and B leagues have been teamed with colored umps," wrote Thompson, "and the contact has been mutually helpful and had far-reaching effects." And Thompson proved right. In late March, Bert E. Gholston became the first black umpire to sign a contract with the East–West.[43]

For Dick Lundy, manager of the Baltimore Black Sox and columnist for the *Afro-American,* the question of competency for black umpires was easily solved. It wasn't that "the colored umpires haven't had the ability but because they haven't been in demand and thus felt it unnecessary to study the fine points and rules of the game." Lundy suggested former players begin umpiring. They knew the fine points and probably needed the money.[44]

But the color of East–West umpires was not the league's only problem. Posey's exclusion of Pittsburgh's other team was calculating, rather than corrupt, but rumors of more serious improprieties dogged the East–West from its inception. Rumor had it that Posey, who had already taken the leadership role for the Detroit Wolves' entry to the league, along with that of his own Homestead Grays, was maneuvering to take a controlling interest in the Cleveland team, as well. The charge that Posey was essentially maneuvering a series of puppet regimes for his own benefit would continue through the coming months, as would Posey's covetousness of players on other teams and in other leagues.[45]

"The war cloud," wrote columnist William "Dizzy" Dismukes, "now grows to more ominous proportions." But as the two fronts of Southern and East–West administrations clashed over the league affiliations of Chicago and Pittsburgh, the Monarchs began spring training in relative calm.[46]

5
Spring Training
The Monarchs, the Crawfords, and the Negro Southern League

"Casino Park is the first word of Monroe and the state of Louisiana," reported the *Shreveport Sun*. "People know Monroe mostly by the Monarchs and the Casino Park, as the Monarchs have played the brand of baseball for the past two years that have attracted the attention of the entire baseball world."[1] There were surely other, more sinister things by which black outsiders knew Monroe. But by March, those concerns were temporarily shunted aside. Spring training began on March 5, and the team was preparing to play its brand of baseball. The air was thick with humidity and expectation for its first major league season. But as the Monarchs stood at the precipice of this new experiment, the full roster had yet to be completed.

On the morning of Wednesday, March 23, Stovall purchased "Red" Murray from the New York Black Yankees. After closing the deal, the Monarchs owner wired his new pitcher transportation money.[2] Murray wasn't a perennial all-star, but he was an accomplished left-handed pitcher. This was dealing on the highest national level, surpassing what the Monarchs would have been able to accomplish in previous minor league years, when attendance receipts kept teams such as the Black Yankees, under new ownership in 1932, out of the red.[3]

The day after the Murray purchase, Gus Greenlee's fifteen-member Pittsburgh Crawfords team arrived in Monroe for a two-game exhibition series, the product of Monarchs publicity and the Crawfords' spring training regimen in nearby Hot Springs, Arkansas. Oscar Charleston and Satchel Paige—the biggest draw in black baseball—drew the curiosity of fans black and white. Part of the grandstand was reserved for white patrons, a policy that would remain necessary throughout the season, even after Paige and the Crawfords had moved on. The sense of celebration was palpable, and Stovall ensured that everyone would feel it, hiring both a local jazz orchestra and a jug band to enhance the atmosphere in and around the stadium.[4]

The Crawfords had an up-and-down year in 1931. Pittsburgh handled the Baltimore Black Sox, the Newark Browns, and Indianapolis ABCs. They split, however, with crosstown rival Homestead and fell flat against cross-state rival Hilldale, not winning a game against the Daisies. On January 16, the team mailed its contracts to players for the 1932 season. More players would be acquired, and some would not sign, but the contract news was significant because it signaled that the team's managerial question would soon be answered. Bobby Williams managed the Crawfords of 1931, but though the team was relatively successful, owner Gus Greenlee had decided to make a managerial change. He chose Oscar Charleston.[5]

Charleston began his career with the Indianapolis ABCs and played for a number of other teams before joining Cumberland Posey's Homestead Grays in 1930. He would not be the only player Greenlee acquired from Homestead. In a sign of controversies to come, Grays star Josh Gibson signed a Homestead contract on Monday night, February 1, and the following morning he signed another with the crosstown rival Crawfords. The second was authorized by a notary public. Though the Grays claimed their contract was legitimate, the Crawford contract won out. (Adding to Posey's frustration, Gibson would hit .490 with thirty-one home runs in 1932.) The following day, February 3, Roy Williams, Gibson's friend and Grays teammate, also signed with the Crawfords.[6]

Posey saw the Crawfords machinations as a threat to his own talent pool and to his proposed East–West Negro Baseball League, but Greenlee insisted that he was not trying to sabotage the East–West. He was just trying to build the best team possible. The statement was necessary—an obvious public relations salvo—but with Pittsburgh snubbed for East–West membership and with the traditional domination of Posey's Grays in western Pennsylvania, Greenlee's player acquisitions were either calculated to sap Homestead strength or a happy accident that produced the same result.[7]

Things had gone well for the newly constituted Crawfords at training in Arkansas. The only snag came when Gibson developed acute appendicitis, forcing the slugger to undergo surgery and keeping him out of preseason games. But the appendectomy was a success, and Gibson's prognosis was good. Harry Kincannon arrived with a sore ankle, but recuperated quickly. John L. Clark, traveling with the team, praised not only the mineral water, but also the Woodmen of the Union Hospital and its doctors.[8]

Members of the club took time to hike and climb the surrounding mountains. They visited the city's famous baths. The southerners, Clark noted, "are not burdened with the rush and hustle of the Pittsburgher, yet they seem to get just as far and acquire just as much." He noticed that in Hot Springs, policemen did not constantly patrol the black neighborhoods. "No bluecoat to peep in your window, batter down your door, intercept strangers or introduce you to the Captain because you have a new car or some flashy jewelry," he wrote. "It seems that the layman and professional man have just a little more in common and cooperate in politics as well as in business."[9] The spring appeared promising for the Crawfords, as did their time in the South.

Here again, as in the 1919 newspaper debate over the Bolden murder, Clark was delineating a difference between the racism of the southern town and northern big city. What African Americans in Hot Springs or Monroe lacked in the cosmopolitan benefits of metropolitan life, they gained in a relative lack of institutionalized police brutality. Of course, police mistreatment of the black population was generally not a punishable offense, and quantified records of those instances do not exist. Clearly, however, Clark interpreted some benefit in a southern life that most in black Pittsburgh would have considered themselves lucky to avoid.

The Crawfords, for their part, found plenty of benefit in the southern life once the team reached Monroe for the exhibition games at the end of March. The jazz band would prove necessary for Monarchs fans, as the home crowd witnessed the visiting Crawfords score six runs in the opening inning, all allowed by Monarchs pitcher Barney Morris. Morris was the most familiar player to Monroe fans, a veteran of the team throughout its short history, but this wasn't his day. Another onslaught in the fifth chased Morris from the game, but at that point the contest was out of hand. Crawfords starter Sam Streeter allowed only two Monroe runs before Satchel Paige pitched a cleanup inning. Pittsburgh won 11 to 2.[10]

Monarchs manager Frank Johnson spent his Saturday assuring the media that he would be far more willing to pull a struggling pitcher in future contests. He had used his rookies in the first game, but on Sunday he would put his strongest lineup on the field. Red Murray had arrived from New York and would see playing time if he felt ready. Charleston countered by announcing Paige as his Sunday starter. The *Monroe Morning World* was impressed: he was "said to throw the fastest ball in negro baseball and that should be plenty fast judging by the hurlers who have performed here in the past."[11]

Both bands returned for the Sunday contest, as did the white patrons. And this time a far more satisfying local product took the field. Though Murray proved unready for his first start, the Monarchs won the game 6–3.[12] This was more than mere consolation. A split with the vaunted Crawfords—even an exhibition split—was a minor coup for little Monroe.

Perhaps the Monarchs' most significant competition, however, would drift beyond the bounds of the Southern League schedule—would, in fact, be a team they would never face. Like most black baseball teams of the day, the Monarchs would jockey for publicity with the town's white minor league team, the Monroe Twins, members of the Cotton States League and residents of artificially lit Forsythe Park. The Cotton States was a Class D white minor league encompassing parts of Louisiana, Arkansas, Texas, and Mississippi. It was far from a first-tier league. In the region, the Southern League, the Southeastern League, and the Texas League all garnered better players. The Cotton States had suffered significantly from Depression-affected attendance, as well as the preponderance of nearby greener pastures, and former member Jackson, Mississippi, had already absconded for the Southeastern. "The Cotton States League," reported the *Birmingham Age-Herald*'s James H. Street, "venerable boll weevil loop that is heavy with baseball tradition, may knock off this season because its finances are weak, although the spirit of fans in these parts is willing." But league president Frank A. Scott was confident that 1932 would be a banner year. Southern League president John D. Martin and Texas League president J. Alvin Gardner each promised aid to the struggling Cotton States, as did St. Louis Cardinals president Branch Rickey, Cleveland Indians president Billy Evans, and St. Louis Browns vice president L. C. McEvoy. The more prosperous minor leagues used the Cotton States as a developmental circuit, and did not want their makeshift farm system to disappear. Even with the aid, however, Monroe's prospect for white baseball seemed doubtful.[13]

Across town at Casino Park, the "three times negro world champions"—Rube Foster's American Giants—arrived on Saturday, April 3, for another two-game series. The team's white owner, Abraham Saperstein, accompanied the team and announced to the media that his American Giants had not been better since the days of Rube Foster. They had, in fact, players comparable to Babe Ruth himself, Saperstein crowed. But these were not the American Giants everyone knew, and they had actually never belonged to Rube Foster. Saperstein was a Chicago booking agent and sports promoter, specializing in "clown" teams, such as the Zulu Cannibal Giants. In 1927, in his native Chicago, Saperstein created the Harlem Globetrotters basketball team (using the name "Harlem" to indicate to towns the team would visit that the players were black), and he spent the winter months of early 1932 traveling through northern states with his barnstorming squad, staying principally in Minnesota and South Dakota. He would later return to baseball, serving as president of the Negro Midwestern League and the West Coast Negro Baseball Association. In 1932, his baseball team, like the Harlem Globetrotters, used a misleading name to create a certain perception. Rube Foster's teams had barnstormed through the South during their Florida-based spring training. Using Foster's name would either lead locals to think they were paying to see the Chicago American Giants or a direct descendant of Rube Foster's teams. Neither was the case, but statements declaring that his team would be better than the days of Rube Foster ensured that curious crowds would come to the ballpark. After touring the South and returning to Chicago, manager Jim Brown would take Saperstein's team to Cleveland, forming the Cleveland Cubs and participating as a member of the Negro Southern League. In March, however, the team was in Monroe, and Frank Johnson countered Saperstein's claims with an announcement that Red Murray would make his debut.[14]

And it was an auspicious debut. Murray pitched eight innings, allowing no runs on only two hits. The Monarchs won 7–0.[15] On Monday, the Monarchs managed an 8–5 victory. Whites attended both games in the segregated grandstands.[16]

Meanwhile, the Crawfords barnstormed through the South and West before returning home in early April. They scheduled their first games of the season against the New York Black Yankees on April 29 and 30. The series would also serve to inaugurate the team's new stadium.[17] Greenlee Field, still under construction through February, was on upper Bedford Avenue in the Hill district of Pittsburgh. L. A. Bellinger designed it, the largest such stadium in western Pennsylvania, at the approximate cost of $75,000. He used seventy-five tons of steel, fourteen carloads of cement, and 1,100 lineal feet of steel fencing. It seated 7,500 for baseball and ten thousand for boxing, with plans for eventual expansion more than doubling those figures. The park was surrounded by high red brick, hiding steel supports. Under the stands, large locker rooms that could accommodate a number of teams shared space with equipment storage rooms and the business offices of the Crawfords. It was designed—through every brick, through all the lathe and plaster—to become the new Mecca of black baseball.[18]

Mayor Charles Kline and other notable city officials attended the park's inaugural game, and the *Pittsburgh Courier*'s Robert L. Vann made a dedication speech and threw out the first pitch. An American flag and Crawfords pennant went up in center field, and Gus Greenlee received a standing ovation. The pomp proved unhelpful, however, as the Yankees won the first Greenlee Field game in front of four thousand fans. Though Satchel Paige struck out ten Yankee batters, an RBI single by center fielder Clint Thomas in the top of the ninth gave New York a 1–0 victory. Still, the stadium was ready and so was the hastily constructed team.[19]

Frank Johnson was becoming more and more confident that his squad, too, was ready. But the team's exhibition pitching clearly worried Stovall, particularly in light of his team's participation in a high-caliber league like the Southern. In early April, he purchased Elbert Williams from the Cuban House of David. Williams was a legitimate star. He had come to the Cubans from Detroit, and the Cubans' barnstorming gave the team broad exposure. He was credited with four no-hit games during the 1931 season, one of those coming against the nearby Shreveport Sports. Again Stovall filled his team's need with high-level national dealing. He hadn't done such things before, and he wouldn't in any subsequent season. But this was the majors.[20]

Williams arrived on Friday, April 8, in time to prepare for the Monarchs' final exhibition series against rival Houston. That morning, the Southern Association of the Amateur Athletic Union (AAU) issued a statement supporting the organization's policy of segregation, making headlines in black communities across the country. In a public letter, the secretary-treasurer of the organization declared, "Negroes are not permitted to compete with white men and women in the South." The official explained that "the general attitude in the South, and this does not apply only to the Southern Association, but to all questions wherein negroes are concerned is . . . against competitive athletics of any kind between blacks and whites."[21] The segregation of sports in the South was certainly not news to any of the Monarchs players, but the public nature of the AAU's announcement and its lack of justification for its policy shocked most African Americans, in North and South. News of the statement was almost certainly known in the Monroe clubhouse.

Yet the exhibition series against Houston had high stakes that helped the teams set aside the news from the AAU. The Houston Black Buffaloes had finished a close second to Monroe in the 1931 Texas-Louisiana League pennant race. After the Buffaloes were eliminated from competition, Stovall added insult to injury by purchasing the services of Houston's center fielder, Roy "Red" Parnell, for Stovall's Dixie Championship Series against the Nashville Elite Giants, winners of the Southern League. Parnell was now back with the Buffaloes, managing the team. Exhibition or no, this was a rivalry. The Houston series was just as meaningful to Monroe fans as were those with Pittsburgh and Chicago. This time, half of the grandstand was reserved for whites.[22]

On Saturday, April 9, Johnson announced that he cut the roster to the required fourteen players. Elbert Williams arrived and warmed up, demonstrating he was ready to pitch against Houston. Though two jazz orchestras aided the opening festivities, rain cooled the heated rivalry. Williams allowed only two hits in five innings, and the Monarchs won the weather-shortened game 1–0.[23]

The second game of the series, on Monday, April 11, was Ladies' Day at Casino Park—"the first ladies' day of the year." Women "accompanied by a paid admission" entered for free. The team celebrated with another victory, their fifth of six exhibition games. The Buffaloes' star first baseman, Chuffie Alexander, had no hits in either game. Still, he was clearly a talent, and his play didn't escape Stovall's notice.[24]

The following weekend, the Monarchs continued their home-and-home with the Buffaloes, as Houston, comfortable in its own park, won 4–3. In the second and final game in Texas, Roy Parnell hit three triples en route to a 10–5 Buffaloes victory. But the Monarchs got a glimpse of their future, as the display put on by Parnell encouraged the team to pursue his services for the full season. The team left Houston without him, but with the hope that he would be along soon.[25]

On Wednesday, April 21, Stovall announced that though Houston took the two final exhibition battles, the Monarchs would win the proverbial war. He purchased outfielder/manager (and sometimes pitcher) Roy Parnell and first baseman Chuffie Alexander from the Buffaloes. Hopes were running high in Monroe. As the season was about to begin, Stovall chartered a bus to carry Monarchs fans to Little Rock, where the team would open its season.[26]

6

The First Half

April–July 1932

The Negro Southern League began its regular season on Easter weekend, and with it came a hope that matched the holiday. As children across the country waited impatiently for the Easter Bunny to arrive, Southern League teams reported healthy ticket sales and appeared confident. They were setting out in an economy that had hidden many eggs, but owners were confident they could find them. "Reports from the different camps of the Southern League are that all clubs have just about whipped themselves into shape," reported the *Louisiana Weekly*. "[Monroe] is considered by some of the baseball experts as the dark horse."[1]

Monroe's dark horse season began at Little Rock's Crump Park, where they swept the hometown Greys.[2] The following weekend, the team traveled to Memphis, splitting a four-game series with the Red Sox, and as the road trip came to a close, Monarchs manager Frank Johnson reported to the media that he and management hoped to secure the pitching services of Robert "Black Diamond" Pipkin, then pitching for the New Orleans Black Pelicans. Though the deal fell through, the attempt indicates an early concern about the constitution of the pitching staff. Still, it was impossible to see the road trip as anything but a success, and it was hoped that the home opener would serve to erase any lingering doubts. If all went well, the Monarchs' first Casino Park game would demonstrate little cause for concern.[3]

The league gave official recognition to the team with the largest opening-day attendance, and though Monroe was by far its smallest market, the club announced it would try to win the prize during its first home game on Friday, May 6, against the Cleveland Cubs, a team it had already beaten as the Rube Foster Memorial Giants.[4] League president Reuben Jackson accepted Stovall's invitation to attend, and his presence only added to the gravity that the black Monroe community attached to the afternoon, the weekend, the season. Businesses in the "Booker T. Washington" district of Monroe closed for the day. A parade preceded the 3:30 game, traveling from Monroe Colored High School to the stadium at noon, and, as it ended, the M.M. Club (a group of local Monarchs boosters) received a prize for the most elaborately decorated float.[5] The *Monroe Morning World* reported that two "negro orchestras" marched in the parade, and the Community Glee Club provided further musical accompaniment. Again, a section of seats was reserved for white fans. Grandstand tickets sold for fifty cents, and box seats for seventy-five.[6]

After the parade had passed and the music died down, the Monarchs experienced a comfortable 6 to 0 victory. They won two more games before the final game of the series, the second of a Sunday doubleheader.[7] Barney Morris, the team's principal holdover from years past, pitched seven innings in that final game without allowing a hit. His teammates stole five bases and scored four runs in those seven innings, and when the game stopped for darkness, the Monarchs had the first no-hitter of the brief Negro Southern League season. "Fans in this section of the country are noticing the Monarchs with interest," noted the *Shreveport Sun,* "as they are looking forward to the pennant being won by the famous Louisiana nine."[8]

But as Monroe demonstrated early success, league trouble continued to loom. In late April, just as the season began, pitcher/outfielder Herman "Jabo" Andrews left the Indianapolis ABCs for territory he presumed more hospitable in the East–West League, joining Posey's Homestead Grays. Jim Taylor, manager of the ABCs, filed an official request with the Southern League that Andrews be forced to return. Jackson sent the request, but Posey failed to comply. Posey, in fact, claimed not to know that Andrews had joined his own team.[9] And so, Jackson announced, all games would be cancelled between the East–West and Southern if Andrews was not returned. It was possible that the early-May series between Detroit and Chicago would not take place. The *Defender* described the controversy as "rivaling the one appearing in the days of Andrew Rube Foster. . . . The trouble, similar in every way with the famous skirmish of 10 years ago."[10] The paper was describing the creation of the Eastern Colored League (ECL), an eastern version of Rube Foster's Negro National League, in 1922. ECL members Hilldale, New York, Brooklyn, Atlantic City, and Baltimore posed no geographical threat to Foster's league, but they raided his National League clubs for talent.[11]

Ten years later, Posey adroitly navigated the negotiations that followed. He responded to Jackson's threats by stating that he would return Andrews, but only if the Detroit-Chicago series went through as planned. At the same time, he put pressure on Jackson by finding four former East–West players in the Southern League. The Crawfords' Rap Dixon began the season with Hilldale. Josh Gibson had originally signed a contract with Homestead. (Though Pittsburgh wasn't in the Southern League, it was an associate member.) James "Sandy" Thompson and Walter "Steel Arm" Davis of Chicago were also East–West property, Posey claimed. In an awkward attempt to remedy the situation, Jackson allowed Thompson and Davis to play in the Detroit series, but under different names. (Davis played as "Williams" and Thompson as "Jones.") But after the tedious negotiations had run their course—and with the series in the books—Posey failed to return Andrews to Taylor's ABCs. "Certainly it looks like Cumberland put over a fast one," wrote the *Defender*'s Al Monroe. "It also looks like the war is just around the corner."[12] The season was one short month old, and now it seemed that the intersectional baseball contest between Detroit and Chicago would be the last of its kind.

On May 12, Jackson announced that all games between Southern League and East–West opponents were cancelled. The East–West teams were poaching players from Southern teams (and vice versa, though Jackson never mentioned it). Furthermore, he argued, Posey never returned Andrews to the ABCs. Knowing the heated rivalry between the owners of the Crawfords and Grays, Jackson placed Gus Greenlee in charge of booking games in the East for Southern League teams. The move was a provocation, leading the *Defender* to describe it "as [the] start of war with Posey." Meanwhile, Robert Cole, owner of the American Giants and vice president of the NSL, expressed his intention to stay above the fray unless events called him to participate.[13]

Through the backbiting of league machinations, Monroe continued its season. Before their weekend reunion with Little Rock, however, the Monarchs played a Thursday exhibition game in nearby Rayville against the town's semi-professional Sluggers. This was a minor coup for the small town of Rayville, Louisiana, which usually watched its team play against the inferior competition of other small area squads and industrial teams.[14] But now the big leaguers had come to town, and Frank Johnson assumed the pitching duties for Monroe, with his regular roster behind him. When his team's scoring began to get out of hand, he moved his pitchers to the infield, and his infielders to the outfield. But however merciful the intent, the Monarchs' talent was too great, and the Sluggers ended their day on the losing end of a 27 to 3 score.[15]

Though the Little Rock Greys put up more of a fight, they still fell three straight to Monroe. On Sunday, May 15, however, as the Monarchs won both games of their doubleheader with Little Rock, events at Casino Park proved less than celebratory for all of the day's paying customers. One of them, Ellen Kennedy, shot Alfred Ewell in the chest, wounding—but not killing—her victim. This violence was accompanied by another incident, as Clara Burns "stabbed another woman at the park five times in the shoulders, back and hips." Neither the *News-Star* nor *Morning World* mentioned the acts with coverage of the baseball games, and one is left to wonder whether play was stopped as the wounded were carried away and the women were arrested. Certainly the violence was rare. The Kennedy and Burns incidents were the first bloody events reported from the so-called Negro amusement park since the drowning during its 1930 inception. And though Casino was not immune to Prohibition violations, no more violent crime would be reported from the park during the remainder of the season. The specifics of the crimes committed that day remain unknown, as do the motives of the assailants, but we do know the consequences of the violence. Clara Burns waived arraignment and pled guilty, ultimately serving sixty days in jail. Ellen Kennedy did, too, receiving a six-month sentence.[16]

As the women waited in the parish prison, the Birmingham Black Barons came to Monroe for a three-game series, the first time the Barons ever traveled to Monroe.[17] Monroe would win two of three from Birmingham, but events in the stands again dominated the white dailies' coverage of the series. Prohibition was the law of the land, but a law little followed in rural northeast Louisiana, where the bootlegger or the bathtub provided a cheap, strong homemade product that remained in high demand. The prevalence of alcohol was such that Fred Stovall had to specifically ban it from Casino Park, and he kept watch for those attempting to smuggle it into the grandstand. Catching one such smuggler while the Black Barons were in town, Stovall carried the perpetrator and his two pints of whiskey from Casino to the parish jail. Upon his arrival, however, he dropped one of the confiscated pints. When he bent to pick it up, his prisoner "swung into a long lope that quickly carried him across the vacant lot at the side of the central fire station, up St. John street and finally into the darkness of Grammont." While coverage of the Monarchs' Sunday doubleheader was buried on the sports page below one in a long line of examinations of the intricacies of Monroe's last-place class-D white minor league team, "the story of how a negro 'got a rabbit in his feet' and escaped while en route to jail" was front-page news.[18]

But with the exception of confiscated liquor and interleague controversy, the NSL season seemed to be operating surprisingly well. "Up to this date," announced president Jackson in early June, giving a brief evaluation of the state of the league, there had been few "fines, suspensions, expulsions and disagreements of any sort coming from the president to any of the teams." He expressed optimism but warned that Memphis had been using players under contract to other teams.

Atlanta's Black Crackers had lost all of their games through forfeit because of the team's use of unofficial league balls, and circumstance portended that Atlanta might not be the only league casualty. "Memphis," warned Jackson, "may be dropped from [the] Southern League family."[19]

Memphis's infractions would eventually and disastrously affect Monroe, but that was yet to come. And as the league did its best to police itself, the Monarchs unwittingly took to the road. When they left town on Thursday, May 26, they left as leaders of the Negro Southern League. Their two-week trip would take them to Montgomery and Nashville, before they returned home for a second series with the Montgomery Grey Sox.[20]

While the big-league club was away during the last week of May and the first week of June, another of Stovall's teams, the Monroe Black Drillers, took over Casino Park, playing a Sunday doubleheader with the Rayville Sluggers (still smarting from their 27–3 beating by the Drillers' big-league counterparts). The Drillers and Sluggers played in a minor area circuit that included teams from the Louisiana towns of Bastrop, Farmerville, Ruston, Shreveport, Winnsboro, and Jonesville, as well as Vicksburg, Mississippi. With a diminished talent pool and without a facility like Casino Park, the smaller local teams took every advantage to play profitable games. The Drillers, for example, announced before the Casino doubleheader with Rayville that "Pork Chop" Chapman, an ex-vaudevillian, would play with the team. Rayville countered that it had a comedian of its own. (The clubs split the Sunday games.)[21]

Stovall used the Drillers—the players all employed at his Drilling Company— as a minor league farm team for his Monarchs ("understudies," the *Morning World* called them), but also as a way to keep his park profitable during the Monarchs' more extensive road trips. After defeating the Monroe All-Stars in the outlying suburb of Brownville on Wednesday, the Drillers returned to defeat the Ruston Lincolnites on Friday. They split a Casino Park doubleheader with Shreveport on Sunday. All told, the Drillers played eleven games, winning nine, during the Monarchs' two-week absence.[22]

The crowds were small. Newspapers were sure to mention beforehand that "'Pork Chop' Chapman will be on hand to clown for the folks." But the Drillers remained a viable part of the broader Casino Park–Monarchs organization, bringing paying customers to the ball field and training possible future talent. The team's business manager, shoe repairman Abraham Rothman, announced on Tuesday, May 31, that Mark Smith and Albert Green, two Drillers outfielders, along with a pitcher named Hardy, would be invited to the Monarchs' spring training the following season. He indicated the following week his confidence

that the Drillers would qualify for the Texas–Louisiana League in 1933, playing for the same pennant that the Monarchs took in 1931. As of early June, black
baseball in Monroe seemed without horizon.[23]

Later in the season, the ever-expanding Black Drillers traveled to New Orleans to take on the New Orleans Elks, a small city team. Though the clubs were
still relatively small-time, their popularity was growing, as demonstrated by the
Missouri Pacific Railroad's willingness to transport the Drillers free of charge.
Taking the ball team for free meant that the accompanying paid admissions of
fans traveling to see the games would be great enough for the railroad to see a
profit.[24] If the Missouri Pacific saw profit in Stovall's industrial team, it stands to
reason that there was an even larger profit in its big-league counterpart. The trip
didn't prove profitable for either team, but it did indicate a level of financial possibility unprecedented in northeast Louisiana's black athletics.

The town's passion was the Monarchs, and its May–June road trip began in
Montgomery, where the team swept a four-game set from the Grey Sox. Monroe's play was impressive, and the *Kansas City Call* appeared confident: "The only
club worrying the Monarchs is the Chicago American Giants and it seems that
there will be no one to move the Chicago team as the Monarchs will not meet
them in the first half [of the season]." As Monroe continued its unlikely rise,
that scheduling discrepancy loomed as another in a long line of controversies.[25]

But Monroe's success, as well as that of its industrial counterpart, wasn't
equaled in the white part of town. On June 3, as the Monarchs engaged the Grey
Sox, Cotton States president Frank Scott announced that his league would allow Sunday doubleheaders. The maneuver, normally discouraged in the Bible
Belt South, particularly among white leagues, was a sign of desperation. Officials hoped that providing two more weekend games would boost attendance.
The Cotton States' season appeared ominous from the outset, as early in the
season the far stronger Southeastern League disbanded.[26] The situation of the
white Monroe Twins was even more dire. The team was losing, remaining near
the bottom of the standings since the season opened. Twins management could
count on dominating the headlines of the local dailies, though their league was
less talented and their record more modest than the crosstown Monarchs, but in
a depression, fans wanted a winning team. The Monarchs were playing to reportedly large biracial crowds at Casino Park, and the Twins needed success to
bring crowds through the Forsythe Park turnstiles. The effort proved less than
successful.[27]

As the Twins and Cotton States League struggled, the Monarchs continued
their early-June road trip in Nashville, where the team managed a split of its own

Sunday doubleheader. They took the first game 4–2 before dropping the second 7–8. Nashville's victory took sole possession of first place away from Monroe.[28]

Meanwhile, as the Monarchs finished up their fourth road series of the season, Cole's American Giants took their first trip away from home, traveling to Indianapolis. At the ABCs' Perry Stadium, Chicago won three of four. The following weekend, the Giants returned home to defeat the Memphis Red Sox in three of five games. The lingering story of the Memphis series, however, was the Giants' two losses. They were not spectacular, but in the plodding weeks to come they would become so.[29]

The Giants' losses to Indianapolis and Memphis gave Monroe an opportunity to catch them in the standings. The Monarchs took full advantage, gaining ground on the league leaders by sweeping a home series with the Montgomery Grey Sox upon their return. (Adding insult to Montgomery's injury, Abraham Rothman announced that the Black Drillers were challenging the Grey Sox to an exhibition game in Bastrop.) The team's success led the far-less-successful Monroe Twins, of the white minor Cotton States League, to attend Monday's series finale. "The Monarchs," said a description of the Montgomery series in the *Louisiana Weekly*, "regret being kept away from a chance to fight it out with the Chicago team in the first half to settle the dispute once and for all, as the Monarchs believe they have a stronger team than the American Giants."[30]

As the Southern League schedule continued, the congregants of Zion Traveler Baptist Church revived and re-revived their back-and-forth over the pastorship of Warner Hill, the origins of which are recounted in chapter 3. In early May, the church's Harmony Club enjoined Hill against preaching at the church, but a majority of the church's congregation had given him a vote of confidence. The Harmony Club spent May in court, arguing that the injunction superseded the vote of some of the church's members. During the second week of May, as the congregation waited for a May 23 court date, another vote demonstrated support for Hill 117 votes to 2. Of course, members of the church's Harmony Club did not participate in the election.[31]

That non-participation would substantially influence the ruling of Judge J. T. Shell, who ruled that Hill was in contempt of court for violating the injunction. A legal reelection to the pulpit, argued Shell, would have nullified the court order, but the absence of the anti-Hill faction at the most recent vote made the election unofficial. No quorum, no validity. Hill would have to leave yet again.[32]

While the Monarchs completed their doubleheader sweep of Montgomery on June 12, Warner Hill tried to force his way back into the Zion Traveler Baptist Church, attempting to preach despite the court's injunction. Tom Jasper, Harmony Club member and anti-Hill congregant, responded by swearing out a warrant against the erstwhile pastor. Hill was arrested and charged with "disturbing public worship," and the arrest only convinced the town's white population that the Zion Traveler scandal was no longer a nuisance. It was a threat. L. V. Tarver, the white superintendent of police, shut down the church indefinitely. As chapter 10 will reveal, he would unlock the doors, regrettably, as the baseball season was coming to a close.[33]

The following weekend, the Monarchs had a pivotal home series with the Nashville Elite Giants, champions of the 1931 Southern League and losers of the Dixie World Series that same year. The Dixie series had been the first of its kind—a championship series between the Southern League and Texas–Louisiana winners to determine a final southern champion (excepting southern states on the Atlantic Coast). Nashville, champion of the Southern League, was a strong favorite, and won the first two games.[34] Monroe, the Texas–Louisiana League champion, tied the Dixie series by taking the next two games, before Nashville won the fifth game for a 3–2 lead. The Monarchs, however, improbably took the final two games and the championship of the South along with them. Those contests in north Louisiana brought fans from all over the state, swelling the crowds at Casino Park to standing room only and giving the Monarchs the necessary notoriety to barnstorm through Mexico in the last months of 1931. The upset by the popular underdogs surely festered with the Elites through the winter. But though the games had gravity because of Dixie World Series memories, they had it for a number of other reasons, as well. Now the Monarchs sat in first place, barely edging out Chicago, who themselves were just above Nashville in the standings. "The Monarchs are leading the league," reported the *Morning World,* "and if successful in taking this series from Nashville, they will have the first half cinched."[35] Furthermore, Nashville never wanted the Monarchs in the league to begin with, and while none of the players were at the league formation meetings, the relatively small size of the organization, along with the bravado demonstrated by Johnson and English in their exclamations to the press, virtually ensured that the Monarchs players understood their initial outsider status. Monroe's small size would only have exacerbated any lingering otherness not removed by resting atop the standings.

Finally, this was the "Emancipation Series," celebrated during all the weekend contests across the league in conjunction with the Juneteenth holiday, marking June 19 as the African American Emancipation Day. Though Lincoln issued his Emancipation Proclamation on January 1, 1863, it was June 19, 1865, when General Gordon Granger announced in Galveston, Texas, that slavery had ended. The announcement sparked celebrations in Texas, Louisiana, Oklahoma, and Arkansas and created the Juneteenth holiday. For the Monarchs, it meant some of the largest crowds of the season, with patrons arriving on trains from throughout the region. With Emancipation Day falling on Sunday, officials moved the ceremonial events to Monday to avoid any religious conflict.[36]

And if the series really was as important as it appeared, the Monarchs showed no ill effects of lingering nerves. On Saturday, the first game of the series, the Monarchs managed sixteen runs on twenty-three hits, compared to eight and five for the Elites.[37] After a doubleheader split on Sunday, the teams played a fourth Monday game to celebrate the holiday.[38] For the Emancipation Day festivities, the Monarchs held their flag-raising ceremony for pennants won the previous year. They first raised their Texas–Louisiana championship pennant, followed quickly by a Dixie World Series championship pennant. Considering the combination of the league participation debates of March, the 1931 championship series, and the close proximity of the two teams in the standings, the ceremony was not something the Elite Giants—or their owner, Thomas Wilson—would be likely to forget.[39]

Thomas T. Wilson started in black baseball in 1914, when he was an instrumental part of the creation of the Capital City League in Nashville, a citywide semipro circuit. Four years later he created his own team, the Nashville Standard Giants, which toured throughout the Tennessee Valley. By 1921, the Standard Giants had become the Elite Giants, and in 1928, Wilson parlayed his team's success into a new ball field in Nashville—Wilson Park—the first stadium in the South owned and operated by African Americans. After briefly moving the team to Cleveland in 1931, Wilson's club returned to Nashville in 1932, where he, along with Reuben Jackson, became a driving force behind the new Negro Southern League.[40]

Monroe won its Emancipation Day contest with the Elite Giants. The 6–4 victory kept the Monarchs in first place and seemed to set the team up nicely for its final two series of the first half, a road contest with Montgomery and a home finale with Memphis. "If the Monarchs are successful in winning the first half," reported the *Morning World,* "there is a possibility that the fans of Monroe and vicinity will see some of the games of the negro world series in Monroe."[41]

The following day, Tuesday, June 21, as the Elite Giants were making their way out of town, the *Morning World* held an open-invitation fight party—complete with a local announcer that could be heard for a square block—so that all in town so inclined could follow the year's signature bout: Max Schmelling versus Jack Sharkey.[42] But as sports-mad Monroe experienced Sharkey's surprise victory and the Southern League played on, the East–West was foundering. "It doesn't necessitate much mental exertion," noted *Philadelphia Tribune* sports editor Randy Dixon, "to apprehend that this East–West League is not the hotsy-totsy idea its originators visualized." Cum Posey purchased a controlling interest in the Detroit Wolves and absorbed the talent from its roster into his own Homestead Grays, eliminating the Detroit entry altogether. No longer were the two clubs simply associated. They were one team. After a league meeting in Philadelphia, led by Posey, East–West officials adopted a set of policies they claimed would remedy the financial sinkhole the league was apparently creating. First, teams would categorically cut player salaries and overhead expenses. They would also revise the league schedule to eliminate midweek games, moving to a weekend schedule similar to the NSL's. Finally (and despite early-season hand wringing over the issue), the league would stop employing salaried umpires. These were, it seemed, desperate times.[43]

But rules changes and salary cuts didn't seem to be enough. If the East–West's season was to continue into its second half, league officials decided, a radical overhaul would be in order. The future was uncertain at best. Sportswriter Bill Gibson expressed increasing pessimism throughout June. When the Washington Pilots took on the Baltimore Black Sox, a usually potent rivalry, the Sunday gross was just over $400. When the strongest clubs in the East were suffering like this, "you can surmise what the second and third-raters are doing," Gibson wrote. John L. Clark could see the same problems. "The first two months have told an unwelcome story to those who make the national pastime," he wrote. "As far as the grandstand patron is concerned, he is getting better baseball, and paying less for it."[44]

As the East–West faltered, the Monarchs played on, next traveling to Montgomery for a four-game series on June 25. The team had won eight straight against the Grey Sox, and hoped to continue the streak. The first half's schedule was winding down. The American Giants continued to jockey for first place. The games in Alabama seemed pivotal to the pennant outcome. With this information—and the pressure that came with it—in tow, the Monarchs took the Montgomery series 3 games to 1.[45]

In early June, with the American Giants and Monarchs tied in the standings, the *Defender* had described Chicago's frustration that the two teams were not scheduled to meet in the first half. "They figure five games with the southern champs would settle the issue beyond all doubts, but they do not play Monroe, leaving the other teams to help them win the flag." The Monarchs were frustrated, too, even more so with the schedule's other major discrepancy, leaving

Chicago to play virtually every Southern League game at home. (This part of the problem was conveniently absent in the Chicago press.) Still, a head-to-head series seemed like a salve for the tension and a solution to the "best team" debate.[46] With the Monarchs now in first place, the team was publicly "peeved because they do not get a chance to fight it out with the Chicago team in the first half to settle the dispute once and for always, as they believe they have a stronger team than the American Giants."[47]

Wilson L. Driver, columnist for the *Atlanta Daily World,* thought Monroe should be careful of what it wished for. Monroe had defeated all comers. They were in first place. "Why worry about meeting the Chicago team as long as they have the chance to pile up a fat percentage and assure themselves of the surest bet of winning the pennant? The chance of meeting the American Giants is coming soon enough and it will be another one of those affairs of over-anxiousness; and bloey! here goes the old ball game, the series AND the pennant hopes. To go still further into the dope, it will be just another case of David meeting Goliath; only Little David won't have the good Lord's help this time."[48]

It was a fair point. But everyone could agree that possession of first place would ultimately be beside the point if the league itself was unable to survive. As June turned to July, the *Defender* reported the potential death of both of the country's "major" black organizations. Though the front-runners in each league were doing well, the rest of the teams were foundering. "While Posey is O.K., the Baltimore Sox good and Monroe and Chicago strong in the Southern loop," reported the *Defender,* "the rest of the clubs comprise merely the field. And this is no year for 'field nags.'" Pittsburgh, the paper noted, was in the best shape, as it was affiliated with both leagues, had a large new park, and had what amounted to a bona fide all-star team.[49]

The Crawfords finished the first half by taking on Tom Wilson's Nashville Elite Giants. One of the games was a charity contest for Roselia Maternity Hospital, and a Fourth of July doubleheader that Monday added two more wins to Pittsburgh's already impressive total. Tom Wilson and the Crawfords' Gus Greenlee already knew each other from the Southern League meetings, but the holiday weekend in close quarters certainly allowed the owners to become better acquainted. And it was ultimately that acquaintance, among others, that would forge the future of black baseball once the 1932 season had run its course.[50]

Across town, Cum Posey was not seeing such success. Attendance was scant at East–West League games, but most of the clubs publicly shrugged off the problems, claiming that cool weather and rain were keeping fans away. They would return soon enough.[51] But on June 30, any lingering bravado—and any lingering uncertainty about the East–West—dissolved: "Due to present conditions that have caused the receipts from operations to shrivel to the point where they are insufficient to meet the carrying charges to operate baseball clubs on a salaried basis, club owners of the East West league have abandoned the first-half schedule, discontinued payment of monthly salaries and adopted the plan, already in effect with some of the leading independent clubs, of forming a working agreement on the percentage basis with players."[52] Officials cited "lack of patronage" as the root cause of the dissolution, as well as travel costs and the distance between league cities, but they expressed optimism that there might still be a second-half schedule. There was not. The league announced that since the Baltimore Black Sox were leading in the standings at the time of the collapse, they would be awarded the league championship, for whatever it was worth. The East–West experiment was over.[53]

On July 1, with his team preparing for its series with the Elites, John Clark published a grand "I told you so," to follow his preseason criticism of the East–West League's formation. Pittsburgh and New York, both left out of the East–West, were maintaining their financial solvency, while the league itself was virtually defunct. "It is evident now," Clark wrote, "that the East–West league sponsors had the wrong conception of baseball conditions of 1932. It must also be evident by now that the motives behind the idea were false and impure." He closed his article with chest out and finger wagging. "All these and other claims were made six months ago. Check up and determine who was right." A softer version of this criticism appeared in the *Defender*. "Reasons and causes for the organization were many and beautiful," Clark wrote, "but not altogether truthful."[54]

Rollo Wilson, who would become a baseball commissioner himself in the years to come, had a more jaded interpretation of the league's demise. He cited Garland Mackey of the *Washington Tribune,* who commented that from the season's inception, Posey and the East–West courted the white dailies in member cities. In so doing, "they sort of high-hatted the sepia scribes." Meanwhile, the white press never gave the black league the coverage that African American newspapers would have devoted. All Posey had to do was not take the black press for granted. But he did, and thus "the inevitable happened. Depression and the lack of publicity in the places where it would do the most good—the race newspapers—forced an abandonment of the daily schedule."[55]

Wilson, however, wasn't the only critic, and Posey's frustration with his failure and the consistent press criticism finally boiled over in a letter to the *Courier* sports editor.[56] "We attempted to operate a league on business principles and provide positions for players. Economically we picked the wrong time," wrote

Posey. But his explanation for the collapse quickly became far more specific. "Perhaps the owners would have been willing to continue salaries a little longer had the critics not been so noisy. This criticism has cost the players their salaries and owners much losses. Now, the critics have nothing to offer the players, but still feel they have reason to gloat over some owner's downfall." Posey's accusations seem like a crude amalgam of sour grapes and passing the buck—and they were—but his attacks then turned toward race, as had all of the East–West's press relationships in 1932: "No Colored baseball club in the country is on such a firm foundation that men who are paid to write news for the public should seek to bring personal animosities before the people. Every sporting editor in the country is boosting sports. It would pay one or two of ours to do the same."[57]

"Ours" were the members of the black press snubbed in favor of white papers for coverage of the East–West. Given the Depression and the color of the players on his team, Posey seemed to be saying, black newspapers owed him. These negotiations on the border of race only made the league's demise more emotionally charged. The Southern League didn't collapse (though it would undergo serious difficulty in the season's second half). Neither did it court the white press. Most of its teams, after all, played in the Jim Crow South. But Monroe stood as the one exception to this generally established rule. The town had no viable black press when the season began, and its owner was a wealthy and prominent member of the community. It was, by and large, the white contact facilitated by press coverage and the reputation of the team owner that brought white and black together in Jim Crow northeast Louisiana for one championship run. Of course, the power of these games being what they were, reputation and coverage had their impact only because there *was* a championship run. Success mattered, too.

And though the East–West didn't have success in 1932, Posey's attitude was certainly not unprecedented. "The ivory atop the necks of some of the owners, if placed end to end would put a crimp in the elephant-hunting industry," wrote Bill Gibson of the East–West's collapse. "The colossal ignorance of some of the moguls regarding ethics, courtesy and business tact would supply all of the leagues in the country."[58] The *Indianapolis Recorder* echoed Gibson's sentiments: "How in the HECK these officials of so-called leagues can entertain any hopes of future possibilities in the diamond classic for the Negro with present day slip-shod methods in management, I can not see."[59]

The Depression was eroding the urban economies that surrounded the newspapers and ball teams. It laid waste to the National League the year prior, leaving sportswriters jaded and ready to warn their readers not to get their hopes up.

"The failure of Negro baseball in this section in measuring up to the required standard is caused from lack of knowledge of ADVERTISING," wrote the *Shreveport Sun*'s Pitman Nedde. African Americans in north Louisiana had nice facilities, good equipment, and strong players. White people even attended their games. But because the games were not marketed properly, "clubs have been broken up that would have been recognized the country over."[60] Of the nineteen newspapers with full surviving coverage for 1932, only five did not include editorials lamenting the uncertain state of professional black baseball. (See tables 1 and 2.) The *Memphis World* was the only of the five to report on a hometown team of any principal significance to the 1932 season, and the late-June and July editions (the precise time when Memphis had ample reason to complain) have not survived. All of the papers with broader national circulations included such criticism.

Entering the Memphis series on Saturday, July 2, the Monarchs had received word that the league had reversed some Chicago losses. Details of the league machinations were sketchy, but they knew something suspicious had taken place—was taking place—and that their only recourse was a sweep of the Red Sox. Once again, a section of the stands was segregated for the white patrons.[61]

Memphis was a strong team, featuring eight left-handed batters, and in the first innings of the first game, either that talent, the Monarchs' frustration, or Casino Park's short right-field wall won the day. Memphis scored three runs in the first. The Monarchs countered with two, and the game was tied by the fourth. Finally, in the bottom of the eleventh, Barney Morris singled with two outs and a man on third, salvaging Monroe's chances at the first-half pennant with a 6–5 victory.[62]

Doubleheaders were scheduled for both Sunday and Monday, but a Saturday rain wreaked havoc with the field. Only one game was played, and that lasted just seven innings. The Monarchs won the mud-shortened game 5–3. The pennant was still possible.[63]

Fourth of July celebrations for white Monroe included a children's bicycle parade through downtown, a "bathing revue," swimming races, and a lantern parade at the town's pool. The Major McGuire rodeo was in its fourth and final day, and the American Legion held its annual dance on the Cherokee terrace of the Hotel Frances. All black Monroe had was the Monarchs, but that, it turned out, was all it really needed. The team didn't disappoint, winning the holiday games 6–1 and 8–2.[64]

The doubleheader was supposed to be the final two games of the season's first half, but that day the *Monroe News-Star* reported that the team would play another game with the Red Sox at Forsythe Park, Monroe's white baseball stadium and the only park with artificial lights. It would be a makeup for the series' earlier rained-out contest, played "by orders of the president of the Negro Southern League" to determine the first-half champion.

No record of the outcome of this makeup game exists. But if it happened, the Monarchs won. The *Chicago Defender* reported that Monroe won five games from Memphis in the series. It was this fifth game that served as the backbone of the *Defender*'s argument justifying the American Giants' first-place finish. The paper portrayed the game as a ploy to boost Monroe's winning percentage above Chicago's. It never reported the Sunday rain-out that reduced the five-game series to four. It also failed to report that even without the mysterious fifth game, the Monarchs' winning percentage still bested that of the Giants. Everything, even the simplest of outcomes, seemed shrouded in controversy.[65]

As the season's first half came to a close, Pittsburgh's John L. Clark, writing for the West Penn Service, felt disillusioned—not by the continuous and increasingly loud claims to a championship by Monroe and Chicago, but instead by the dilapidated state of the game. "Sixteen baseball clubs started at the tape on 1 May in an organized form," he wrote. But team owners chose to ignore the hard realities of the Depression. "Fat wallets are not so fat, and many owners are about to call the whole thing a bad job." He highlighted Homestead, Washington, and Baltimore in the East–West, Monroe and Chicago in the Southern, and independents Pittsburgh and New York as the season's most financially successful teams—perhaps its only financially successful teams.

Syd Pollock, owner of the Cuban Stars, responded to Clark the following week, demonstrating a promoter's optimism. He acknowledged the difficulties brought by the Depression but argued that "Negro baseball has not fallen by the wayside." If people were patient, the coming years would "bring back the awaited better times."[66]

The Negro Southern League, however, wanted better times in 1932. The pressure to sustain the league, in the face of a depression and the East–West collapse, was great. A prominent, large-market franchise could carry the group, as long as that franchise won the league's championship. And so, as the first half ended, Southern League officials sought to sustain themselves by making a champion of their most prominent team.

Table 1. 1932 Black Press Sample Set, Divided by Region of Origin and Circulation Category[1]

South	North	Border	West
Memphis World	*Indianapolis Recorder*	*Louisville Leader*	*California Eagle*
Shreveport Sun	*Chicago Defender*	*Kansas City Call*	*Houston Informer*
Louisiana Weekly	*Pittsburgh Courier*	Baltimore *Afro-*	
Atlanta Daily World	New York *Amster-*	*American*	
Birmingham Reporter	*dam News*		
	New York Age		
	Negro World		
	Philadelphia Tribune		
	Boston Chronicle		
	Cleveland Gazette		

National Editions	**Regional Editions**
Atlanta Daily World	*Memphis World*
Chicago Defender	*Shreveport Sun*
Pittsburgh Courier	*Louisiana Weekly*
New York *Amsterdam*	*Birmingham Reporter*
News	*Indianapolis Recorder*
Baltimore *Afro-*	*New York Age*
American	*Negro World*
California Eagle	*Philadelphia Tribune*
	Boston Chronicle
	Cleveland Gazette
	Louisville Leader
	Houston Informer
	Kansas City Call

Table 2. Presence of Editorials Decrying the State of Baseball

Editorials Decrying the State of Baseball	Editorials Absent
Indianapolis Recorder	*Memphis World*
Shreveport Sun	*Houston Informer*
Louisiana Weekly	*Negro World*
Atlanta Daily World	*Cleveland Gazette*
Chicago Defender	*Louisville Leader*
Pittsburgh Courier	
New York *Amsterdam News*	
New York Age	
California Eagle	
Philadelphia Tribune	
Boston Chronicle	
Kansas City Call	
Baltimore *Afro-American*	
Birmingham Reporter	

Table 3. Newspapers' Demonstration of Choice for a First-Half Pennant

Chicago American Giants	Monroe Monarchs	None
Houston Informer	*Memphis World*	*Indianapolis Recorder*
Chicago Defender	*Shreveport Sun*	*New York Age*
Pittsburgh Courier	*Louisiana Weekly*	*Negro World*
California Eagle	*Atlanta Daily World*	*Boston Chronicle*
Kansas City Call	New York *Amsterdam News*	*Cleveland Gazette*
Baltimore *Afro-American*	*Philadelphia Tribune*	*Birmingham Reporter*
		Louisville Leader

Table 4. Pennant Choice Based on Newspaper Location

Chicago American Giants	Monroe Monarchs	None
West	South	North
North	South	North
North	South	North
West	South	North
Border	North	North
Border	North	South
		Border

Table 5. Pennant Choice Based on Circulation Quantity

Chicago American Giants	Monroe Monarchs	None
Regional	Regional	Regional
National	Regional	Regional
National	Regional	Regional
National	National	Regional
Regional	National	Regional
National	Regional	Regional
		Regional

Table 6. Articles about the 1932 Negro Southern League by African American Publications

Note: Abbreviation "NS" means "no source," indicating the unavailability of source material for that month.

	JAN	FEB	MAR	APR	MAY	JUN	JUL	AUG	SEP	OCT	NOV	DEC	Total
Memphis World	0	[NS]	1	9	5	2[I]	[NS]	1	2	0	0	0	20
Indianapolis Recorder	[NS]	[NS]	[NS]	[NS]	6	4	7	1	2	0	0	1	21
Louisville Leader	0	0	0	0	0	0	1	0	2	0	0	0	3
Shreveport Sun	0	0	2	5	2	1	1	0	9	1	0	0	21
Louisiana Weekly	0	0	2	3	4	5	3	3	2	1	0	0	23
Atlanta Daily World	0	1	9	16	22	18	13	4	9	0	0	[NS]	92
Chicago Defender	3	0	6	5	15	14	21	12	12	4	0	0	92
Pittsburgh Courier	2	0	5	7	8	10	8	7	11	2	0	0	60
New York Amsterdam News	0	0	2	0	0	2	0	1	1	0	0	0	6
New York Age	0	0	0	0	1	0	0	0	0	0	0	2	3
Negro World	0	0	0	0	0	0	0	0	0	0	0	0	0
California Eagle	0	0	0	2	0	0	1	0	1	0	0	0	4
Philadelphia Tribune	1	0	4	3	3	3	1	1	1	0	1	0	18
Boston Chronicle	0	0	0	2	0	0	0	0	0	0	0	0	2
Cleveland Gazette	0	0	0	0	1	1	0	0	0	0	0	0	2
Kansas City Call	3	3	6	12	6	9	5	6	4	3	2	2	61
Baltimore Afro-American	1	1	2	7	4	4	5	2	4	0	1	1	32
Birmingham Reporter	1	1	5	14	6	0	2	0	2	0	0	0	31
Houston Informer	0	0	0	1	0	0	0	2	1	0	0	0	4
TOTAL	11	6	44	86	83	73	68	40	63	11	4	6	504

Table 7. Production of Articles about the Southern League Quantified by Location

Note: Abbreviation "NS" means "no source," indicating the unavailability of source material for that month. Abbreviation "I" means "incomplete," as only partial coverage for the month still exists.

	JAN	FEB	MAR	APR	MAY	JUN	JUL	AUG	SEP	OCT	NOV	DEC	Total
SOUTH													
Memphis World	0	0	1	9	5	2[I]	[NS]	1	2	0	0	0	20
Shreveport Sun	0	0	2	5	2	1	1	0	9	1	0	0	21
Louisiana Weekly	0	0	2	3	4	5	3	3	2	1	0	0	23
Atlanta Daily World	0	1	9	16	22	18	13	4	9	0	0	[NS]	92
Birmingham Reporter	1	1	5	14	6	0	2	0	2	0	0	0	31
TOTAL	1	2	19	47	39	26	19	8	24	2	0	0	187
NORTH													
Indianapolis Recorder	[NS]	[NS]	[NS]	[NS]	6	4	7	1	2	0	1	1	21
Chicago Defender	3	0	6	5	15	14	21	12	12	4	0	0	92
Pittsburgh Courier	2	0	5	7	8	10	8	7	11	2	0	0	60
New York Amsterdam News	0	0	2	0	0	2	0	1	1	0	0	0	6
New York Age	0	0	0	0	1	0	0	0	0	0	0	2	3
Negro World	0	0	0	0	0	0	0	0	0	0	0	0	0
Philadelphia Tribune	1	0	4	3	3	3	1	1	1	0	1	0	18
Boston Chronicle	0	0	0	2	0	0	0	0	0	0	0	0	2
Cleveland Gazette	0	0	0	0	1	1	0	0	0	0	0	0	2
TOTAL	6	0	17	17	34	34	37	22	27	6	1	3	207

Continued on the next page

Table 7. Continued

	JAN	FEB	MAR	APR	MAY	JUN	JUL	AUG	SEP	OCT	NOV	DEC	Total
BORDER													
Louisville Leader	0	0	0	0	0	0	1	0	2	0	0	0	3
Kansas City Call	3	3	6	12	6	9	5	6	4	3	2	2	61
Baltimore Afro-American	1	1	2	7	4	4	5	2	4	0	1	1	32
TOTAL	4	4	8	19	10	13	11	8	10	3	3	3	96
WEST													
California Eagle	0	0	0	2	0	0	1	0	1	0	0	0	4
Houston Informer	0	0	0	1	0	0	0	2	1	0	0	0	4
TOTAL	0	0	0	3	0	0	1	2	2	0	0	0	8

Table 8. Production of Articles about the Southern League Based on Paper Circulation

Note: Abbreviation "NS" means "no source," indicating the unavailability of source material for that month.

NATIONAL	JAN	FEB	MAR	APR	MAY	JUN	JUL	AUG	SEP	OCT	NOV	DEC	Total
Atlanta Daily World	0	1	9	16	22	18	13	4	9	0	0	[NS]	92
Chicago Defender	3	0	6	5	15	14	21	12	12	4	0	0	92
Pittsburgh Courier	2	0	5	7	8	10	8	7	11	2	0	0	60
New York Amsterdam News	0	0	2	0	0	2	0	1	1	0	0	0	6
California Eagle	0	0	0	2	0	0	1	0	1	0	0	0	4
Baltimore Afro-American	1	1	2	7	4	4	5	2	4	0	1	1	32
TOTAL	6	2	24	37	49	48	48	26	38	6	1	1	295

REGIONAL	JAN	FEB	MAR	APR	MAY	JUN	JUL	AUG	SEP	OCT	NOV	DEC	
Memphis World	[NS]	0	1	9	5	2[I]	[NS]	1	2	0	0	0	20
Indianapolis Recorder	[NS]	[NS]	[NS]	[NS]	6	4	7	1	2	0	0	1	21
Louisville Leader	0	0	0	0	0	0	1	0	2	0	0	0	3
Shreveport Sun	0	0	2	5	2	1	1	0	9	1	0	0	21
Louisiana Weekly	0	0	2	3	4	5	3	3	2	1	0	0	23
New York Age	0	0	0	0	1	0	0	0	0	0	0	2	3
Negro World	0	0	0	0	0	0	0	0	0	0	0	0	0
Philadelphia Tribune	1	0	4	3	3	3	1	1	1	0	1	0	18
Boston Chronicle	0	0	0	2	0	0	0	0	0	0	0	0	2
Cleveland Gazette	0	0	0	0	1	1	0	0	0	0	0	0	2
Kansas City Call	3	3	6	12	6	9	5	6	4	3	2	2	61
Birmingham Reporter	1	1	5	14	6	0	2	0	2	0	0	0	31
Houston Informer	0	0	0	1	0	0	0	2	1	0	0	0	4
TOTAL	5	4	20	49	34	25	20	14	25	5	3	5	209

Table 9. Newspaper Coverage Patterns, by Region and Circulation, with the Availability of a Second-Half Schedule

Relatively Consistent Coverage	Substantial Coverage Stopped by Aug	Sparse Coverage Throughout	Second-Half Schedule
Louisiana Weekly			NO
Chicago Defender			YES
Pittsburgh Courier			YES
Kansas City Call			YES
Baltimore Afro-American			NO
	Memphis World		N/A
	Shreveport Sun (resumed for World Series)		NO
	Atlanta Daily World (resumed for World Series)		YES
	Philadelphia Tribune		NO
	Birmingham Reporter		NO
	Indianapolis Recorder		NO
		Houston Informer	NO
		Louisville Leader	NO
		New York Amsterdam News	NO
		New York Age	NO
		Negro World	NO
		California Eagle	NO
		Boston Chronicle	NO
		Cleveland Gazette	NO

South (Regional)
North (National)
North (National)
Border (Regional)
Border (National)

South (Regional)
South (Regional)
South (National)
North (Regional)
South (Regional)
North (Regional)

West (Regional)
Border (Regional)
North (National)
North (Regional)
North (Regional)
West (National)
North (Regional)
North (Regional)

Table 10. The *Monroe Morning World*'s Portrayal of African American Life in 1932

January		Positive Coverage	
Negative Coverage		Church-related	0
Crime		Other	3
Murder	2	*Total*	3
Robbery	1	Ratio	5.666
Other	0		
Drunkenness	0		
Other	0	*April*	
Total	3	Negative Coverage	
Positive Coverage		Crime	
Church-related	1	Murder	11
Other	2	Robbery	9
Total	3	Other	9
Ratio	1.000	Drunkenness	0
		Other	9
February		*Total*	38
Negative Coverage		Positive Coverage	
Crime		Church-related	8
Murder	1	Other	7
Robbery	4	*Total*	15
Other	6	Ratio	2.533
Drunkenness	1		
Other	5	*May*	
Total	17	Negative Coverage	
Positive Coverage		Crime	
Church-related	1	Murder	6
Other	2	Robbery	21
Total	3	Other	20
Ratio	5.666	Drunkenness	2
		Other	7
March		*Total*	56
Negative Coverage		Positive Coverage	
Crime		Church-related	9
Murder	5	Other	16
Robbery	2	*Total*	25
Other	6	Ratio	2.240
Drunkenness	0		
Other	4		
Total	17		

June
   Negative Coverage
      Crime
         Murder   8
         Robbery   5
         Other   18
      Drunkenness   12
      Other   7
      Total   50
   Positive Coverage
      Church-related 11
      Other   13
      Total   24
        Ratio   2.0833

July
   Negative Coverage
      Crime
         Murder   2 (1)
         Robbery   8
         Other   9
      Drunkenness   6
      Other   7
      Total   32 (33)
   Positive Coverage
      Church-related 1
      Other   4
      Total   5
        Ratio   6.400 (6.600)

August
   Negative Coverage
      Crime
         Murder   1 (5)
         Robbery   7
         Other   4
      Drunkenness   2
      Other   2
      Total   16 (21)

Continued on the next page

Positive Coverage
   Church-related 1
   Other   4
   Total   5
    Ratio   3.200 (4.200)

September 1–12
(the Crawfords series ended on
September 12)
   Negative Coverage
      Crime
         Murder   1 (5)
         Robbery   3
         Other   3
      Drunkenness   3
      Other   1
      Total   11 (16)
   Positive Coverage
      Church-related 1
      Other   0
      Total   1
        Ratio   11.000 (16.000)

*September: the remainder of the
month*
   Negative Coverage
      Crime
         Murder   5
         Robbery   7
         Other   3
      Drunkenness   1
      Other   6
      Total   22
   Positive Coverage
      Church-related 1
      Other   2
      Total   3
        Ratio   7.333

Table 10. *Continued*

October				*Positive Coverage*	
Negative Coverage				Church-related	1
Crime				Other	6
Murder	7			Total	7
Robbery	9			Ratio	5.571
Other	8			*December*	
Drunkenness	2			Negative Coverage	
Other	9			Crime	
Total	35			Murder	11
Positive Coverage				Robbery	8
Church-related	1			Other	7
Other	2			Drunkenness	2
Total	3			Other	8
Ratio	11.666			*Total*	36
November				Positive Coverage	
Negative Coverage				Church-related	0
Crime				Other	0
Murder	17			Total	0
Robbery	3			Ratio	36.00
Other	6				
Drunkenness	3				
Other	10				
Total	39				

Table 11. Top-Line Headline Coverage Comparison of a White and Black Daily, May 1932

	Monroe Morning World	*Atlanta Daily World*
Total Articles	147	153
COVERAGE LOCATION		
Local	52	79
National	60	54
State	26	7
Regional	4	8
International	5	5
POLITICS	83	29
Democratic Campaign	7	0
Taxes and Budget	19	0
Prohibition	11	1
Scottsboro	0	2
VIOLENCE/CRIME	41	67
Lindbergh	12	8
SPECIAL INTEREST	23	57
Church-Related	0	24

Table 12. Newspaper Choice of a Legitimate 1932 Negro League Champion, by Paper, Region, and Circulation

"Dixie" Series	Monroe v. Pittsburgh	None	Both
Houston Informer	*Memphis World*	*New York Age*	*Indianapolis Recorder*
Chicago Defender	*Shreveport Sun*	*Negro World*	*Louisville Leader*
	Louisiana Weekly	*Boston Chronicle*	*Atlanta Daily World*
	New York *Amsterdam News*	*Cleveland Gazette*	*Pittsburgh Courier*
	California Eagle		*Philadelphia Tribune*
	Baltimore *Afro-American*		*Kansas City Call*
			Birmingham Reporter
West	South	North	North
North	South	North	Border
	South	North	South
	North	North	North
	West		North
	Border		Border
			South
Regional	Regional	Regional	Regional
National	Regional	Regional	Regional
	Regional	Regional	National
	National	Regional	National
	National		Regional
	National		Regional
			Regional

7
The Southern against the South
The First-Half Pennant Controversy

Long before the season began, before any of the Monarchs' first-half victories, their application for league membership had been a point of significant contention among the teams from other, larger cities. "Chief among the problems and issues discussed [at the Nashville meeting] were the fates of Louisville, which city did not choose to enter league baseball, and the attempt of Monroe, La., to force its way into the body over the protest of the other teams," reported the *Atlanta Daily World*. "Argument against Monroe was that its location made travel from the other cities too much of a financial burden. While this battle was going on Chicago changed its plans and moved in as a regular member instead of merely associating with the group as was first planned." The anti-Monroe faction was not disclosed in newspaper reports, but the available evidence points to Thomas Wilson and the Nashville group as the principal instigators. Atlanta, Birmingham, Chicago, Indianapolis, Little Rock, Louisville, Memphis, Montgomery, Monroe, and Nashville were voted franchises. Little Rock, Memphis, and Montgomery had reasonable journeys to Monroe and played the Monarchs more than any of the remaining NSL clubs. Indianapolis had long distances to travel for all Southern League games. Louisville was a late inclusion into the league, as was Chicago. Birmingham, Atlanta, and Nashville were each far from northeast Louisiana, and each could have complained about the trip. Though the Birmingham Black Barons were eventually voted a franchise, however, the *Birmingham Reporter* and team officials could not get word from the league office on their status for weeks. They didn't have a manager until late March. Atlanta was never even given a complete first-half schedule of games. Both left the league in June, before the first half was ever completed.[1]

This leaves Nashville. The previous year, the Monarchs "won the title of champions of the south," the unofficial minor league championship known as the Dixie World Series, by defeating the Nashville Elite Giants.[2] And as the new season began, Reuben Jackson, Southern League president, stressed the need for a boost in attendance and actively courted big-name out-of-South teams like the Chicago American Giants, a club that became the most widely reported of all the NSL squads. Monroe was by far the smallest of the included cities and could have been seen as a potential detriment to the league's "major" status.

Reuben Jackson lived in Nashville. Born in Sparta, Georgia, he had been a college football star at Morris Brown before attending Meharry Medical College in Nashville. He took an MD in 1926, becoming a general practitioner and establishing an office at 1123½ Cedar Street. Jackson drifts in and out of the historical record. He began his life after medical school with a clear plan for success, marrying Bertha L. Allen, establishing a general practice, and buying a home on Nashville's Second Avenue—a comfortable situation he maintained throughout his year-long tenure as NSL president and through 1937. During the 1932 season, he also served as medical examiner for the Nashville Colored City Schools. In 1934, he began a venture with fellow doctor Henry C. Floyd, the Ever Ready Service Station, which survived until 1941. When this business is considered along with his ventures in sports, Jackson appears to be a man of many interests (and, subsequently, many streams of income). In 1938, however, Jackson's general practice office moved, and the doctor was boarding with a widow named Cleo D. Moore. By 1940, he had abandoned Nashville altogether. He returned in 1942 and remarried in 1946. Dr. Floyd died that year, but Jackson did not actively participate in the funeral. In 1958, he drifted from the record forever. All those Jackson came in contact with through his tenure in Nashville—and particularly through his early success—eventually fell away. Whether Jackson's sins caught up to him or hard luck drove him away is impossible to know, but Floyd's death prompted a two-page obituary in the *Nashville Globe* chronicling the community's admiration for him—an accolade his former business partner certainly never received. Jackson's $8,500 in 1933 taxable real estate holdings fell to $1,080 dollars by 1948, and the taxes of the latter were delinquent. Throughout, however— and particularly in those early years—Jackson maintained an active interest in sports.[3]

That interest and his early rising status in the community led to his relationship with Thomas T. Wilson, owner of the Nashville Elite Giants. The son of two medical doctors, Wilson grew to become a "numbers man," a gambling magnate, along with his dealings in baseball, football, hotel, and nightclub ownership. He founded the Elites and their home field, Wilson Park, but also staged games at the white park, Sulphur Dell, when Wilson's almost eight-thousand-person seating capacity threatened to be inadequate. Wilson's Elite Giants joined the Negro National League in 1930 and the NSL when the National folded. This was the logical move for Wilson, as his friend and business partner was president of the new league. Together, Wilson and Jackson also owned the Nashville Elite Giants professional football team. As did their Negro Southern baseball league, their Negro Southern football league featured Jackson as president and Wilson as treasurer. NSL football meetings took place in Jackson's medical office, as the two decided on franchises to be awarded and other league minutia. In the NSL baseball meetings, Jackson's presidency and Wilson's position as treasurer acted as bookends to the newly awarded vice presidency of Robert Cole, new owner of the Chicago American Giants and cash cow to the infant league. The Negro Southern League was a for-profit business emanating from Nashville, Tennessee, and there wasn't much profit in a small-town team in northeast Louisiana.[4]

No record exists disclosing how the entry dispute was resolved, but it was, and Monroe received its franchise in the NSL.[5] If indeed Nashville was the principal opponent to Monroe's entry, Little Rock, Memphis, and Montgomery probably came to the Monarchs' defense. Little Rock and Memphis had both been strongly considering membership in Stovall's original Tri-State League. Montgomery, like Monroe, was making its first jump into "major" league baseball. Though Jackson's experiment could have functioned without Monroe, it could not have functioned with only five teams.

Of course, Jackson and Wilson did have a legitimate reason to worry about the possible stability and profit potential of a new baseball league. Declining revenues had caused the Negro National League to collapse. Meanwhile, the East–West League opened in controversy, acting as a hopelessly unstable vehicle for Cum Posey. Posey did what Jackson and Wilson could not do—exclude teams that did not serve his financial or political interest. But controversy would have its way nonetheless, and, as seen in chapter 6, the East–West collapsed by the end of June.[6]

By the time of its collapse, however, the problems of the East–West League had left their imprint on the Southern. The Herman Andrews interleague controversy in early May, followed by Southern and East–West backbiting over other players with rival league contracts, sent Jackson into a panic about his own aggregation's legitimacy. In response, he "declared off" all games between the Southern and East–West leagues. "Posey should be a man of his word," stated Robert Cole, "and not show signs of getting there at any cost." It would not be the only time that organizational instability caused confusion for league teams, and it would not be the only time that Jackson's solution to league administrative problems would include "declaring off" games. From early June to mid-July, he would collude with Wilson to steal a pennant from the Monroe team that neither wanted in the league to begin with.[7]

On June 3, Jackson released a statement to the major black weeklies and dailies suggesting that the Memphis Red Sox would be dropped from the Southern League. "The trouble, one gathers from the telegram," reported the *Chicago Defender,* "came through the Tennessee nine's failure to return players, unnamed, taken from other teams in the same organization." In other words, the player contract disputes that caused the rift between the Southern and East–West leagues weeks prior were replayed by teams within the NSL. Memphis's misdoings remained unnamed, but in early May the *Memphis World* had reported that Red Sox manager Homer Curry expected several new additions to sign up before the team's return from a road trip. Nine days later, Memphis signed "Shifty" Jim West, a Birmingham first baseman who impressed the manager in exhibition games between the teams. Also, the *World* reported, "Manager Curry has been in communication with several other stars who will likely join the team before they finish their next home series." The *Pittsburgh Courier* described "an embarrassing situation" with the Memphis team. "West is now the property of Memphis since he has been properly released from his former owner which was Birmingham." Even before the West signing, however, the Red Sox had stepped on the Black Barons' toes. They signed Birmingham's Clarence Lewis, who claimed that the team's inability to pay him in 1931 made him a free agent. Meanwhile, Thomas Wilson claimed that his own stake in Birmingham's team gave him the right to sign Lewis for the Nashville Elite Giants. But Memphis would win that battle, too. Monroe was 33–7 on the Fourth of July (though the league listed them at 32–8. Chicago's nine losses and thirty wins kept them slightly behind the Monarchs. But two of the American Giants' losses were to Memphis.[8]

"All is not well in the Southern League," lamented the *Defender.* Two weeks after his initial early-June telegram—the one intimating that the Red Sox had acted illegally—Jackson ruled that some of Memphis's games were invalid, due to its use of players claimed by other teams. The ruling, naturally influenced by the Posey troubles from earlier in the season, called for more than a simple forfeit, however (which would have kept Monroe in first place). Jackson ruled that Memphis's two wins against Cole's American Giants would be counted as losses, a decision that conveniently gave Chicago one fewer loss than Monroe. His decision to change losses to wins (rather than void the games) came at the final administrative meetings of the first half of the season, thus taking the pennant from Monroe and handing it to the league's large-market revenue vehicle in Chicago. The intermission meetings took place on June 29 and 30 at the Negro Board of Trade in Nashville. "I am expecting you to be present without fail," Jackson told team officials. "This meeting means everything."[9]

After everyone arrived, Jackson put on an optimistic front, "regardless of the cry of depression and other hard luck stories." Jim West was finally ruled the property of Memphis after being formally released by Birmingham.[10] Atlanta, Birmingham, and Little Rock were dissolved as league members.[11] "Well," lamented the *Birmingham Reporter*'s William J. Moore, "it looks like the end of Negro baseball for the season of 1932." For uncharacteristically struggling Birmingham, that was certainly the case, but Jackson maintained his confidence for those who remained. "It is an undisputed fact," he argued, "that organized baseball will have full precedence over unorganized baseball as long as the spirit of cooperation exists in the Southern League family."[12]

But as the *Louisiana Weekly* noted, it was precisely league baseball that seemed unorganized. "The fans of Monroe and Louisiana are watching the results of the Chicago Defender to see just how the Defender will give the final standing. Protests are being mailed. . . . All the southern papers as well as some of the northern and eastern papers carry the standing just as it is . . . and naturally, the fans are not fooled."[13]

The *Defender*'s results didn't alleviate southern skepticism. The paper reported five Monroe wins in the final series with Memphis but still credited Monroe with only thirty-one victories (the *Morning World* listed thirty-three). The paper's standing list even came with a caveat:

Monroe	31–7	0.816
Chicago	33–8*	0.805
Nashville	24–13	0.545
Montgomery	22–17	0.534
Memphis	22–22	0.500
Louisville	13–17	0.433
Indianapolis	14–19	0.424

*One game lost to Louisville under protest[14]

It seemed that every different source carried different results, leaving everyone with a team loyalty or axe to grind with numbers that could meet their own individual arguments. Since the *Defender* had such an axe, and it had one of the loudest voices in the black community, its results would necessarily be influential. But they weren't correct. "The miracle of miracles has occurred," Al Monroe's article below the standings began. "Cole's American Giants, officially the winners of the pennant in the first half of the Southern league race Saturday morning are now mere runners-up to the Monarchs of Monroe, La., according to R. B. Jackson, president of the association." The *Defender* also reported that "the official results, already announced as Chicago first and Monroe second, were ordered changed when Monroe won all of five games played with Memphis. The schedule called for Monroe and Memphis playing three days, July 2, 3 and 4, but through some queer arrangement the extra games were played and the league officials announced Monroe and Chicago tied for first place. While this was going on, however, it became known that Chicago had two postponed games with Louisville and that by winning both could come out on top. These games are now being played in Chicago."[15] Though the standing listed Monroe in front, Al Monroe described the Monarchs as "only a short distance behind." He described Robert Cole's consideration of an official protest if his team was not given what he felt they rightly won. "At the same time the league admitted that it was ready to listen and might even order a play-off of the first half of Monroe and Chicago."

Al Monroe closed the article by mentioning a league problem with Memphis, foreshadowing the NSL's eventual solution to the pennant dispute. "Memphis is in bad with the league and all its games are forfeited to the opposition, even though the revised standings do show the Tennessee nine credited with victories that were given them since the last standings were released."[16]

It was a cryptic description, to be sure, and initially the majority of the black press ignored the win-reversals and unequivocally declared the Monarchs winners of the first half. The *Louisiana Weekly* acknowledged the league ruling on the games, but declared Monroe the victor anyway, listing the team's 31–7 record as superior to Chicago's 31–9. The paper's coverage noted a series of protests mailed to the league office by Monroe fans, arguing that the NSL attempted "to give the Chicago nine something they have not rightfully won." Neither the press nor the fans were gullible enough to fall for the Southern's dirty tricks. The *Atlanta Daily World* listed Monroe's 31–7 and Chicago's 31–8 as the "official standing" of the league in its July 8 edition. "If you've noticed the league standing of the Negro Southern league," wrote Wilson L. Driver, "you'll find that the Monroe club of Louisiana came out on top in the first half of the league race, and the Chicago Giants in second place." It described the NSL's final administrative meeting in depth, including attendance prizes, umpire status, franchise transfers, and player acquisitions. Monroe, it reported, won the first-half pennant.[17]

Two weeks later, however, the *Daily World* reprinted an open letter from president Jackson, released following a league meeting with Robert Cole in Chicago. It read as follows:

Ending the first-half of the split season around July 4, we were faced with a very complex decision, that is, a statement in regards to which team really attained the highest percentage of the close of the first half. All of the clubs connected with the Southern League have played good ball. Most of the clubs are featuring real baseball artists, naturally such qualifications are to be considered. However, there are ideals yet to be cultivated for the preservation of good organized baseball. This year has been one of depression for the clubs to carry on both morally and financially with success. Those composing the league have managed to strain and keep up. The fans apparently are well satisfied at seeing the baseball attractions. To be frank and without prejudice, one or two teams are fooled, little chesty. Maybe a bit of over-confidence and their test for ability is yet unforeseen. Organized baseball is just now in its making and will take some time for the game to return to the old standard which it once held. There are many ideals to be adjusted, however, they all are very simple. For example, the most of our teams do not pay, do not give attraction, [are] not managed correctly, fanchise [*sic*] and registration fee[s] are too limited, moral conduct of players overlooked, league affiliations not guaranteed, inefficient umpires, zoning and distant [*sic*] problem[s], and a number of other details not mentioned but with cooperation and organization these few obstacles can be easily cleared away.

Cole's American Giants are winners for [the] first-half, this team played and won more games, presenting the best attraction qualities, and above all, their individual respect for league affiliation is unsurpassed. In the output (Beginning of season) all laws made by league members were approved and especially those guarding the rules governing the title winner for league honors. When the test came for a show-down, Cole's American Giants have qualified. This telegram, and every form of communication, have flooded the office of the president requesting information and filing protest[s] concerning the right standing, but util [*sic*] every inch of the rules had been met with and a general check-up made of all games won and lost, there was no release of official standing. However, some few sport writers have over-zealously accepted reports of games won and averaged a percentage for publication. Some things to be considered in averaging a team's percentage, especially two ore [*sic*] more clubs averaging about the same number of games won: the use of the official league ball, using disqualified players, clubs missing their schedule dates, clubs giving a breach to some of all rules in baseball. Thus this official percentage standing was somewhat delayed. An official trip to Chicago for pacific business, purposely to adjust such affairs was necessary. The schedule for [the] second-half has been released and every team will be expected to carry on. In the event any club finds it impossible to meet the requirements of the league, especially the engagements as to schedule, said club automatically eliminate[s] itself WITHOUT A VOTE.

All of the clubs have played good ball as mentioned before, but such clubs as the Monroe Monarchs, Nashville Elite Giants, Memphis Red Sox, Indianapolis ABCs, Montgomery Grey Sox, and the Louisville Black Caps are in the run for winning honors for the second half.[18]

Jackson's letter subtly distorts the nature of his decision, and some specific passages merit consideration. In saying, "This year has been one of depression for the clubs to carry on both morally and financially with success," Jackson acknowledges the financial burden of the league, in what sounds almost like an initial apology for everything that follows. The list of generic problems with teams leaves almost infinite room for an official to maneuver in his ruling on the merit of games. In his declaration of Chicago's victory, Jackson cites wins, "the best attraction qualities," and "respect for league affiliation" as valid reasons for the pennant. While this seems suspicious on its face, it also functions as an agent of misdirection. "This team played and won more games," he writes. But in an era where night baseball was rare, and games sometimes ended in ties due to darkness, the pennant came to the team with the highest winning percentage, not the team with the most wins (notice that Chicago also played more games). Jackson later cites "using disqualified players" in his final calculation of winning percentages, among a long list of vague factors for meriting a loss versus a *true* win. He also mentions the distance problem as a factor in league decisions. Distance, of course, was precisely the Nashville argument against Monroe in March. Finally, and possibly most incriminating, is his admission that he visited Chicago to aid in the decision process: "Thus this official percentage standing was somewhat delayed. An official trip to Chicago for pacific business, purposely to adjust such affairs was necessary."

No more about this meeting in Chicago between Jackson and Robert Cole is known, but it was prompted by a threatened protest of the Monarchs by Cole's team. Cole was the owner of Chicago's Metropolitan Funeral System Association when he took over the American Giants in 1932. Like Nashville's Thomas Wilson, he was also a gambler. The following season, Cole and Wilson combined with Gus Greenlee, owner of the Pittsburgh Crawfords, to preside over the newly reconstituted Negro National League and found the East–West All Star game, which would become a staple of black baseball for years to come. (Each would contribute equally for promotional expenses.) Columnist Rollo Wilson noted later in the year that Greenlee, the acknowledged driving force behind both the new league and its showcase game, "hoped to surround himself with men of financial strength who would be willing to count any losses as an investment, an investment which would pay dividends in the years to follow." But the relationship between the three (Cole, Wilson, and Greenlee) began in 1932, facilitated by president Jackson. Later in the year, Cole would field an American Giants football team in Jackson and Wilson's professional league. Regardless, his position and continued involvement in Nashville-based sports enterprises, along with his team's unquestioned prominence, were more than helpful for Jackson and Wilson's entrepreneurial endeavors.[19]

"The decision worked wonders with Cole's American Giants of Chicago," reported the *Defender,* "who now move back into first place as a result." The immediate addition of two Chicago wins and subtraction of two of its losses pleased the columnists of the *Defender,* but Monroe, who played and defeated Memphis more than any other team, did not receive the benefit of loss reversals. The *Monroe Morning World* described the Memphis situation as the result of the league president's dubious motives. "Monroe has won more games and lost less than Chicago but in order to give the Chicago team the break it was ruled to throw out some of the games Chicago lost." The *Defender,* for its part, described the frustration of both teams at not being able to have a head-to-head series to decide the winner, as well as its frustration with the Monarchs taking on what it saw as extra games with Memphis to compensate for the league ruling. The *Defender* described "some queer arrangement" by which "the extra games were played." It argued that "[t]his thing of scheduling four games and playing five and six is all rot. . . . So why not remove all doubts by drawing up a schedule and holding the teams to it. . . . Let's wake up and do this thing in a business way.

What say?" Cole's threatened protest of the Monarchs resulted from the extra Monroe games, but his concerns found an easier remedy through the Nashville-based administration, which miraculously realized that two games with Louisville had been previously postponed. After winning those games, the Giants claimed the pennant. This was a four-game swing for Chicago in a forty-game first half—a full 10 percent of the season artificially constructed to give Cole's team the championship.[20]

After the disputed early-July Memphis series, the *Monroe Morning World* confidently announced, "The victories gave the Monarchs undisputed possession of the first half of the Negro Southern League." The paper also reported that the team protested the decision to reverse two of Chicago's losses to Memphis. A just forfeit for Monroe fans would have given "neither team credit for them. Even though the games were thrown out Chicago would have won 26 and lost seven with a percentage of .787, 38 points behind the Monarchs."[21] For the remainder of 1932, both of the town's white dailies would refer to the Monarchs as champions of the Southern League.

That kind of advocacy is telling. The *Monroe Morning World* and *Monroe News-Star* covered the majority of Monarch games, particularly those played at home. They also commented on the state of the Negro Southern League standings. They were the only white papers in the region to do so. The white weeklies of the surrounding areas in northeast Louisiana never mentioned the Monarchs. They rarely, if ever, mentioned *any* news of the black community. Only one, for example, included coverage of the Zion Traveler Baptist Church controversy. In that kind of cloistered, myopic climate, there was no chance that any of the other regional newspapers of northeast Louisiana would mount a defense of the Monarchs' supposed pennant.[22]

But the *Morning World* and *News-Star* can also be favorably compared to larger white newspapers. The *Louisville Courier-Journal, Arkansas Gazette, Arkansas Democrat,* and *New Orleans Times-Picayune* each carried two black baseball articles through the entire year. The *Chicago Tribune* carried three articles about its local team. The *Austin Statesman* carried four, as did the *Austin American*. The *Nashville Banner* and *Birmingham Age-Herald* held no coverage of their respective local teams. The *New York Times* and *New York Herald Tribune* carried no news of black baseball, either, though articles appeared on their sports pages reporting on the results of fishing, rugby, lacrosse, cricket, outboard motorboating, clay target shooting, Gaelic football, airplane racing, fencing, archery, snooker, and table tennis, among other sports. Even the *Memphis Commercial Appeal,* which included a far broader scope of coverage for black baseball, did not come close to reaching the reporting level of the Monroe dailies.[23]

This seeming aberration cannot be credited to a rogue "race man" inside the *Morning World* sports office. The sports editor for both the *Morning World* and *News-Star* was George V. Lofton, who began his career with the papers two years prior to the Monarchs' championship season in 1930. In the 1940s, after the merging of the two editions, he became the new entity's managing editor and served in that position until 1952. He dominated the paper's sports and news coverage through much of the city's Jim Crow era and did not demonstrate an overt sympathy for the black cause. The white dailies' coverage of the Monarchs, then, was not the result of Lofton's civil rights sympathies. Civil rights sympathies, in fact, were nowhere to be found in Monroe's white dailies. It was, instead, a representation of white Monroe's internalization of the black team's success. As the season began, Monroe's white dailies provided brief write-ups of the games of the "Negro Monarchs," but as of the season's halfway point, they were defending the rightful championship of "Monroe."[24]

Monroe's Monarchs organization was busy defending itself, as well, and it responded to the pennant controversy by offering an unsuccessful protest to the league concerning the American Giants' use of unofficial baseballs in a series with the Montgomery Grey Sox. A week after the first-half press release, president Jackson made a statement concerning the official ball: "We have rules which each team must respect, especially the rules governing regular[ly] scheduled series which are to be played with the official league baseball as long as we have an organized league. As it appears now, only a few of the clubs are using the official ball, namely, Chicago, Nashville, Louisville and Monroe." The team, however, did not submit their protest in writing. "Had Monroe complied with this request there is no telling what would have happened in the flag race," commented the *Defender.* Jackson noted Monroe's failure to officially notify the president's office about protests of Montgomery games. Since the Monarchs' management did not use proper procedures, he claimed, the team's protest went unacknowledged. "A bitter war involving the Monroe and Chicago ball clubs and Dr. R. B. Jackson, president of the Southern league, occupied the back offices of the local clubhouse this week and the bomb shells were still smoking as Dr. Jackson left the city," wrote the *Defender*'s Al Monroe.[25]

Dual reports of the first-half standings led to uncertainty. (See table 3.) The *Defender*'s first-half standings gave Chicago first place with thirty-four wins and seven losses, while Monroe had thirty-three wins and seven losses.[26] The

Morning World reported that the Monarchs' thirty-three wins and seven losses trumped Chicago's twenty-eight wins and nine losses.[27] "The Monarchs won the first half of the Negro Southern League and will coast along until time for the play-off in September," claimed the *Morning World.* "The Monarchs have been granted permission to play any teams they desire in the second half and the fans of Monroe will see the Monarchs in action with teams of other leagues until the play-off." But the paper's declaration of a broader scheduling initiative also disagrees with other competing accounts. Both the *Chicago Defender* and *Pittsburgh Courier,* for example, list a full schedule for the second half of the season. While the Monroe press would prove more accurate in the long run, the contradictory messages coming from different news outlets only exacerbated confusion about who was the rightful pennant winner and just how that decision was reached.[28]

Meanwhile, various papers took various stances on the debate. When the papers' first-half choices appear within their location and coverage areas, a distinct regional pattern emerges. (See tables 4 and 5.) With the exception of the *Birmingham Reporter,* whose hometown team had already abandoned league play, all of the southern papers declared Monroe the first-half champion. This should come as no surprise. Just as southern black baseball took a perennial backseat to northern black baseball, so too did the southern black press. Southern baseball's semi-colonial relationship with the North stemmed from several interrelated factors—smaller cities, a predominantly rural black population, Jim Crow and the legacy of a racism that had permeated the South since the arrival of slavery in seventeenth-century Virginia, and, of course, money. Without an urban, industrial infrastructure, a strong black middle class was unable to rise and corral the minds of its economic inferiors into one understood standard. And black baseball thrived on the existence and stability of the black middle class. The same could be said for black newspapers. In a predominantly rural area without the panoply of urban hubs fostered by industrialization (and thus without a dominant middle class) the southern black press was seen as being in a consistently minor league, its voices drowned out even in its own region by large-circulation northern papers like the *Chicago Defender* and *Pittsburgh Courier.* Southern journalism had an axe to grind, as well. Significantly, however, the bulk of national coverage (or, coverage from northern papers with national circulations) centered on the American Giants. The New York *Amsterdam News* mentioned Monroe as the first-half winner but never adamantly argued the team's case.[29] As a consequence, every subsequent historical mention of the 1932 Negro Southern League first half has deemed Chicago the winner.[30] The bulk of southern coverage, however, chose differently.

"The Monarchs and Chicago are in the throes of a red hot race for the first half pennant," announced a Monroe press release published in the *Kansas City Call*. "Monroe has won 31 and lost 7, while Chicago has won 27 and lost 9. The Louisiana team, however, holds the inside track and general consensus is that the Monarchs will win the flag." The *Call*'s coverage is significant, and two aspects of it merit attention. First, the article carries a Monroe byline and was almost certainly sent by Monarchs management, making "consensus" a nebulous concept. This was a calculated attempt by Stovall and English to broaden the scope of their message. But, second, that did not matter. The message carried the authority of the influential *Kansas City Call* and was read as such. The same can be said for each paper to make similar assertions. When the sports cannot be seen, reports of them dictate public opinion. And when different papers publish different verdicts, confusion is the only possible result.[31]

The confusion was not unprecedented. During the NSL fiasco of 1932, the largest white minor league organization in the South, the Southern Association, experienced similar problems. With the Chattanooga Lookouts' winning percentage behind that of the Memphis Chicks by a very slim margin, Chattanooga argued that it should be allowed to make up a game with Knoxville. League president John Martin ruled that the game should be played, but the league's board of directors vetoed his decision. The Lookouts appealed to Kenesaw Mountain Landis, the commissioner of Major League Baseball, who ruled in Chattanooga's favor. The game was played, and the Lookouts won and eventually secured the pennant, though Memphis finished the season with more wins and fewer losses than its rival.[32]

Furthermore, the 1932 season would not be the last time either Cole or Wilson proved their willingness to manipulate situations to suit their own ends. In 1934, the Negro National League championship series between the Chicago American Giants and Philadelphia Stars ended in controversy, with league commissioner Rollo Wilson refusing to suspend Philadelphia players for striking umpires after questionable calls. Acting dually as owner and National League treasurer, Cole used his power to oust the commissioner.[33]

Following the conclusion of the 1932 season, Wilson proved his own devotion to his financial sustenance, moving the Elite Giants from Nashville to Detroit, hoping to become more accessible to the East Coast–based National League (since it was larger and more profitable than the NSL). The next year he moved the team to Washington, D.C. In 1936, the capital city version of his Elites had another first-half controversy. Wilson scheduled two makeup games with the Philadelphia Stars in order to gain ground on the first-half leader, but when Stars losses put them in second place behind Washington, Wilson refused to play. When league commissioner Ferdinand Morton ruled the games to be necessary, and Washington subsequently lost, Wilson claimed that the games' immediacy limited his ability to field a proper team. His protest ultimately succeeded, and a September makeup game gave Washington the first-half pennant. The controversy angered many, but it proved a valuable case study of Wilson's willingness to manipulate the rules to bring himself success. In 1938, Wilson moved the team to Baltimore.[34]

And so these sorts of championship debates were common. Even in the most well-organized seasons, league schedules were rarely considered sacrosanct, and the inevitable extra and cancelled games led to disputes in which clear pennant justifications were rare (if not impossible). For Monroe, however, the dispute was not common. It was not trivial. 1932 was the team's only major league experience. Monroe's fans did not undergo the internecine disputes of previous major league seasons, and they did not accept the league decision. Black newspapers chose sides along regional lines, only contributing to Monroe's sense of justified outrage.

Of course, Chicago's fans were outraged, as well, and they made reasonable arguments to defend their position. Historian Neil Lanctot describes Thomas Wilson as "usually low key" and "usually silent," and Phil Dixon and Patrick J. Hannigan portray him as "a long time Negro league backer."[35] He was. But Wilson's association with Jackson and Cole in the 1932 Negro Southern League season produced an illegitimate first-half pennant winner and deprived Monroe, Louisiana, of its rightful place in baseball's historical memory.

8

The Second Half

July–August 1932

Everything seemed to be chaos. The confusion engendered by the first-half champions debacle bred confusion throughout the rest of the season. Its remainder seemed in doubt, as only four black newspapers published a second-half schedule for the league.[1] Only five papers maintained consistent baseball coverage through the rest of the season. "Every day the papers chronicle the dropping out of some team in some league," reported *Afro-American* sports editor Bill Gibson, "or of the folding up of entire leagues because of the fact that the fans are conspicuous by their absence. North, South, East and West, the plaint is the same. The Pittsburgh Crawfords constitute the only team able to make the turnstiles click. But even they have years to go before bringing in enough dough to pay for their $75,000 park."[2]

The monthly article tally for available newspapers demonstrates clearly the effect of press criticism for the confused first half of the Southern League season. (See table 6.) The bulk of NSL coverage was in April, May, and June, showing a palpable interest in the season and its progress. July coverage, by contrast, was limited to league pennant meetings and the choosing of a champion. In August, the total dropped again, before the various convoluted championships that closed the season generated a flurry of September articles in various papers in the sample set—some reporting on the games, others arguing for the validity of one pennant or the other, as we shall see in chapter 9. After September, only twenty-one more articles exist for the rest of the calendar year, as assorted reports on the possibility of a season in 1933 offered editorialists a final soapbox from which to fret over the state of baseball.

When broken down into regional location, the numbers become more telling. (See table 7.) The August coverage drops significantly in the South, particularly in the South's largest black newspaper (and the only black daily paper in the country), the *Atlanta Daily World.* Also, the coverage decline begins much earlier in the South. New Orleans, home of the *Louisiana Weekly,* and Shreveport did not have teams in the NSL. Memphis's June and July tallies have not survived. Atlanta's and Birmingham's teams stopped league play prior to the Monroe-Chicago controversy of early July. Southern newspapers, in other words, had no more local incentive to pay attention. The first-half pennant controversy only exacerbated their apathy. Instead, the northern papers with a surviving stake in the outcome of the Southern League—the *Indianapolis Recorder, Chicago Defender,* and *Pittsburgh Courier*—remain truest to the pattern set by the broader national coverage trends. Notably, those three publications carry the most Southern League coverage in a regional category without many concerned newspapers. In the border region between North and South, the *Kansas City Call* and Baltimore *Afro-American*—playing to a large circulation but without a direct hometown interest in the outcome—kept a generally consistent (though smaller) coverage pattern throughout. Meanwhile, the West's coverage existed almost entirely in the form of wire service reprints.

When those papers are broken down into national and regional circulations, the pattern remains constant. (See table 8.) Notably, of the papers with significant ball clubs in 1932, only the *Kansas City Call* had a higher number of August articles than it did July articles. That paper's hometown team, the Kansas City Monarchs, took the opposite route of the other teams in Negro League baseball for 1932. The Kansas City Monarchs did not field a team for the first half of the season, and when they did begin play, they barnstormed independently. In August, their opening games against the Chicago American Giants counted toward the Giants' second-half record, and so are included in the sample's August total. If those contests are eliminated, the August numbers become markedly lower.[3] (The same cannot be said for the national total when Chicago's Kansas City coverage is eliminated. The American Giants lost the series, and the *Defender's* only article on the games announced that they would take place—no reports of the outcomes were printed. Journalistic disillusionment only grew with the increased confusion of the second-half schedule.)[4]

And so the full range of black newspapers largely gave up on the second half of the baseball season, and the same southern papers that argued for Monroe's pennant stopped any kind of consistent, substantial coverage by August, as the turmoil of July caused them to focus on other events. (See table 9.) The summer of 1932, for example, was an Olympic summer. Two black track stars, Eddie Tolan and Ralph Metcalfe, sprinted to gold and silver medals. Their victories dominated the headlines of every black paper in the nation, but only some chose to use the remaining column inches for baseball coverage.[5]

Like baseball, the Olympics demonstrated the tenuousness of the relationship between the press and black athletics. The dominance of Tolan and Metcalfe was palpable, but as historian Mark Dyreson has argued, "the mainstream media simply refused to draw conclusions about the shattering of any American racial mythologies at the Los Angeles Olympics." David B. Welky notes that white coverage that did praise the sprinters consistently attached racial designations to their descriptions. They were never champions; they were Negro champions. African American papers such as the *Kansas City Call* and *Atlanta Daily World* called specific attention to the tendency in the white press to downplay the achievements of Metcalfe and Tolan.[6] It all looked suspiciously familiar to baseball fans. Still, some African Americans were more optimistic about the coverage these Olympic athletes received. In late August, Edwin B. Henderson, head of the Department of Health and Physical Education for Junior and Senior High Schools, released a newspaper column titled "Race Hatred Tends to Decrease in the Olympics." African American athletic achievement, he argued, was making social equality possible. The Olympics in particular promoted "a broader international and interracial sympathy," wrote Henderson. "Races of men the globe over have used these games to gain racial and spiritual respect." And though many mainstream papers chose to ignore the feats of America's black sprinters, those that did cover them were the proof of progress. "I don't know when the New York Times has given first column prominence and headlines to a colored man for whatever feat or fame as it did to Eddie Tolan last week."[7] But in the black weeklies, accolades for Tolan and Metcalfe were not exceptions. They dominated the sports pages, and even the front pages. And they served as an adequate replacement for the controversy and skepticism bred by the baseball season.

But when the white dailies of Monroe covered black athletics, they covered the Monarchs. The fans believed their team was the champion, and the team knew it had more games to play. Of course, the theft of the first-half championship clearly had its lingering effects, and as the second half began, the Monarchs struggled to regain their early-season form. Monroe began its new schedule on a three-week road trip, covering Memphis, Chicago, and Louisville. Even as the games got under way, the scheduling discrepancy again appeared blatant. Chicago, already rested from its early-season lack of travel, wouldn't take to the road until August.[8]

As the Negro Southern League muddled through, seemingly plagued by controversy, corruption, and a growing apathy among the press, the white Cotton States League died a more definitive death. After a July 4 doubleheader, De-Quincy, Arkansas, announced that it could not sustain a baseball team in 1932. DeQuincy had taken the place of the Cotton States' Port Arthur, Texas, team when it folded in June. League president Frank Scott rushed to find a replacement. But he couldn't. He wired the National Baseball Association for a loan to sustain the league. The loan was refused. "I see nothing to do," Scott announced, "but close the season."[9] Two days later, the Associated Press reported that "the South's historic Cotton States League has closed the gates. Opening this season with a struggle, battling financial handicaps almost from the start, it succumbed finally with four stalwarts of the six-club circuit dying hard."[10] The Monroe Twins were one of the four. The Monarchs now played the only game in town.

But as the second half started, the Monarchs were playing it away from home. And they weren't playing it very well. In Memphis, Monroe began a dramatic slide, demonstrating the lingering effects of the pennant controversy by losing three of four to the Red Sox. Manager Homer "Goose" Curry took the mound in the first game, allowing ten hits but holding the visitors to six runs. It was a series that would contain a number of memorable plays—errors, double steals, and even a triple play—but none seemed to go the Monarchs' way. In the second game, the first of a Sunday doubleheader, Monroe managed its only victory, hitting four home runs on its way to a 15–2 win. But the Monarchs would lose the nightcap, and they would lose the Monday finale.[11]

Chagrined by Memphis, Monroe then limped to Chicago for what they must have felt to be the most important series of the season. League president Reuben Jackson, in Chicago to determine the first-half winner, stayed and watched the Monarchs-Giants series in the owner's box at Cole Field—a fact not lost on anyone following the games back home in Louisiana.[12] Fraught with the symbolic importance such a series between the two first-half contenders held, the pressure on the small-town team was immense. And this time, they proved unable to rise to it.

Saturday's game, the first between the two teams, proved to be the close contest everyone expected from the first-half pennant race. Willie Foster pitched for the Giants, and Elbert Williams for the Monarchs, and during the first eight innings neither team managed a run. Williams, in fact, allowed only one hit through the first eight. Foster, meanwhile, had nine strikeouts. In the top of the ninth, Monroe managed to plate one run and seemed on the strength of the prior eight innings to have a victory well in hand. But in the bottom of the inning, Chicago managed two hits, the second coming with two outs, scoring the Giants' second run. The Monarchs lost 2–1.[13]

Sunday featured a doubleheader, and Monroe came out to save face in the opener. The Monarchs' Dick Matthews pitched versus the Giants' Willie Powell. Matthews was another Stovall purchase, this time from in-state rival the New Orleans Black Pelicans. His acquisition didn't draw the headlines of, say, Red Murray, but Matthews's arm had been dependable throughout the season. And he pitched well on Sunday, allowing four runs on eight hits, while Powell faltered early and never gained momentum. In the sixth, with the score tied 2–2, he allowed six Monarch runs. Chicago never recovered, and Monroe took the game 9–4.[14]

That victory, however, would be the last of the series for the Monarchs. In the second game of the doubleheader, Melvin "Put" Powell pitched scoreless baseball for the American Giants until the seventh. He allowed only two runs in the final three frames, making Chicago's four runs plenty to take the game. Monroe then lost games on Monday and Tuesday. The Monarchs were outmaneuvered in the first-half pennant negotiations, but in the second series of the season's second half, they were outplayed.[15]

As Monroe took its lumps, other teams began more auspiciously. Nashville sports columnist Luther Carmichael proudly trumpeted the Elite Giants' undefeated second-half start. The club won seven in a row, and he was "expecting the Giants to give somebody a heck of a fight for the bunting before this hectic second half comes to a termination."[16]

The Crawfords, too, continued on, dropping three of four in an early July series with the Black Yankees. Those games were a blip on an otherwise continuous line of success, but success on the field did not always match success at the box office. On July 15, new grandstand prices took effect at Pittsburgh's Greenlee Field, falling from fifty to forty cents.[17] An undaunted Gus Greenlee, however, kept spending. With the East–West League defunct, and its dictates no longer holding players to contracts, the acquisitions began in earnest. In mid-July, the team announced its first of the spoils of the East–West collapse. Jud Wilson, who played third base for the Homestead Grays until the league's dissolution, signed a contract with the Crawfords. Judy Johnson, with Hilldale at the East–West's inception, also joined after his club faltered. Herbert A. "Rap" Dixon then arrived from Baltimore. The all-star team was recruiting more all-stars.[18]

As of July 12, the Crawfords had played ninety-four games in 109 days, including the preseason, beginning with their first contest with Monroe on March 25. The team's traveling bus had logged more than seventeen thousand miles. By season's end, the Crawfords would tally their record at 96–34–4 in 134 games.[19]

But as Pittsburgh continued to win, Monroe continued to stumble through its early paces. Defeated in two straight series, the Monarchs traveled from Chicago to Louisville for a scheduled contest with the Black Caps. The team had experienced a rocky first half, but on July 7 announced its plans to play out the remainder of the season as scheduled by the Southern League. The series, however, did not go as scheduled. Two short weeks after Louisville assured fans that it would play out the second half, the club disbanded. Management chose not to publicly announce the decision until Monroe arrived, so when fans reached the ballpark on Saturday, a sign greeted them at the entrance: "No game today." The Black Caps' players, left in the lurch by management's decision to close operations for the season, moved temporarily to another local Louisville team, the Red Birds, creating a two-team amalgam that looked much like the now-defunct Southern League aggregation. The Monarchs split a Sunday doubleheader with the new, gerrymandered group.[20]

From Louisville, the Monarchs limped home in late July for their first series of the second half in Casino Park. With rain on Saturday, the four-game set with Memphis featured doubleheaders on Sunday and Monday. The Red Sox (now forgiven by the league for their early-season misdeeds) had bolstered their lineup after the break and were hovering near the top of the second-half standings, and Monroe dutifully reserved part of the stands for white patrons. Adding to the games' intrigue, a Monroe sweep could put the team back in the Southern's second place. A sweep, however, was not to be. The Monarchs lost both games on Sunday. But on Monday, they looked impressive in two victories.[21] It appeared possible that the team had regained its first-half form and was poised to demonstrate to the Southern League why it deserved its rightful pennant. But they wouldn't get the chance. The Memphis series would constitute the Monarchs' final official games with a Southern League opponent.

On July 29, Jackson released a statement preaching the necessity of using official league baseballs, and the declared winner of the games based on that rule: "Naturally offenses of this kind will cause a misunderstanding when the official standing is released. However, the standing as found with this communication is official: Nashville vs. Indianapolis, nonofficial balls, Nashville, three games; Nashville vs. Columbus, nonofficial balls, Nashville, four games." Nashville was undefeated, but—despite Luther Carmichael's optimism—the team's perfect 7–0 record in the second half was the result of forfeits due to Indianapolis's and Columbus's use of improper equipment. Jackson again awarded an ally victories and again defended the decision, much as he did for Chicago in the first half. This decision, too, would lead a competing team to suspect foul play—the Indianapolis ABCs did not lose all of their games against Nashville, and in a few short weeks, ABCs manager Jim Taylor would publicly question Jackson's motives.[22]

Meanwhile, in early August, instead of continuing their league schedule, the Monarchs announced that the team would play the New Orleans Black Pelicans for an unofficial "state championship" of Louisiana. As proclaimed by the Monroe newspapers in early July, the Monarchs played under the assumption that they were winners of the Southern's first half, and that, as such, they were free to play any schedule they saw fit.[23] Such claims of victory, by the Monroe press or the Monarchs themselves, could have been genuine, or they could have masked a more calculated defiance of league policy in response to the first-half championship machinations. Either way, this was the team's public policy, and the rest of their season consisted of a graduated set of makeshift "championships," beginning with this initial series with the Pelicans.

The intrigue of the Pelicans series, however, was not solely peripheral. The team was managed by their star left-handed pitcher, Robert "Black Diamond" Pipkin (whom the Monarchs had courted early in the season). The *Morning World* called Black Diamond "one of the greatest negro hurlers in the entire country." In addition, the two teams played a similar series in 1931, won by the Monarchs. The rivalry, the championship label applied to it, and a Pelican roster that featured five former Negro National League players made the series interesting to both white and black. Stovall and English reserved half of the grandstand for white fans.[24]

Prior to Sunday's doubleheader, the new management of the New Orleans team announced that the squad's name had changed along with its leadership. They were now the Algiers Giants. Owned and operated by Sam Calderone, the Giants had traded players with the Pelicans all season, and the two teams were fierce New Orleans rivals.[25] Though the Monroe press cited a name change, however, the first game between Monroe and Algiers happened while the New Orleans Black Pelicans were losing a thirteen-inning contest to visiting Mobile. The team that came to Monroe, in fact, contained players from both the Giants and Pelicans. Furthermore, when the series moved to New Orleans for its second half, the teams played in West Side Park, Algiers (a New Orleans suburb). Announcements encouraged fans to purchase tickets at Sam Calderone's Pharmacy at 114 Teche Street in Algiers.[26]

During the week of that return series, *Louisiana Weekly* sports editor Earl Wright publicly decried the practice of "team jumping" among players on New Orleans baseball teams, which often shifted the makeup of a local team in an instant, only for that makeup to change again in days or weeks. "For years," he wrote, "this sort of thing has been a nuisance."[27] And if his analysis was correct, then players probably switched teams when the possibility of a better percentage of the gate was possible. Monroe never played a Pelican team that changed its name. That team might have resembled the Pelicans, but it was always Algiers.

The Giants acquitted themselves well, and managed a split of the Sunday doubleheader. The situation now surely seemed ominous for Monroe. The Monarchs' play had been inconsistent at best in the season's second half, and in the third game of the Louisiana championship series, Black Diamond took the mound for the visitors. If there was concern, however, it was quickly dispelled. Monroe scored one in the first, four in the fourth, then chased Black Diamond in the sixth with three more. They won 10–1, giving them a two-games-to-one lead. The series would continue in New Orleans, it was announced at a press meeting, and dates would be forthcoming. At this same press meeting, the Monarchs announced that they had won the right to play in the Negro World Series against the so-called Eastern League champions. Those dates, too, would soon be announced. Whoever the opponent, transportation would be provided for all those who wanted to see the games.[28]

As with the second-half schedule discrepancies, the proclamation that the Monarchs would play in the World Series could have been a swipe at NSL officials. After all, the Southern did not acknowledge the Monarchs' first-half championship, so there was no governing body to bestow such a "right." In addition, the Eastern League champions did not exist, because there was no Eastern League. More likely than vindictiveness or retribution, however, is the possibility that Stovall or English was in contact with the Pittsburgh Crawfords management. Both teams opened their preseason schedule against each other in Monroe. Pittsburgh was unaffiliated with the East–West League, and thus survived the group's midseason collapse. The first-half pennant controversy made the Monarchs appear to be a viable league champion, yet without a commitment to a league championship series. It was, it seemed, an auspicious confluence of opportunity and availability for both teams.

But the press conference wasn't over. Monroe had clearly abandoned the Southern League schedule, but nonetheless officially announced that scheduled games for the weekend of August 12–14 had been cancelled. "The schedule of the negro southern league has been changed," reported the *Morning World,* "which forces the Monarchs to enter the negro world series earlier than was planned." Instead, the team would travel to New Orleans to finish its state championship series with Algiers. On the way, the club would stop in Alexandria for a two-game Thursday–Friday exhibition series with the town's Lincoln Giants. They would then, after completing their scheduled games with New Orleans, engage the Austin Black Senators in another "Dixie Series." Only then would the Monarchs play the "World Series." Unsurprisingly, it was only two short days after its initial announcement that the team produced a full schedule of World Series games. Pittsburgh would be its opponent.[29]

Meanwhile, the *Defender* speculated on August 13 about the possible demise of the NSL. Montgomery, Atlanta, and late replacement Alcoa, Tennessee, had folded, it reported. The article noted that Monroe had not participated in a league series in several weeks, though that claim was false. The status of Memphis, too, was uncertain, reported the *Defender*. The Red Sox had missed a series with Chicago, but only because Chicago didn't travel south.[30]

In fact, the American Giants had also abandoned league play. In mid-August, the team split a home doubleheader with the Homestead Grays, now playing independently after the collapse of the East–West. It dropped the other two games, however, losing its first series at home all year. The Giants next lost a series with the Kansas City Monarchs, then another to the Grays, before finally refinding their form against two white teams—the House of David, featuring Grover Cleveland Alexander, and Buck Weaver's All-Stars.[31]

In its report of August 13, the *Defender* noted, "The Monroe Monarchs are preparing for the big series with Chicago or some team in the East. Several thousand additional stands are being built [at Casino Park] for this series." The report was obviously filed by a Monarchs press agent. The article continued by arguing that all southerners would demand a championship series because of the theft of their rightful first-half pennant. "The interest has been worked up so high in the South that the I.C. railroad offered a round-trip fare of $9 from Monroe to Chicago and vice versa with a four-day stay in the town." Thousands of Louisiana fans, the paper claimed, would make the trip to Chicago. "[The Monarchs] are asking the press to demand this as fair play must be given."[32]

Monroe, however, wouldn't return to Chicago. And the team had more immediate concerns. As previously announced, before engaging Algiers in the second half of the Louisiana Series, the Monarchs stopped in Alexandria to play exhibition games with the Alexandria Lincoln Giants, splitting the two contests before continuing on to New Orleans. "Beating the Monroe Monarchs," wrote Pitman Nedde, congratulating the Alexandria squad, "is an achievement worthy to any ball team, as we all know by now that the Monarchs truly know their onions when it comes to performing on a diamond."[33]

That Sunday, the New Orleans Black Pelicans returned to Alexandria, as well, losing to the home team. Reports of the contests listed the crowd at more than two thousand, mirroring earlier reports of similar crowds at Monroe Black Drillers' games. Earl Wright, *Louisiana Weekly* sports editor, found the claims laughable, and his account sheds light on a further enigmatic layer obscuring reports of the 1932 season. Wright described telling the Pelican players about the attendance claims in Alexandria reports (which his sports section printed in the same edition). "Some of the ball pursuers laughed long and loudly while others simply shook their heads." It didn't happen. It couldn't have happened, Wright noted. "According to the Orleanians some 500 shoved real honest-to-goodness money through the window while some 200 more came in on passes," he wrote. "The park is unable to accommodate 1500 people."[34]

This would not be the last time that the Pelicans accused Alexandria of dishonesty. The team returned to the town two weeks later and dropped a three-game set to the Lincoln Giants. When they returned home, the Pelicans cried foul to the New Orleans press, claiming that Alexandria umpire Sylvester Cotton "robbed them in every way except with a gun." They accused the entire organization of dirty play and argued that the infractions were so blatant that "the majority of the white fans left the game and threatened to stay out of the park if such was the procedure."[35] The accusations are interesting because they highlight the sectional rivalries and prejudices within the state. But more interesting is the language the team used to make its claims. The dissatisfaction of the white patrons was the measuring stick of fair play, indicating that through their sure resentment of white racism, black baseball men still respected white baseball opinions, at least to some degree. It was the early-season umpire controversy all over again.

But in New Orleans, black and white witnessed the Monarchs make relatively quick work of Algiers. A 17–2 Sunday drubbing of the Giants followed a Saturday shutout, 5–0. Monroe lost on Monday but rebounded on Tuesday, and the state champions returned from New Orleans on Thursday morning after spending an extra day in the Crescent City. That night they departed for Austin. Again, team management announced that Monroe had won the Negro Southern League pennant, and that it was that fact alone that qualified them to play Pittsburgh in the World Series. "This is the first time," the *Morning World* reported, "a team from the south has won the right to take part in the Negro World Series." That it was. It was the first time a team from the South would play in any world series, black or white.[36]

On Friday, the Monarchs won the rain-shortened first game of the Dixie Series by topping Austin 5–2. The following day, however, the Senators evened the series tally. Though Monroe managed eight hits to Austin's five, a young pitcher named Hilton Smith allowed the Monarchs only two runs in a very impressive outing. The Senators won 3–2. In the third and final game of the Austin portion of the championship, the Monarchs rallied to a 5–4 victory.[37]

Before the Monarchs' return engagement with Austin at Casino Park, however, and with Memphis long out of contention in the Southern League's second half, Stovall demonstrated that he, like Greenlee, could take advantage when other clubs faltered. He acquired Red Sox pitcher/manager Homer "Goose" Curry, as well as left-hander Bob Harvey, to help the Monarchs compete with Austin and Pittsburgh. On Friday, August 28, the day after Frank Johnson announced the team's new acquisitions, he told the media that he wanted to win two in a row, finishing off the Senators and getting the Monarchs on their way to Pittsburgh a day early. Half of the grandstand, he assured reporters, would be reserved for white patrons. Newspaper advertisements for the game billed the Monarchs as "Negro Southern League Champs." Tickets remained fifty cents for the grandstand, and seventy-five for box seats, as they had all season. In a year of declining revenues and collapsing leagues—a year in which even the Crawfords had to lower ticket prices—the Monarchs' financial viability never wavered.[38]

Still, Johnson's hope for a quick victory at home went unfulfilled. Hilton Smith started his second game of the series, and with his win the previous weekend, the young hurler was 29–0 on the season. In his thirtieth, Smith allowed just one earned and one unearned run en route to a 4–2 Senators victory. Stovall and Doug English looked on with covetous eyes. With the series now tied, however, there were more immediate concerns. The Monarchs would need to win the next two games.[39]

On Monday, the Monarchs' hurler Elbert Williams took over the pitching duties in the ninth inning of a 2–2 tie, holding the Senators scoreless. In the bottom of the ninth, he hit the game-winning RBI single. Williams was one of Stovall's big-name spring purchases, and the return on his investment was palpable. Williams proved to be the team's iron man the following day as well, taking the mound in the Dixie Series' final game. As in previous seemingly tenuous situations, the Monarchs responded well to pressure. Williams allowed only three scattered hits in a complete game shutout of visiting Austin. "The Monarchs," reported the *Morning World,* "looked the part of champions yesterday and it seems that they will give the Pittsburgh Crawfords . . . plenty of trouble in the negro world series." The following morning, Wednesday, August 31, the Monarchs set off for Pittsburgh and the Negro World Series.[40]

Again, the team had strong advocacy from Monroe's white dailies, an unprecedented phenomenon in the region. In 1909, Monroe's *Evening News* and *Daily Star* combined to form the *News-Star.* Then Colonel Robert Ewing, publisher of the *New Orleans States* and *Shreveport Times* came to Monroe in 1929 and created the *Morning World.* In 1930, Ewing bought the *News-Star,* as well, making it the afternoon counterpart to the *Morning World* and giving him a virtual monopoly on mainstream white news in the region.[41]

Coverage of the black community in Ewing's *Morning World,* the Monarchs excepted, was generally negative, consisting primarily of arrest reports, Prohibition violations, and patronizing caricatures of the southern black dialect (to say nothing of advertisements for visiting minstrel shows and cartoons featuring exaggerated black features—two additional mechanisms for creating a negative black image in the white mind). Positive portrayals of black life revolved exclusively around religious and civic meetings. Still, the Monarchs' impact on the paper's non-sports pages was palpable, as the success of the team had a reciprocal effect on the *Morning World's* coverage of black life. Negative coverage of the black community grew steadily in the paper from January to April, finally peaking in May. (See table 10.) When murder, robbery, and other crime statistics are added to reports of drunkenness, bootlegging, and general condescension, the total monthly negative stories for the first five months of 1932 start at three in January, and then go to seventeen, seventeen, and thirty-eight, with a high of fifty-six in May (minstrel show advertisements and cartoons are not included in the sample). Positive portrayals of the black community's church and civic meetings remained infrequent, beginning at three in January, and running to three, three, fifteen, to twenty-five in the subsequent months.[42]

Some of the murder incidents reported did not occur in Monroe or Ouachita Parish. But that was really beside the point. The portrayal of the criminality of the black populace did not rest on regional variation. Negative depictions of what it meant to be black contributed to the white image of African American inferiority and the need for continued segregation. But as the Monarchs' season progressed, the frequency of those negative depictions markedly decreased. From June through August, the negative coverage numbers ran from fifty to thirty-two to sixteen. The Monarchs' series with the Crawfords would ultimately end on September 12, and the negative portrayals decreased to eleven in the first half of that month. Additionally, the reports of Prohibition violations, or drunkenness, for this time span numbered twenty-three, as the violent crimes of murder and robbery decreased to their lowest totals in months. (The *Morning World* reported only thirteen other African American Prohibition violations for the eight-and-a-half other months of the year.) The negative coverage numbers again increased after the season's conclusion, from the second half of September to the New Year, moving from twenty-two, thirty-five, and thirty-nine to, finally, thirty-six in December. The number in December was accompanied by *no* positive coverage in the month.[43]

These numbers demonstrate the ability of sports to serve as, in the words of Michael Lomax, a "unifying element" for black fans of black baseball. The African American community responded to its team's success with a dramatic decrease in violent crime.[44] But that unifying element was broader than race. The white newspaper decreased its negative representations of the black community as the Monarchs continued to win. The *Morning World*'s numbers are the only ones available, but they show a positive correlation of black coverage with team performance. The willingness of white Monroe police officers to make arrests decreased, and the likelihood that the white newspapers would find such action newsworthy diminished, as well. As the Monarchs accumulated victories, Sherman Briscoe—a teacher and football coach at Monroe Colored High—gave the African American community the *Southern Broadcast,* its first black weekly newspaper of the decade. Stovall added seats to Casino Park, which signaled his belief that the black community could afford the fifty-cent entry fee. Whether black fans responded to baseball success with better citizenship or the white press simply found itself disposed to treat them more fairly in its pages, there is no question that the black population of Monroe was doing better.[45]

Still, though the Cotton States' Monroe Twins lost consistently in a white league that would not survive the summer, stories of its camp, its trades, its games, and its league dominated the *Morning World* and *News-Star* headlines, leaving write-ups about the Monarchs to languish below the fold. They were there, but they were always secondary. Ollie Burns, an African American college student at the time, recalled the coverage discrepancy in the mainstream Monroe dailies, but understood the time and place in which she lived. "It wasn't important to print in the paper," she noted, "even though this was a World Series team. It was the thirties. A different day." The slight could be frustrating, "but we couldn't let it get us down in our thinking."[46]

Pitman Nedde bemoaned a similar balance of power in Shreveport sport. The town "doesn't seem to be interested in a baseball team enough to support it through a full season. And especially this is true of Negro teams that are organized here. On the other hand, the Sports (white team) can go through a full season at the bottom of the league (as is usually their standing), nevertheless they have almost as many Negro fans in the bleachers attending their games as whites." Shreveport not only had a larger black community than Monroe, but its mouthpiece, the *Shreveport Sun,* had been operating successfully since 1920. Such advantages made the problem all the more puzzling for Nedde. "The question before us is, why Negroes of Shreveport will flock to the Biedenharn park to see ball games, and won't go to Negro ball games at all."[47]

It was a fair question, and one with no clear answer. Yet there was something to be said for winning. The *Morning World* coverage of the 1932 Monarchs far exceeded the coverage the white papers offered in the "minor" years prior. Throughout the late 1920s, only a rare national boxing match between black opponents merited coverage by the white papers of Monroe. Only one—a notice of Jack Thompson and Joe Dundee's 1928 Comiskey Park bout—took up more space than an advertisement one year prior for a special meeting of the Ku Klux Klan at the Monroe Woodmen of the World Hall. After the Monarchs' founding in 1930, coverage of the team was sparse, but generally available following victories. When the club was successful—and this remained true when it came to black weeklies, as well—the team became newsworthy.[48]

White and black papers both liked to report on winners. Winners sold newspapers. But otherwise, the black and white presses were very different. The divide between them becomes even clearer when the news priorities of Monroe's *Morning World* and the black population's only daily, the *Atlanta Daily World,* are evaluated. (See Table 11.) An analysis of the top line of each front-page column in the newspapers for the sample month of May 1932 demonstrates far different above-the-fold priorities. The *Morning World* emphasized politics. The *Daily World* emphasized crime and religion. The *Morning World* cared about the Democratic primary. The *Daily World* cared about the Scottsboro boys. This kind of coverage discrepancy demonstrates that the white and black audiences were receiving two different messages—were developing (or continuing to develop) two different mindsets. But beyond those headlines, beyond the front page, it was obvious that every southern press, every southern audience, cared deeply about sports.[49]

"The greatest and most successful newspapers both white and black have followed the trend of the human mind and are devoting more space, and more careful attention to their sports and theatrical sections than ever before in the history of journalism," wrote Harry Levette, sports editor of the *California Eagle.* Black newspapers were the last to get involved. But that was only because of their arrogance. "Year by year sports took a greater hold on the nation and brainy men found in them not only the foundation for the health of the nation's offspring but the development of mental qualities gained by clean competition, manliness, fairness and consideration of others." Levette noted that the larger papers devoted at least two pages to sports coverage, revealing "the importance in which they are held as pabulum of reader interest."[50]

Sports were certainly important for Monroe residents, black and white, in 1932, and most of them lived those contests through the newspaper press. Such writing facilitates memory, and the influence of that coverage would allow the Monarchs' season to resonate with the population even after the newspapers fell silent. So, too, would controversy. But in a season flush with it, the controversy had yet to run its course.

Two weeks prior to the Monarchs' trek to Pittsburgh, Reuben Jackson and Southern League officials announced that they were calling the second-half race in favor of league leader Nashville, despite the fact that the bulk of its league victories had come through forfeit. The Elite Giants would meet Chicago for the Southern League championship. The *Chicago Defender* reported that the winner of the series would play Posey's Homestead Grays, mistakenly referring to the team as champions of the East–West League. For the *Defender,* this was the World Series—the only World Series.[51] Regardless, the NSL championship series would reunite Jackson, Wilson, and Cole. Jackson informed Monroe and the other NSL franchises that Nashville would be awarded the second-half crown without playing out the remainder of the schedule. This again appears to be rank opportunism from Jackson, a hallmark of his presidential reign. The Southern League teams, whether they adhered to the mandated schedule or not, showed no signs of the financial collapse or disastrous attendance demonstrated by the East–West League. But Jackson saw Tom Wilson's Elite Giants in first place; he saw an opportunity to stage a championship gala between his league's two largest franchises and his two partners in the first-half pennant scandal (and his two partners in the Negro Southern Football League). And so with Nashville in the second-half lead, it became time for the postseason.[52] Jackson hoped to secure a contract for the winner to play either Homestead, Pittsburgh, or New York in a world series that would only further legitimize his fledgling league. The president announced that he expected the heads of all teams represented at the series. Fred Stovall, however, would be busy.[53]

9
The World Series
September–October 1932

The Monarchs were working through a series of graduated championships in August. They were the state champions of Louisiana. They were Dixie Series champions. And as they climbed each rung of that hastily constructed ladder, the fans of Monroe—particularly the black fans of Monroe—basked in the reflected pride of those victories. The team lived there, of course, and as such moved in the circles of local black culture. But devotion to the team didn't rest on personal relationships. In the most unlikely of places, a group of black men with "Monroe" emblazoned on their chests were proving to be the best at what they did—in the state, in the area known as Dixie, and soon, they hoped, in the world.

As Monroe prepared for its "world" championship, however, preparations for the Negro Southern League's own hastily constructed championship pitting Nashville against Chicago came into question. The weekend prior to the Southern's mid-August series announcement, the vaunted Elite Giants, Jackson's choice for second-half champion, fell victim to a sweep at Memphis against the Red Sox. The Elites seemed far less potent when their victories weren't bestowed by forfeit, and the "championship" appeared more and more suspect.[1]

Then Jim Taylor had his say. The Indianapolis ABCs' leader, frustrated by inexplicable forfeits and win reversals, made a strong denunciation of league decisions, which he clearly found corrupt. He cited Indianapolis wins over Nashville that were not counted by the league office. "There have been some protests and legislations through the office of the president and some club owners to give or make certain teams win the pennant," Taylor wrote. He noted that Monroe won more and lost fewer games in the first half, and that by his count Chicago had managed the feat in the second half. Of course, neither Jackson, Cole, nor Wilson wanted Chicago as second-half champion. Since the president gave the

American Giants the first-half pennant, a second Chicago win would mean no championship series, no claim against the legitimacy of the Monroe-Pittsburgh contest. So Nashville was unfairly given the second-half title, Chicago the first.[2]

But Jackson remained undaunted. The week following his Southern League championship announcement, he had more concrete plans to report. September 2 would be the official last day of the season. September 3—the day of the Monroe-Pittsburgh opener in the World Series—would also open the Dixie Series in Chicago. Three games in Nashville would follow the three up north. If the championship was still tied, a seventh game would be played in Detroit or Kansas City. Jackson announced that NBC and CBS would broadcast the games on national radio. He promised prizes such as diamond rings, wristwatches, silk hose, bicycles, gasoline, and even one hundred pounds of sugar. To further conflate the importance of the series, he announced that Nashville mayor Hilary Ewing Howse, Tennessee governor Henry Horton, and various other state luminaries would be on hand for the Nashville games.[3]

Jackson congratulated Monroe, Indianapolis, Memphis, Louisville, and Montgomery on successful seasons, "but due to the depression and for plans already consummated, they were ordered to begin and prepare for next season's aggregation. Financial status, low administration fees, poor attendances are some of the chief causes why such orders were given from the executive headquarters." The statement sounds familiar—much like Jackson's first-half explanation announcement. At the end of the season, however, protest letters concerning the president's behavior would have no effect.[4]

Clearly, there was some gamesmanship between organizers and supporters of both series. When Monarchs business manager Doug English reiterated in late August that his team would play Pittsburgh in the World Series, his interpretation of Monroe's qualifications clearly broke from the official NSL line. He argued that the Monarchs won the first-half pennant, that no one won the second half because of the stoppage of league play, and thus that Monroe was the Southern League champion. But Jackson's announcement said differently. "Immediately after this official verdict had been announced," the *Louisiana Weekly* reported, "hundreds of protests, it is said, from fans all over the South, flooded President Jackson's office. They painted the ruling as a daylight hold-up of the Monroe team and didn't give him a minutes [*sic*] rest from the matter." English claimed that Jackson wrote him a letter rectifying the first-half controversy, declaring Monroe the league champion, and authorizing them to play in the World Series against Pittsburgh. Jackson's public claims, to say nothing of his organization of and appearance at the Southern League championship series between Chicago and Nashville, seem to invalidate this report. English was, more than likely, lying. But his explanation's prominent place on the *Louisiana Weekly*'s sports page surely convinced many—if anyone in Louisiana still needed convincing.[5]

"The Negro World Series in which the Pittsburgh Crawfords of Pittsburgh, Pa., and the Monroe Monarchs of Monroe, La., are vying for honors," reported Charles Isaac Bowen, writer for the Associated Negro Press, "will just about wind up the baseball interest in the Negro Major leagues this season." Lending the Associated Negro Press's declaration of legitimacy to the Monroe-Pittsburgh series added weight to Monroe's claims. Pittsburgh press agent John L. Clark—surely more biased—referred to the Monarchs as "dixie champions" in his reporting. "This aggregation of players is said to be the best the South has produced in years."[6] According to the *Pittsburgh Courier,* Monroe carried nine players with batting averages of at least .300 in league play.[7]

Most papers followed the lead of the *Courier* and the Associated Negro Press. The New York *Amsterdam News* and *California Eagle,* for example, reprinted wire-service reports declaring the Monroe-Pittsburgh series the only legitimate championship. (See table 8.) Even those who covered both series referred to the Pittsburgh contest as the "World" Series and the Chicago contest as the "Dixie" Series. But some, like the *Louisville Leader,* remained jaded by the awkward development of the season. "Winning this title will not settle the question of the championship team," it reported. "The disorganized state of affairs among Negro baseball clubs prevent[s] such a settlement with only one series." William "Dizzy" Dismukes, writing in late December and reviewing the season that was, summarized the confusion that clouded baseball. "Monroe, La., boasted the highest percentage in the first half of the Southern league split season. Chicago had the distinction of winning the second half, yet Nashville and Chicago advertised and engaged in a playoff for the championship." It seemed that even the experts were confused. Still, with few exceptions, the majority of the sample papers described the two series by advocating one or the other as preeminent. When the "World Series" finally ended, the *Memphis World* argued that the final game "closed the series in which the Crawfords and Monarchs battled for the Negro World Championship."[8]

But as the papers debated legitimacy or viability or both, the Monarchs took the field in Pittsburgh. "Returns of the games at Pittsburgh," announced the *Monroe Morning World,* "will be given at Tenth and Desiard Streets every day starting about 2 o'clock."[9] And though people, white and black, flocked to downtown Monroe for updates on Saturday, September 3, the South's first World Series began inauspiciously. The Monarchs lost game one by a score of 7–3. Elbert Williams allowed only six Pittsburgh hits, but an RBI triple by Johnny Russell and two costly errors by second baseman Augustus Saunders gave the Crawfords seven total runs. Ted "Double-Duty" Radcliffe pitched the opener for Pittsburgh, allowing eight hits, including an RBI triple by Roy Parnell, but those hits amounted to only three Monroe runs.[10]

The second game, however, saw the Monarchs put up a far greater effort. Pitcher Barney Morris started for Monroe. Nerves appeared early, as right fielder Ted Page opened the bottom of the first with a leadoff walk, then a stolen base, and a single by Jud Wilson. The Crawfords took a 1–0 lead. But the early trouble passed and Morris settled down, holding the Crawfords scoreless through the eighth inning. Meanwhile, Roy Parnell's RBI double in the seventh evened the score at one. Tied in the ninth, Murray Gillespie entered to pitch an inning, but after striking out Oscar Charleston, manager Frank Johnson pulled him in favor of Williams, who carried the game to a tenth. Shortstop Leroy Morney led off the extra frame with a double, and after outs by Parnell and Porter Dallas, right fielder Zollie Wright's single scored him from second. Williams continued to pitch in the bottom of the tenth and closed the game by retiring the Crawfords in order. The small-town team had tied the star-filled Crawfords at one game apiece.[11]

"The hustling whole-hearted assault of the Monarchs, even though behind," reported the *Pittsburgh Courier,* "made a hit with Greenlee Field fans." Their efforts drew great applause on Monday, Labor Day, as well, as the hometown fans showed their appreciation for the southerners' attempts to rally. The capacity crowd celebrated "Louisiana Day" to honor the visitors. In the first game of a doubleheader, Monarchs pitcher Murray Gillespie suffered early and often at the hands of the Crawford hitters. Ted Page tallied four singles against the former Memphis Red Sox hurler, Ted Radcliffe had three, and Johnny Russell and Jake Stevens had two apiece. Augustus Saunders's two singles were no match, as the Monarchs fell 2–7.[12]

The nightcap proved no better for Monroe, as Satchel Paige took the mound for Pittsburgh. "No, Elmer, not an Ethiopian war dance," the *Bismarck Tribune* once described, "just Satchel winding up that steel spring in his right arm."[13] Leroy Robert Paige had joined the Chattanooga Black Lookouts, members of an earlier incarnation of the Negro Southern League, in 1926. That year he won twenty-six consecutive games. He then had stints with the Birmingham Black

Barons and Nashville Elite Giants. When Nashville folded midway during the 1931 season, Paige joined the Cleveland Cubs before following Gus Greenlee's pocketbook to Pittsburgh. He went 23–7 in 1932.[14]

"The elongated and colorful Satchel was a monarch of all the Monarchs he surveyed in the early frames," wrote the *Courier*'s sports editor, Chester L. Washington. Paige allowed four hits and no runs through the first five innings of the day's second game, but faltered slightly in the sixth. A leadoff single to center field by Homer Curry began the frame, followed by an RBI double by Roy Parnell. Zollie Wright followed with another single to drive in Parnell. But third baseman Porter Dallas grounded into a fielder's choice, taking Wright from the base paths. Augustus Saunders struck out, then Chuffie Alexander—one of the Monarchs' late-season additions from Houston—lined out to first.[15]

Meanwhile, the Crawford bats again came to life. In the second inning, Josh Gibson doubled to deep center, and a Parnell error allowed him to advance to third. An error at shortstop by Leroy Morney allowed Judy Johnson to reach safely; then Gibson scored from third on a wild pitch. The Crawfords then managed two more runs in the fourth. After six innings the score was 4–2, and the Monarchs remained at that distance until the eighth, when Bob Harvey began to tire, allowing five more Crawford runs. The final score was 9–2. Monroe had gained the admiration of Pittsburgh fans, but they would return to Monroe down three games to one in the World Series.[16]

At the same time, the Southern League championship began. With five thousand reportedly in attendance, the American Giants took a 5–1 lead into the ninth inning of game one, but Nashville managed five runs in the frame to stun the home team 6–5. The following day (this time in front of a reported 7,200 fans) in the first of a Sunday doubleheader, nine innings would not be enough, as the teams took a 1–1 tie into the fifteenth inning before Nashville won again. In the second Sunday game, Melvin Powell pitched a successful game for Chicago, giving the home team its sole home victory, 5–3. The teams would rest the following weekend, then resume the series in Nashville on September 18.[17]

"These Southern lads went into Chicago and snatched two of the three battles engaged in and thereby removed a bit of confidence from the Cole men," reported the *Defender*. But when the series continued in Nashville, Chicago cruised to a 10–5 victory in game four, tying the series at two games all. Weather won the rest of the weekend, and the Chicago victory proved the only game played, but when the rain subsided, the teams played two more games, splitting them to tie the series at 3–3. "This town is baseball crazy," wrote Al Monroe. "In the days when Meharry was good at football and Fisk was even stronger, there was a sportive unrest at certain times of the year, but not even those approaching spec-tacles matched the interest that centers here now on the eve of the final game." Monroe was almost certainly exaggerating—reports from Nashville had been fabricated all season long—but even the city's faux enthusiasm would not be re-warded. Chicago defeated Nashville 9–2 in the finale, taking the Dixie champi-onship. There was no further series in a larger tournament. No Homestead. No Baltimore. No Hilldale. There was, in the larger national media, a lack of rec-ognition for the importance of the series.[18] What interest remained in the 1932 baseball season was directed solely on a small town in north Louisiana.

"Sunday," wrote Pitman Nedde, "thousands of baseball fans will pour into Monroe from all parts of the south and east to witness this all-important ath-letic event, never played in the south before."[19] The Crawfords and Monarchs ar-rived in Monroe on Thursday night, September 9. The *Morning World* reminded readers that the 1931 Dixie Series witnessed the Monarchs returning to Monroe down to Nashville, a contest they eventually won. Surely they could do it again. "This is the first time a WORLD SERIES BASEBALL GAME has ever been played in the south," reported the *Shreveport Sun,* "among white or colored, and to miss this opportunity is to miss a rare treat that probably will not come again in a lifetime." Southern leagues had always been minor—as had southern cul-ture, southern literature, southern business, southern everything. But now the South had proven its worth. It was finally besting the North at its own game. It was no longer a colonial dependent. It was a legitimate competitor.[20]

On Friday, team officials announced that one of Pittsburgh's Labor Day victo-ries was, in fact, an exhibition contest—a fundraising game for charity. And so, with only a simple ride back south, the Monarchs made up a game on the Craw-fords. The series was now two games to one. The Monarchs also announced more good news. The young Austin Black Senators pitcher that managed to twice befuddle the locals was now a part of the Monroe team. Stovall, English, and the entire organization had been mesmerized by the talent of Hilton Smith, and the day after Monroe's final victory over Austin, the Monarchs' owner got his revenge on a successful opponent the way he had all season. He bought him. By the time the Pittsburgh series returned to Louisiana, Smith had, too. He would start the first home game of the series. "That was the first time I saw Josh Gibson and Satchel Paige," Smith later recalled. He wasn't the only one who was drawn by the awe of celebrity. Heavy attendance was expected, and officials made ar-rangements with area railroads running from Shreveport, Alexandria, New Or-leans, and Little Rock.[21]

So Monroe was not the only place excited about the prospect of a world series played locally. "The fans of Louisiana and the entire south are stirred over this series and hope for Monroe to win," reported the *Louisiana Weekly*. Booster clubs were organized throughout the region. "Letters have come in from points in Texas, Arkansas, Mississippi and Tennessee that they will be here for the series."[22]

For Pittsburgh fans anxious to see all the games of the series, the Baltimore & Ohio, the Illinois Central, and the Pennsylvania railroads agreed upon a flat round-trip discount rate of $26.25 to carry Pittsburghers to Monroe. The Illinois Central also offered $1 round-trip rides from Shreveport to Monroe for the Louisiana games of the series—in Pitman Nedde's words, "this most remarkable event ever to happen in the south." The games were standing room only, with patrons paying grandstand price for standing space.[23]

Prior to the first Monroe game, the Monarchs held a Negro Southern League pennant-raising ceremony in front of an enthusiastic overflow crowd, rewarding themselves for something not all in the league thought they deserved. Hilton Smith pitched his first game in a Monarchs uniform, lasting five and two-thirds innings, allowing six hits and four runs. He struck out two. Of course, two of those runs came on a deep home run to left field by Josh Gibson. "There was a train on the track [behind the left field fence] at the time," recalled Monarchs' second baseman Augustus Saunders, "and we always said the ball carried on to the next town." It seemed for most of the afternoon that Smith would suffer his first loss in thirty-one chances. Harry Kincannon and Satchel Paige had combined to keep the Monarchs in check. Entering the ninth inning, with the skies rapidly darkening, the score was 4–2 Pittsburgh. Then the Crawfords scored two more in the top of the ninth. But as the darkness continued to creep in, the Monarchs began to rally. Reaching the bottom of his order, and knowing he was up against Paige, Johnson began substituting pinch hitters. The makeshift offense managed four runs in the ninth to tie the ball game, just as darkness dictated that there would not be extra innings. The fifth game of the series ended in a tie. Pittsburgh still led 2–1, with one tie and one official exhibition.[24]

The late rally was desperate and hard-fought. It was, perhaps, too desperate, too hard-fought. Monarchs pitcher Bob Harvey started the following day's game but faltered early, allowing two runs in the first and another early in the second. An anxious Frank Johnson pulled him after only one and a third, handing the ball instead to Barney Morris. Though Morris was able to quell the Crawford bats, allowing only one additional run by the close of the seventh, Monroe remained behind 4–2. But this was no longer Saturday, and the Monarchs' determined late-inning effort of the previous afternoon gave way to collapse on Sunday. The Crawfords would win 11–4.[25]

Johnson appeared before the press undaunted. There was still a chance to come back, and he would use every pitcher available to stem the tide of Pittsburgh's hitting. This was no reason to panic. But on Monday, panic seemed more than reasonable. Monroe pitchers combined to allow nine runs on eleven Crawford hits. Pittsburgh gave up six runs on eight hits. Each team had four errors, falling out of form as the series wound its way down and the effects of the long season took their toll. The Monarchs fell to the Crawfords 9–6. The World Series was over.[26]

Monroe listed the three-game attendance at over fifteen thousand. "Fans turned out to a greater extent here than in Pittsburgh. Standing space was unavailable as the two teams drew the largest crowds ever to see a Negro baseball game in this vicinity."[27]

Early reports from Pittsburgh indicated that the Crawfords might immediately follow the series with a trip to New Orleans before their autumn barnstorming schedule. Instead, though, on the Tuesday morning following the final series game, both the Crawfords and Monarchs traveled to New Orleans, where they played an exhibition game for the fans of south Louisiana before finally parting ways. In the exhibition, the Crawfords abused Barney Morris and Bob Harvey for seventeen runs, though many resulted from fielding errors. Josh Gibson put yet another ball over the left field fence, and the final score was 17–5.[28]

"If the Crawfords are successful in winning the series from the Monarch team," Pittsburgh had announced before the series, "they will probably play the winner of the Dixie series. Should the Crawfords win this tilt, they will challenge the Homestead Grays for the city title." This wasn't an organized tournament, but Pittsburgh, unaffiliated and with all-stars at almost every position, clearly saw the opportunity for more publicity, more games, and more gate receipts. After the series win over the Monarchs, Pittsburgh reiterated its desire to take on either Nashville or Chicago. "But," the *Courier* reported, "they're hoping it's Chicago."[29]

That series, however, never happened. The majority of the black press portrayed the Monroe series as more significant than the Chicago-Nashville series, so Pittsburgh had little to gain by playing the winner. The Crawfords opted against the anticlimax, instead returning home relatively quickly to face the crosstown rival Grays one last time, eventually losing three of four to Cum Posey's team.[30]

But as black baseball's postseason progressed, African Americans also made inroads into white baseball's postseason. Alvin E. White reported for the Associated Negro Press from the press box at the (white) World Series between the New York Yankees and Chicago Cubs. Alvin White estimated that one-fifth of the crowd at Yankee Stadium was African American, "occupying seats in boxes, grandstand, and bleachers." The Baseball Writers of New York City, the organization handling press assignments for Yankee Stadium, officially recognized black reporters for the first time.[31]

The World Series they witnessed became legendary, as Babe Ruth headlined the four-game Yankee sweep with his famed "called shot" in Chicago. White's interpretation of the home run credited a black fan as its impetus. "An irrepressible colored bleacherite," Amos "Loudmouth" Latimer, heckled Ruth unmercifully after the slugger's first-inning two-run home run. When he spoke, "the Babe pointed at Latimer and gave him his promise." According to White, Ruth doffed his cap before his at bat in the third inning, waving it at Latimer. "The Babe held up one finger, signifying that it only took one swing to hit the apple." The 440-foot home run that followed supposedly missed Latimer by three feet and tallied as the longest home run in the young history of the Cubs' home field.[32]

Not all of white baseball's decisions, however, were as inclusive as the opening of its press box. In late September, after the championships had run their course, Major League Baseball decided to cancel postseason exhibitions between the races. "For the first time in many years," reported the *Chicago Defender,* "there will be no games between teams composed of Race players and all-star club[s] recruited from the major leagues, and fandom is wondering why. That is, there will be no games played in cities where major clubs are located, according to information just received. . . . The decision of the majors to pass up playing before Race fandom is quite a shift in things from what has occurred in the past." The paper noted that the Chicago Cubs had risen to first place in the National League, and speculated that the Cubs, "a lily-white organization, would be at the root of such a move if the thing came up for consideration at either of the league or interleague meetings." Robert Cole tried scheduling other white all-star teams for his park, but failed. In August, his American Giants defeated the House of David and Buck Weaver's All-Stars, but neither team was affiliated with Major League Baseball. It could have been the doing of the Cubs, or, the *Defender* speculated, it could have been the doing of Commissioner Landis. Whoever was originally responsible, the crucial fact for black baseball fans was that traditional postseason exhibition games between white and black teams would not take place in 1932.[33]

Such could never have happened in the South, anyway. The southern devotion to college football and the Jim Crow hegemony that dominated the region would have made such autumn interracial all-star contests unprofitable and dangerous—if not outright impossible. Besides, baseball fans in Monroe were still concerned with the Monarchs. As Monroe finished its series with Pittsburgh, Alexandria successfully finished a series with Algiers, prompting the Lincoln Giants to rechallenge Monroe for yet another state championship. The games, of course, were exhibitions, not championship games, but the Monarchs agreed, hoping, like Pittsburgh, to capitalize on their newfound fame. Monroe played the games with a vastly diminished roster, as several players moved on to other teams to barnstorm following the season, and over two weekends the team split its four-game series with Alexandria.[34]

Even with a group of lesser players, however, there was one more series to play. Little Rock returned to Casino Park on October 9 and 10. The Greys' season fell apart early, but the team had managed a modicum of success after abandoning league play. They acquitted themselves well in a September tournament with teams from Arkansas and Oklahoma, and their late-season success even brought a group from Arkansas's capital city to Monroe to cheer the Greys to victory. Prices were reduced from their normal fifty cents, and box seats were not reserved for their usual additional quarter. The jazz orchestra returned, however, and half of the grandstand was still reserved for white fans. Barney Morris and Red Murray would take their respective halves of the Sunday doubleheader, and Homer Curry would pitch the following day. On Monday, there would be one final Ladies' Day. All women were admitted free.[35]

The series was a "thank you" exhibition for the fans who had supported the Monarchs in their most successful season. Reduced prices, no box seat markups, free entry to women, and the orchestra virtually assured that the usual game-day profit wouldn't come. But profit, this time, was beside the point. Stovall, noted by historians and contemporaries alike as both generous and savvy, said "thank you" to black and white Monroe. And Monroe, almost surely, reciprocated.

10

After September
The Season, the Monarchs, and Monroe
in the Popular and Historical Mind

When the World Series concluded, it was harvest time in northeast Louisiana. "'Twenty cents a hundred pounds, and one meal; twenty-five cents a hundred pounds, and feed yourself!' is the theme song of the poverty-stricken army of cotton pickers who are now beginning their annual assault upon the snowy locks of Old King Cotton," wrote the Associated Negro Press.[1]

But the local papers had more dire events to report. On August 31, while the Monarchs prepared for the World Series, superintendent of police L. V. Tarver reopened the Zion Traveler Baptist Church. He warned the waiting members of the congregation that no more disturbances would be tolerated, then left the keys to the building with deacon Alec Johnson. Tarver wasn't acting out of kindness. He was responding to a congregation-wide vote on a resolution created by a special committee. In a contentious but "official" vote, church members agreed to bar Warner Hill from the church. He would be replaced by M. J. Foster, principal of Monroe Colored High School.[2]

This, it was assumed, would be the end of the year-long controversy. But four days later, while the eyes of most were focused squarely on Pittsburgh and the Monarchs' second game of the World Series, Tarver's decision proved disastrous. As Foster began his Sunday sermon on September 4, four female congregants, supporters of Hill, walked to the pulpit and asked him to stop. Though the protest was calm, the reaction was not, and the congregation of Zion Traveler grew very violent very quickly. Hill supporter James Dugans responded to the chaos by pulling a pistol. Seeing the gun, George Daniels, president of the Harmony Club, ran to the house next door, where he had planted a gun before the service. He claimed after the furor that he hid the gun because he expected Hill's supporters to "shoot up the church if Foster preached."[3]

That they did. While Daniels was away, Dugans shot Daniels's daughter Patsy in the stomach. She was still alive, but bleeding profusely on the church floor when her father returned with his pistol. Daniels saw his daughter, and then he saw the smoking gun of Dugans turned quickly upon him. Dugans fired at Daniels, wounding him, but the shot did not incapacitate the shattered father enough to keep him from firing back. Dugans was hit, and as he fell he began firing wildly—striking Robert Sam Lee, Mattie Levy, and Clarence Burrell— before dying on the church floor.[4]

Police and rescue workers arrived soon, rushing Patsy Daniels and Mattie Levy, both in critical condition, to the same colored ward of St. Francis Sanitarium that housed George Bolden so many years ago. While Levy survived, Patsy Daniels died on Monday afternoon.[5] On September 11, the day before the final game of the World Series, George Daniels was arrested and charged with carrying a concealed weapon. He paid his bond and was released. In September 1932, criminal hearings were held for bad checks, manufacturing whiskey, forgery, disturbing the peace, assault and battery, breaking and entering, and burglary. But Daniels's crime was only a misdemeanor.[6] There are two explanations for this kind of treatment: either Negro shootings were not considered so egregious, or retribution for a murdered daughter seemed reasonable enough. The second explanation seems most plausible. Superintendent Tarver stated at the scene that Dugans was to blame for the incident.[7]

After the debacle, Tarver again closed the church, but on November 6, the doors to Zion Traveler would open one more time. All church offices were open to new elections, and Hill was barred from all of them. Instead, Warner Washington Hill and those who sided with him started their own church, Triumph Baptist.[8]

Only weeks earlier, on a night in late August, Clark Griffith sat in his owner's box in Griffith Park, home of the American League's Washington Senators, and watched the Pittsburgh Crawfords play the Washington Pilots. He expressed his confidence that Negro League baseball could be successful, but that it needed league stability to survive. In an interview with the American Negro Press, he argued that organization gave fans a proprietary interest, an assurance that there would be a full conclusion to the season. And, of course, the baseball had to be good. "Negroes," he said, "no longer are willing to pay to see just any kind of ball."[9]

The baseball was assuredly good, but league stability was still a work in progress. At the close of 1932, John L. Clark denounced secrecy and "skullduggery" in league machinations. Black baseball needed a commissioner to regulate player acquisitions, contract disputes, and schedule completion. And Clark would soon get his wish. On December 14, baseball officials met in Indianapolis to plan the 1933 season. The group—including delegations from Chicago and Nashville, Kansas City, Detroit, Pittsburgh, Cleveland, and Indianapolis—elected Robert Cole chairman of the committee and agreed to meet again on January 10 in Chicago. Monroe was not invited.[10] As negotiations continued, Gus Greenlee became more and more involved. When the group eventually created the new Negro National League (NNL), he would become its president and help sustain it during an inevitably tumultuous inaugural season. The American Giants would also be part of the National League in 1933, but problems with the team's home stadium led Cole to temporarily move the organization to Indianapolis. That season, Cole's Indianapolis version of his Giants finished a half-game in front of the Pittsburgh Crawfords. With a measured dose of comeuppance, however, Greenlee, acting as president of the NNL, awarded the pennant to his own team. Still, controversy or no, the new Negro National League created by Cole, Wilson, and Greenlee struggled through its first season and only grew stronger as the 1930s progressed. Even in the face of a crippling depression, the new league established an institutional strength that would remain until baseball's integration, a period—beginning in 1933—that the Negro Leagues Baseball Museum calls the "Golden Years" of black baseball.[11]

Monroe would see none of this success. As the new National League negotiated without them in 1933, Stovall's Monarchs issued a press release in early October calling for a new Dixie League the following season. Clearly imagining a return to a slightly lesser status, Monroe expected representatives from Shreveport, New Orleans, Algiers, and Alexandria from Louisiana; Longview, Tyler, Dallas, and Fort Worth from Texas; and Little Rock, Jackson, Vicksburg, Memphis, and Montgomery from other southern states. "The Negro Southern league this year was composed of eight clubs," explained Monarchs management. "The Monroe Monarchs won the first half pennant and Cole's Chicago American Giants copped the second. However, this year's league was not composed of only teams representing southern cities as is the main objective of the officials of the new organization." The early meeting attempted to bring certainty to the start of the 1933 season, an attempt to assure fans that the league would be stable. Without the trickery of northern teams, things would surely go more smoothly.[12]

The subsequent meetings took place later that month, with the goal of creating a league "which will compare with the southern white league, both in financial matters as well as strength of teams." Monarchs management called the

Monroe-Pittsburgh crowds "the largest that ever attended Negro baseball games in the South," but knew that the broader baseball picture for 1932 was bleak. "A general listlessness was prevalent throughout the 1932 season which greatly hampered the success of the organization."[13]

No officers were elected and no towns were chosen, but the meeting, chaired by J. B. Martin of the Memphis Red Sox, mandated an eight-team league and a $1,000 bond (or a $100 deposit) to secure a place in the group—a charge separate from any pending franchise fees. The league decided that the schedule would include weekday games instead of solely weekend stints, bringing the potential team schedule to as many as 130 games. Officials promised that there would be another meeting soon. Final decisions had to wait for the white Southern League to hold its winter meetings, as many black southern squads used vacant white parks as their home fields.[14]

At an eleven-hour session in Memphis on January 28, the new Dixie League accepted Monroe, Memphis, and Little Rock from the former season's Southern League, the Crescent City Stars and Algiers Giants from New Orleans, and the Shreveport Sports. Monarchs business manager H. D. English was voted secretary, a position with which he was inordinately familiar. In early February, teams from Jackson, Mississippi, and Alexandria, Louisiana, joined the aggregation to round out the eight-team roster. The league initiated a salary cap and assured the fans that National League teams would barnstorm through the Dixie. Thomas Wilson, owner of the Elite Giants (now members of Greenlee's new Negro National League), attended the meeting and assured the group that the winners of the new league would earn the right to play the National League winners for a national championship. It is doubtful that anyone in Monroe believed him, but hopes remained high.[15]

At the final league meeting in late February, in New Orleans's Astoria Hotel, the Dixie changed its name to the Southern, and the teams finally agreed to play daily games—a revolutionary move for a Depression-era circuit that had historically played only weekend series. Meanwhile, Indianapolis, Chicago, and Nashville attempted to revive the original Southern League, hedging their bets against the possibility that the National League wouldn't work at worst, and hoping to create a viable minor league at best. Two Southern Leagues and the risky policy of daily games combined to sour the optimism of black southern newsmen.[16]

Though league games were scheduled to begin in late April, no news from league officials about the games reached the press. The *Louisiana Weekly,* echoing its calls of early 1932, blamed English. "The clubs lose when this information is not released to the public and the newspapers lose a certain amount of prestige when [they are] unable to dish out the dope." The paper argued that Monroe's *Southern Broadcast* was given preference over other league papers, and argued that "the ultimate result of such a seemingly partial procedure will be that the sports editors of the larger newspapers will tire of this spasmodic receipt of the league's news and grant the loop doings a scarcity of space. And no one will be able to truthfully blame them."[17] English, argued sports editor Earl Wright, was "hoarding the Southern League news." He was selfish, Wright claimed, and he was trying to give the Monroe press a monopoly on information. The practice "can end but one way. The other papers will reach the point where they will be sending every line concerning the league on a non-[s]top flight to the waste paper basket."[18]

Finally, in early May, English bowed to public pressure and released the league standings, which demonstrated that Memphis led the way. Their six and one record barely topped Little Rock's six wins and four losses. Monroe followed closely behind at five and six.[19]

But confusion again would ultimately have its way. Less than two weeks after the first standings appeared, Monroe pulled out of the league, causing it to collapse. Stovall and English chose to instead send the Monarchs on a barnstorming tour, hoping to make a profit by exploiting the team's 1932 success. "The whole thing in a nutshell," wrote a cynical Wright, "is Stovall, English and the other powers that be in the Monarch ranks are disappointed over the showing the Monarchs are making in the league play and don't want to be kicked around by the other big boys." Monroe had abandoned the Tri-State League in early 1932 and were just doing it again. "The folk up Monroe way are simply running true to form." The theory seems more than plausible, but that didn't stop the league from folding, nonetheless. League president J. B. Martin tried to salvage the circuit but was not able to hold it together. After stuttering attempts to continue to play out the remaining schedule, dwindling gate receipts, coupled with the loss of the league's most prominent team, caused the aggregation to disband.[20]

But new baseball leagues were not the only postseason plans of Negro League moguls. As the 1932 baseball season closed, Reuben Jackson and Thomas Wilson created a new Southern League, the Negro Southern Football League. Jackson owned a Nashville Black Bears football team in 1931 that went 13–3. Wilson's participation in Jackson's football endeavor gave him co-ownership of the team, and co-ownership gave the Black Bears a new name—Wilson's trademark Elite Giants. The new 1932 Southern League was organized in Nashville with Jackson as president and Wilson as treasurer, the same setup the two used for the governance of the Negro Southern baseball league. The Elite Giants, Atlanta Bears, Chattanooga Wolverines, and Memphis All Stars joined football teams from Birmingham, New Orleans, Montgomery, and Jacksonville to form the eight-team loop.[21]

But for black Monroe, it was college football, not its professional offshoot, that made postseason news. On Armistice Day 1932, in Monroe's Casino Park, the Southern University Bushmen from Scotlandville faced the Tigers of Grambling's Louisiana Negro Normal and Industrial Institute for the first time. Southern was the major power, the grandfather of the state's African American academic institutions. Negro Normal was a two-year school, smaller and younger than the mighty four-year Southern, and had taken up football only in 1926.[22]

It was, more than likely, the exposure created by the Monarchs' national and statewide baseball success that convinced promoters to bring the Southern-Normal football game to Monroe. The big draw was Southern. The Bushmen represented the largest and most celebrated black educational institution in the state. The team constituted for black audiences what Louisiana State University did for whites—it was a source of state pride and identity. On Monday, March 21, as the Monarchs were embarking upon their only major league season, Dr. Joseph Samuel Clark, president of Southern, had made the trip from Scotlandville to speak at Monroe Colored High School, accompanied by the Southern University Quartet. The auditorium was full.[23] Clark's stature among the African American population of Louisiana was supreme, both feeding from and contributing to the stature of Southern itself. And now the football team was coming.

The practice was far from rare. Many teams traveled to play de facto home games in various parts of the state in order to give a wider range of fans the opportunity to see them play. The LSU Tigers, for example, played the Mississippi State Aggies at Ouachita Junior College's Brown Stadium. The Golden Band from Tigerland marched up Monroe's Desiard Street, and the Tigers' victory delighted the sold-out crowd.[24]

For black Monroe, however, the biggest draw was Southern. "All eyes will be focused on the grid battle to be played Armistice Day," wrote Ralph Jones in the *Shreveport Sun,* "between the mighty Bushmen of Southern University and the Tigers of La. Colored Normal." Ralph Jones was not a reporter for Shreveport's black weekly. He was Normal's head football coach, and his report made it clear that he thought his team capable of giving the Scotlandville powerhouse a run for its money. But Jones's confidence was misplaced. The Bushmen won 20–0.[25]

Baseball, however, was still king, and the teams of 1932 left different legacies in the seasons to come. In 1933, the Cubans won more than 125 games, and late in the season owner Syd Pollock made a case for the integration of baseball. He argued that the Depression necessitated drastic measures to keep the sport afloat. To include black players while avoiding racism against individuals, "my solution is simple." He argued that one black team should be included in the National League and one in the American. "Imagine the drawing power of a formidable colored aggregation. . . . Imagine the interest they would stimulate by their colorful playing and dash around the diamond. Imagine the increase in attendance."[26]

Of course, integration was still years away, and the largest legacy for veteran teams of the 1932 season was debt. White major league attendance fell to 3.5 million, almost 70 percent below 1930 attendance rates. The majors reported losses of $1.2 million. In the South, both the white Southeastern and Cotton States leagues collapsed before completing full seasons. Even the mighty Crawfords remained $16,000 in the red for the season. Greenlee Field welcomed 119,384 paying customers in its first year, 69,229 of those for baseball. And it still hemorrhaged money. Still, though the team was operating at a loss, Gus Greenlee added artificial lights for his stadium in August, at a cost of $6,000. The spending on margin would eventually catch up to Greenlee and his club. The Crawfords' franchise, in fact, would not last much longer than the Monarchs. Greenlee was instrumental in pioneering the new Negro National League, and his team remained successful through 1936. But all of its stars moved to other teams, and in 1937 and 1938, the club was a shell of its former self. 1938 would be its last season.[27]

Cole's Chicago American Giants reached what was billed in south Louisiana as a "World Series" the following season, in 1933, defeating the Crescent City Stars of New Orleans, and then continued play without similar success in the immediate years to come. To revive flagging interest in the team, H. G. Hall, president of the American Giants in 1937, helped create the Negro American League (NAL), which became a western complement to the eastern National League. From 1937 to 1952, the Giants played in the NAL, though they never won another championship.[28]

Monroe not only missed another championship, it never again played major league baseball. Still, at the end of the 1932 season, *Courier* sports editor Chester L. Washington interviewed Cumberland Posey about his choices for an "All-American" team, including the best players at each position. His selection for right field was Roy "Red" Parnell of Monroe. Posey noted that Parnell "has not the aim of some of our other fielders . . . but his bat and base running rates him over the others."[29]

The Monarchs would rejoin the Southern League again in 1934—minus former stars like Parnell—joined by the newly formed Indianapolis Monarchs and a returning Louisville Black Caps.[30] But the team would never reach its 1932 success. The tenuousness of the 1934 league again led the Monarchs to spend much of that summer barnstorming. They played other black teams but also moved outside of the South, playing integrated outfits such as the Bismarck, North Dakota, Cubs and all-white teams such as the Lincoln, Nebraska, Links. After 1934, the team abandoned league affiliation altogether and barnstormed independently. It continued in that fashion through 1935 and much of 1936 before finally dwindling away. The last Monarchs game reported in the Monroe dailies was a July 12, 1936, contest against an all-star team from Marshall, Texas. Sherman Briscoe's *Southern Broadcast* speculated in early August that former Monarchs stars would return later that month to moonlight with the Monroe team. Hilton Smith, Barney Morris, Harry Else, and Leroy Morney, among others, were expected, but the reunion never materialized. The paper reported a final home series in late August with the Montgomery Grey Sox, and the team played again the following weekend, the beginning of September, against Shreveport's Acme Giants. The team was a shell of its former self, the only two links remaining to the 1932 championship team being Stovall and manager Frank Johnson. The *Broadcast* instead resorted to publishing Negro National and American League stories featuring former Monroe players.[31]

Though the Monarchs finally collapsed, however, they left a palpable legacy for southern teams in similar tenuous financial and racial situations. During Monroe's final season of 1936, the Claybrook Tigers were having one of their most successful. Twenty miles southwest of Memphis, Claybrook was once an Arkansas town built around the logging industry of John C. Claybrook, a black entrepreneur and landowner. To keep his workers (and workers' families) happy, Claybrook formed a company baseball team in 1929. Though the club existed in 1932 and 1933, it did not become well known and successful until the mid-1930s. Claybrook began by playing other semipro company teams such as the Dubisson Tigers (a Little Rock club sponsored by mortician Daniel J. Dubisson).[32] But by 1935, Claybrook was facing the Cuban Stars, the Pittsburgh Crawfords, and the Chicago American Giants, among other teams. That year, the Tigers also joined the again-minor Negro Southern League, and won the pennant. The following year, John Claybrook, hungry for wins, lured Ted "Double Duty" Radcliffe—who had played for the Crawfords in the 1932 World Series—to his tiny lumber town. And again Claybrook won the pennant. But when Radcliffe left, success followed him, and by 1938 the team was gone. Claybrook himself left in 1940, and soon after the town was abandoned. Still, it is hard to imagine that the Tigers' mid-thirties run of success could have happened without the precedent set by Monroe.[33]

After the dissolution of the Monarchs, Casino Park played host to a number of city events. City-league softball and baseball championship series occupied the rest of July, August, and early September. In October 1936, the Monroe Colored High Bulldogs football team began its season in Casino, as it had every year since the stadium's founding.[34]

In December of that year, J. Walter Morris, new president of the reconstituted white Cotton States League, called a meeting in Greenville, Mississippi. Teams from El Dorado, Pine Bluff, and Helena, Arkansas, joined club representatives from Jackson, Greenville, Greenwood, Clarksdale, and Cleveland, Mississippi. Monroe hadn't fielded a white baseball team since the Cotton States folded in 1932, but after the first Cotton States meeting, Gladewater, Texas, oil magnate R. W. Burnett purchased the Cleveland franchise and moved it to Monroe. R. D. Swayze, Commissioner of Streets and Parks, and George Lofton, *Morning World* sports editor, met with Burnett and convinced him of the viability of a Monroe team. "We all believe Monroe is a good baseball town," announced league president Morris, "and I am pleased that Mr. Burnett selected this town instead of others he was considering." There was even, it turned out, an available stadium. Forsythe Park had long since fallen away, so Burnett announced a $1,500 renovation project for Casino Park that would include the building of a new fence and a new row of box seats. He would repair the grandstand and push the diamond ten to fifteen feet toward the stands. The park would also receive a new floor in front of the grandstand, a new clubhouse below it, and, for the first time, a women's rest room. The whole park would be painted orange. Of course, Casino now housed white baseball, but the park still belonged to Stovall, who approved Burnett's renovations. Between 1937 and 1941, Stovall leased the park yearly to Monroe's minor league white teams, which changed year to year, the last being the 1941 Monroe White Sox.[35]

The fates of the Monarch players themselves varied. Homer "Goose" Curry, the left fielder and pitcher from Memphis, later enjoyed a long and distinguished career with the Baltimore Elite Giants, the Philadelphia Stars, and again with the Memphis Red Sox. Catcher Harry Else went on to play in the mid-1930s with the Kansas City Monarchs, making the East–West All Star game in 1936. Monroe's shortstop, Leroy Morney, moved on to Posey's Homestead Grays following the 1932 season and continued a well-traveled but substantial all-star career for a variety of Negro National League teams through 1944. Pitchers Barney

Morris and Samuel Thompson also enjoyed success after leaving Monroe, Morris with the New York Cubans and Thompson with the Philadelphia Stars and Chicago American Giants. Right fielder Zollie Wright was another former Monarch to become an East–West All Star, playing for Baltimore, New York, and Philadelphia. Roy Parnell played center field and pitched for the Monarchs. He played on a variety of minor southern teams before coming to Monroe, but his most productive years came with the Philadelphia Stars in the 1940s, and his success earned him candidacy for a special Negro and Pre-Negro Leagues election to the National Baseball Hall of Fame in 2006.[36]

Hilton Smith would remain with the team until 1935, when he went to Bismarck, North Dakota, to join the Bismarck Cubs. Satchel Paige was playing for the integrated team, as was fellow former Monarch Barney Morris. After that season, Smith moved to Kansas City, where he remained until 1948. There he compiled a 204–65 win-loss record and became the first former Monroe Monarch to enter the National Baseball Hall of Fame.[37]

On November 14, 1936, a large headline on the front page of Monroe's *Southern Broadcast* announced, "METCALFE COMING HERE." The Louisiana Colored Teachers' Association met in mid-November at Monroe Colored High, and its featured guest would be Olympic track star Ralph Metcalfe. He was now a professor of physical education at Xavier University, but he would always be the "celebrated trackman" from the 1932 Summer Games.[38] Those games still resonated with Monroe's black population—with every black population. Of course, the success of the Monarchs resonated in 1936, as well, but in the years that followed, Monroe's memory of the team ebbed and flowed.

The club's success would remain with those who were there to witness the feat, but for the broader population, memory of the Monarchs disappeared when the team itself disappeared. Depression-era Monroe was busy surviving a difficult economic situation. "Those were tough times," recalled Ollie Burns, a Southern University college student home in Monroe for the summer of 1932, "but we all enjoyed going to games at the ballpark and cheering for the Monarchs. They made quite a splash in the life of the people of the city." More than seventy years later, however, there is only one photograph of the team on file in the special collections of the Ouachita Parish Public Library. It carries the caption "The Monroe Monarchs won the 1932 pennant in the Southern League. They played the winners of the pennant in the National League, the Pittsburg [*sic*] Crawfords, in the 1932 Negro World Series." Of course, the Crawfords hadn't won the National League title, because no National League existed in 1932. So memory of the team resonated, but in a significantly diminished form. "I guess," says Jean

Stovall Lee, Fred Stovall's granddaughter, "people had other things on their minds besides baseball."[39]

One principal architect of the revival of Monroe's memory of its championship team was Paul J. Letlow, former sports editor of the *News-Star*. In 1992, Letlow interviewed Monarchs' second baseman Augustus Saunders, four years prior to his death. Saunders was the only member of the 1932 team to settle in Monroe after the conclusion of his baseball career. Letlow's resulting story on the team appeared in mid-August and became the first in an intermittent series of articles on the club, usually prompted by outside events—Saunders's death, the 2001 induction of Hilton Smith into the National Baseball Hall of Fame, or the 2006 Hall of Fame induction of Willard Brown, a player on the 1934, '35, and '36 teams.[40]

The other instigator of the Monarchs' rejuvenation was Roosevelt Wright, editor of Monroe's black weekly, the *Free Press*. In 1996, Wright wrote and staged *The Game: A Black Heritage Drama in Two Acts*. Based on his own interviews with Saunders, Wright crafted the story of Saunders's experience in Monroe and the team's championship season. The play is periodically revived at the city's civic center, playing to grade-school audiences from throughout the parish.[41]

Today houses have been built on the empty lot that was Casino Park, but the community now remembers. The Monroe Monarchs Historical Commission, created in 2005 by Jeffrey Newman and Scott Greer, raised awareness about the existence of the team and money for the improvement of a local little league field, now named in the Monarchs' honor. After an exhaustive lobbying effort, Newman and Greer convinced the city to participate in the project. In June 2006, with Letlow, Newman, Greer, Mayor Jamie Mayo, and Fred Stovall's granddaughter Jean Stovall Lee attending, the first game was played on the new field, by two teams of African American boys wearing Monarchs uniforms. In ceremonies before the game, a historical marker was unveiled, as the city government officially and publicly declared its recognition of Monroe's most successful sports franchise. The marker, if nothing else, ensures that the town's memory will never completely ebb—that the kings of Casino Park will, in one form at least, never leave Monroe again.

Conclusion

"We Have Yet to Find a Moses": Monroe as the Exception to Various Rules, Baseball and Otherwise

At the close of 1932, William "Dizzy" Dismukes, writing for the *Pittsburgh Courier,* lamented the loss of Rube Foster. Things had not been the same since his retirement in 1926 and death in 1930. "His guiding influence was keenly felt by his fellow league members the moment illness forced him out of active contact with league matters," Dismukes wrote. "Six years have actually passed. We have yet to find a 'Moses.' Baseball misses Rube."[1] He then briefly reviewed the baseball landscape and found only frustration. "One of the troubles of Negro baseball, aside from the disastrous effects of the depression is that so few new players are being developed. New faces are needed."[2] John L. Clark was even more pessimistic. "More unusual incidents, disappointments and failures will dot the 1932 record than for any previous year. . . . Financially, the season was a total failure." It was especially so for the players, who played more games for less pay. "Organizations of owners failed before the season was half finished." They were too ambitious in troubled times, he believed. "At no point in this year's baseball story is there an encouraging statement."[3]

The next year, the Negro National League would return—created by Robert Cole, Thomas Wilson, and Gus Greenlee, whose association largely developed through the 1932 Monroe pennant controversy—and profits would slowly begin to return. Still, Clark's Crawfords operated at a loss for 1932, as did almost every team in Negro League baseball. There was adequate call for Clark's frustration. But though Monroe's financial records no longer exist, circumstantial evidence points to the team's economic success—to a singular rebuttal to Clark's dire lament. Casino Park "held some people," said Monarchs second baseman Augustus Saunders. But not enough. "They had people out there listening to the announcer over the radio who couldn't get in the park. They'd put them out there as far as they could so it wouldn't interfere with the outfield. We made the money." Reports from Monroe indicated that Casino Park was usually filled to capacity.[4]

Jean Stovall Lee, Fred Stovall's granddaughter, has portrayed the team as her grandfather's hobby and passion—the sort of project for which one would be willing to suffer financial loss if need be. The players always received their pay. They had comfortable living quarters and their own cook. Stovall had more in mind than mere profit. But, significantly in the difficult summer of 1932, he did, it seemed, have profit. Even someone who passionately directed a professional baseball team would have given it up if his financial solvency was at stake.[5] And in a season that witnessed far more established major league teams with far more famous players lose money—most not even surviving the summer—that solvency demonstrated a success just as palpable as a trip to the World Series.

Another sort of profit was garnered by Monroe's black population, who watched as their team and their town won national recognition for being one of the best teams in the most popular sport in the country. And the black population responded. At the end of the season, black crime was down, the community had its own newspaper, and the white dailies were carrying more black sports coverage than they ever had before (or would again for the next quarter century).

And so the Monarchs weren't just exceptions to the Depression baseball rule. They were exceptions, however limited and however brief, to the assumptions of the Jim Crow South, even in the heart of the "lynch law center of Louisiana." On October 28, 1932, for example, the University of Iowa football team traveled to Washington, D.C., to George Washington University. The Hawkeyes' two black players, Wilbur Wallace and Voris Dickerson, sat on the bench in street clothes during the game after being barred from playing by the home team. Though "officials at George Washington denied that they knew colored football players were on the Iowa team," GW's usual black patrons "refused to attend after learning that the university was barring the colored players."[6] Monroe was far less cosmopolitan than Washington, D.C. Its Northeast Louisiana Junior College, in fact, had just been founded the previous year and was no academic match for George Washington. But in the summer of 1932, fans filled the white sections of Casino Park's grandstands to cheer on nine black players with "Monroe" emblazoned across their chests. They were, for the span of nine innings, proud to be represented by African Americans.

But, realistically, that pride did last only nine innings. Coverage of the Monarchs in Monroe's dailies was remarkable, but also significantly lacking compared to the town's unsuccessful white minor league team. Monroe remained a Jim Crow stalwart during and after the 1932 season. It largely remains a segregated society in the twenty-first century. "We knew it," said Ollie Burns, "but we couldn't let it get us down in our thinking. We had, as I've said from time to time, we had to live in two worlds." The success of the hometown team, however, made that life lived in transition more palatable. "I know there were people who thought what went on was more important than what went on at Casino Park. But I didn't let it bother me. This is my world and the world in which I moved. Not that I was satisfied to be in two worlds, but I was comfortable." When it came to those whites who didn't attend the ballgames—those who chose to follow the fledgling white minor league team that season—Burns blamed a mere lack of understanding: "It was a matter of people who had control not knowing the people on this end of town and not understanding. So they had a tendency to make this insignificant."[7]

What people did understand, white or black, South or North, was baseball. The reception of the Monarchs' play gave the team substantial cultural worth in the local community as well as in the broader black baseball world. The team mattered. And in the "lynch law center of Louisiana," this might be the Monarchs' most important historical contribution.

"A few years back, along in 1928," wrote the *Shreveport Sun*'s Pitman Nedde in 1932, "if one would ask an easterner, northerner, or a gentleman from the far west, of the town of Monroe, Louisiana, pertaining to its geographical location, the answer would probably bring about some mean words—words that you probably wouldn't take from dear old dad—but now, the name of MONROE stands out in letters twenty times the point of the ones printed in this article."[8] Even more importantly, around the time of 1932, if one would ask a gentleman from across Desiard Street, in the comfort of his segregated white neighborhood, the name MONARCHS would stand out just as high.

1932 Monroe Monarchs Schedule and Results

Date	Opponent	Home/Away	Win/Loss	Score
		March		
25	Pittsburgh (exhibition)	Home	Loss	2–11
	(no box score available)			
27	Pittsburgh (exhibition)	Home	Win	6–3
		April		
3	Chicago[1] (exhibition)	Home	Win	7–0
4	Chicago (exhibition)	Home	Win	8–5
10	Houston (exhibition)	Home	Win	1–0
11	Houston (exhibition)	Home	Win	5–2
17	Houston (exhibition)	Away	Loss	3–4
18	Houston (exhibition)	Away	Loss	5–10
	(no box score available)			
	—SEASON BEGINS—			
22	Little Rock	Away	Win	6–1
	(no box score available)			
23	Little Rock	Away	Win	6–3
	(no box score available)			
24	Little Rock	Away	Win	15–6
	(no box score or pitcher tally available)			
	Little Rock	Away	Win	8–3
	(no box score or pitcher tally available)			
30	Memphis	Away	Win	6–1
		May		
1	Memphis	Away	Loss	2–3
	Memphis	Away	Loss	2–3
2	Memphis	Away	Win	9–1
6	Cleveland	Home	Win	4–3

7	Cleveland	Home	Win	5–2
8	Cleveland	Home	Win	6–0
	Cleveland	Home	Win	4–0
12	Rayville (exhibition)	Home	Win	27–3
	(no box score available)			
14	Little Rock	Home	Win	7–1
15	Little Rock	Home	Win	6–1
	Little Rock	Home	Win	8–2
16	Little Rock	Home	Win	4–3
21	Birmingham	Home	Loss	1–5
22	Birmingham	Home	Win	2–0
	Birmingham	Home	Win	1–0
28	Montgomery	Away	Win	12–2
	(no box score available)			
29	Montgomery	Away	Win	10–6
	(no box score available)			
	Montgomery	Away	Win	4–2
	(no box score available)			
30	Montgomery	Away	Win	8–1
	(no box score available)			

June

5 (The *Monroe Morning World* lists the Monarchs at 22–5, meaning they had assumed four games against Nashville. One may have taken place on June 5.)

6	Nashville	Away	Win	4–2
	Nashville	Away	Loss	7–8

7 (The *Monroe Morning World* lists the Monarchs at 22–5, meaning they had assumed four games against Nashville. One may have taken place on June 7.)

11	Montgomery	Home	Win	3–0
12	Montgomery	Home	Win	4–2
	Montgomery	Home	Win	3–2
13	Montgomery	Home	Win	7–2
18	Nashville	Home	Win	16–5
19	Nashville	Home	Win	3–2
	Nashville	Home	Loss	0–5
20	Nashville	Home	Win	6–4
25	Montgomery	Away	Win	6–3
26	Montgomery	Away	Loss	1–7
	Montgomery	Away	Win	8–1
27	Montgomery	Away	Win	2–0

July

2	Memphis	Home	Win	6–5
3	Memphis	Home	Win	5–3
4	Memphis	Home	Win	6–1
	Memphis	Home	Win	8–2

—FIRST HALF ENDS—[2]

9	Memphis	Away	Loss	6–7
10	Memphis	Away	Win	15–2
	Memphis	Away	Loss	7–13
11	Memphis	Away	Loss	7–8
16	Chicago	Away	Loss	1–2
	Chicago	Away	Win	9–4
	Chicago	Away	Loss	2–4
18	Chicago	Away	Loss	1–6

(no box score available)

19	Chicago	Away	Loss	1–2

(no box score available)

24	Louisville	Away	Win	4–1

(no box score available)

	Louisville	Away	Loss	3–4

(no box score available)

31	Memphis	Home	Win	2–0
	Memphis	Home	Loss	0–1

August

1	Memphis	Home	Win	10–0
	Memphis	Home	Win	5–4
7	Algiers (New Orleans)	Home	Win	4–2
	Algiers	Home	Loss	2–3
8	Algiers	Home	Win	10–1
11	Lincoln Giants (Alexandria)	Away	Win	7–3

(no box score available)

12	Lincoln Giants	Away	Loss	1–3

(no box score available)

13	Algiers	Away	Win	5–0

(no box score or pitcher tally available)

14	Algiers	Away	Win	17–2

(no box score or pitcher tally available)

15	Algiers	Away	Loss	2–6

(no box score available)

16	Algiers	Away	Win	(no known score)
	(no box score or pitcher tally available)			
20	Austin	Away	Win	5–2
	(no box score available)			
21	Austin	Away	Loss	2–3
	(no box score available)			
22	Austin	Away	Win	5–4
	(no box score available)			
28	Austin	Home	Loss	2–4
29	Austin	Home	Win	3–2
30	Austin	Home	Win	10–0

September

3	Pittsburgh	Away	Loss	3–7
	(no box score or pitcher tally available)			
4	Pittsburgh	Away	Win	2–1
5	Pittsburgh	Away	Loss	2–7
	Pittsburgh	Away	Loss	2–9
	(no box score available)			
10	Pittsburgh	Home	Tie	6–6
11[3]	Pittsburgh	Home	Loss	4–11
12	Pittsburgh	Home	Loss	6–9
	(no box score available)			
13	Pittsburgh (exhibition in New Orleans)		Unknown	Unknown
	(no box score or pitcher tally available)			
17	Lincoln Giants (exhibition)[4]	Away	Loss	10–26
	(no box score available)			
18	Lincoln Giants (exhibition)	Away	Win	9–6
	(no box score available)			
25	Lincoln Giants (exhibition)	Away	Win	4–3
	(no box score available)			
	Lincoln Giants (exhibition)	Away	Loss	1–2
	(no box score available)			

October

6	Little Rock (exhibition)	Home	Unknown	Unknown
	(no box score or pitcher tally available)			

Little Rock (exhibition)   Home   Unknown Unknown

(no box score or pitcher tally available)

7   Little Rock (exhibition)   Home   Unknown Unknown

(no box score or pitcher tally available)

Win/Loss Totals

	Wins	Losses	Ties	Winning Percentage
Exhibition:	8	5	0	0.615
Regular Season:	51	20	0	0.718
(Month by Month)				
(April)	(5)	(0)	(0)	(1.00)
(May)	(15)	(3)	(0)	(0.833)
(June)	(11)	(3)	(0)	(0.786)
(July)	(8)	(9)	(0)	(0.471)
(August)	(12)	(5)	(0)	(0.706)
World Series:	*1*	*5*	*1*	*0.143*
Total:	60	30	1	0.659

Win/Loss Breakdown by Team

	Wins	Losses	Ties	Winning Percentage
Algiers Giants	5	2	0	0.714
Austin Black Senators	4	2	0	0.667
Birmingham Black Barons	2	1	0	0.667
Chicago American Giants	3	4	0	0.429
Cleveland Cubs	4	0	0	1.00
Houston Black Buffaloes	2	2	0	0.500
Lincoln Giants (Alexandria)	3	3	0	0.500
Little Rock Greys	8	0	0	1.00
Louisville Black Caps	1	1	0	0.500
Memphis Red Sox	10	6	0	0.625
Montgomery Grey Sox	11	1	0	0.917
Nashville Elite Giants	4	2	0	0.667
Pittsburgh Crawfords	2	6	1	0.222
Rayville Sluggers	*1*	*0*	*0*	*1.00*
	60	30	1	0.659

Monroe's Original First-Half Schedule as Announced by the Negro Southern League in March 1932[5]

Dates	Opponent	Home/Away
April		
23, 24, 25	Little Rock	Away
30	Memphis	Away
May		
1, 2	Memphis	Away
6, 7, 8	Cleveland	Home
14, 15, 16	Little Rock	Home
20, 21, 22	Birmingham	Home
28, 29, 30	Montgomery	Away
June		
5, 6, 7	Nashville	Away
10, 11, 12	Little Rock	Away
18, 19, 20	Nashville	Home
25, 26, 27	Little Rock	Home
July		
2, 3, 4	Memphis	Home

Monroe's Original Second-Half Schedule as Announced by the Negro Southern League in July 1932[6]

July		
9, 10, 11	Memphis	Away
16, 17, 18	Chicago	Away
23, 24, 25	Louisville	Away
30, 31	Memphis	Away
August		
1	Memphis	Away
6, 7, 8	Knoxville	Home
13–16	OPEN	
21, 22, 23	Memphis	Home
28, 29, 30	Nashville	Away
September		
3, 4, 5	Louisville	Home
10, 11, 12	Montgomery	Away

Comparative Tallies of Other Sources

Robert Peterson's *Only the Ball Was White* and Dick Clark and Larry Lester's *The Negro Leagues Book* both give Monroe's first-half total as follows: thirty-three wins and seven losses, for a percentage of 0.825.[7]

John Holway's *The Complete Book of Baseball's Negro Leagues* offers a season total for the Southern League teams, and seems incredibly mistaken with its tally of twenty-six wins and twenty-two losses, for a percentage of 0.542.[8]

The *Monroe Morning World*'s first-half standings were thirty-three wins and seven losses, for a percentage of 0.825.[9]

The *Pittsburgh Courier* did not print any final first-half standings, but its standings as of (and including) July 3 seem to match my count: thirty-one wins and seven losses, for a percentage of 0.816.[10]

As part of its pre–World Series coverage, the *Courier* printed its breakdown of all of Monroe's games:[11]

Team Played	Total Games	Wins	Losses
Memphis	13	8	5
Little Rock	12	12	0
Montgomery	12	11	1
Nashville	8	5	3
Louisville	2	1	1
Birmingham	3	2	1
J. Brown's Chicago	5	1	4
New Orleans	7	5	2
Austin	3	2	1
Cleveland	4	4	0
Cole's Chicago Giants	3	3	0
Houston	5	3	2
Crawfords	2	1	1
Alexandria	3	2	1
	82	60	22

APPENDIX 2

Timeline of 1932 Player/ Personnel Acquisitions

February 27: Monroe is admitted to the newly formed Negro Southern League at its Nashville meeting.[1]

March 23: The Monarchs purchase "Red" Murray, pitcher, from the New York Black Yankees.[2]

March 27: The Monarchs purchase Dick Matthews,[3] pitcher, from the New Orleans Black Pelicans.[4]

April 7: The Monarchs purchase Elbert Williams, pitcher, from the Cuban House of David.[5]

April 9: The Monarchs reduce the team to the required fourteen-player roster.[6]

April 19: The Monarchs acquire Roy "Red" Parnell, pitcher and infield, and Chuffie Alexander, outfield and infield, from the Houston Black Buffaloes.[7]

May 14–16: The Monarchs add Leland Foster to the pitching staff.[8]

July 9–19: The Monarchs acquire Samuel "Sad Sam" Thompson, pitcher, from Indianapolis.[9]

August 11: The Monarchs acquire Homer "Blue Goose" Curry and Bob Harvey, pitchers, from the Memphis Red Sox.[10]

August 20–22: The Monarchs acquire Red Murray, pitcher, from the Memphis Red Sox.[11]

August 31: The Monarchs acquire Hilton Smith, pitcher, from the Austin Black Senators.[12]

APPENDIX 3
Monroe Monarchs Roster Breakdown and Comparison

In the comparison of Monarchs rosters shown below, the roster compiled by the author precedes those presented by three other sources. When considered with the acquisition list from appendix 2 and the statistical analysis from appendix 4, the presentation of the following rosters constitutes an inherent argument for the author's version of the team's list of players. This should *not* be construed as an indictment of the other versions, however.

These different versions of rosters demonstrate the ease with which inconsistencies can develop. The confusion of the season has led to historiographical discrepancies. Additionally, the final three lists appear in reference books containing the rosters of hundreds of Negro League teams. Here, the author has focused on one team in one season.

Discrepancies will never fully disappear. The author's compilation below is not (and *cannot be*) definitive, but it seeks to provide a more accurate count of the contributing players.

1932 Monroe Monarchs Roster as Compiled by the Author

Core Position Players

Morney, Leroy	shortstop
Saunders, Augustus	second base
Wright, Zollie	right field
Dallas, Porter	third base
Else, Harry	catcher
Walker, W.	left field
Alexander, Harvey "Chuffie" (or "Chuffy")	first base
Parnell, Roy	center field, pitcher (reserve third base)
Curry, Homer	left field, pitcher (late addition)

Core Pitchers

Matthews, Dick   pitcher
Murray, "Red"   pitcher
Morris, Barney   pitcher
Williams, Elbert   pitcher
Harvey, Bob   pitcher (late addition)

Reserves

Harris, Samuel   reserve outfield (all positions), third base,
                                        and pinch hitter
Walker, Hoss[1]   reserve catcher, left field
Johnson, Frank   reserve left field, manager
Sheppard, Ray   reserve infield (all positions), pitcher,
                                        pinch hitter
Gillespie, Murray   reserve pitcher (first half; returned for
                                        World Series)[2]
Smith, Hilton   reserve pitcher (late addition)
Thompson, Samuel   reserve pitcher (acquired midseason)

Players of Brief Consequence

Heller, (first name unknown)   preseason first base
Burnham, Willie   preseason pitcher
Markham, Johnny   preseason pitcher
Sias, George   preseason third base
Carter, Marlin   preseason second base
Sanders, Samuel   preseason pitcher
Foster, Leland   reserve pitcher (appeared for ⅔ inning against
                                        Little Rock on May 16, and ⅔ inning
                                        against Birmingham on May 21)
Purvis (or "Pervis"),   reserve pitcher (appeared in the second game
(first name unknown)   of a May doubleheader against Montgomery,
                                        earning the win)

1932 Monroe Monarchs Roster adapted from *The Negro Leagues Book,* edited by Dick Clark and Larry Lester[3]

In the list below, the spelling and rendering of players' names and nicknames are shown as they appear in Clark and Lester's book. The editors included a question mark for first names that were unknown to them.

? Alexander (Chuffy)	1b
Homer Allen	p
Willie Burnham	p
Marlin Carter (Mel)	ss
Homer Curry (Goose)	of
Porter Dallas (Big Boy)	3b
Harry Else	c
Leland Foster	p
Murray Gillespie	p
Samuel Harris	of, p
Bill Harris	c
David Harvey (Bill)	p
Frank Johnson	of
James Liggons	p
Dick Matthews	p
P. D. Moore	c
Leroy Morney	ss
Barney Morris	p
Harold Morris	p
? Murray	p
Roy Parnell (Red)	cf, p
? Pervis	p
Bob Saunders	2b
Ray Sheppard	1b, 3b
Hilton Smith	p
Samuel Thompson (Sad Sam)	p
H. Walker	c, lf
W. Walker	of
Graham H. Williams	p
Zollie Wright	rf, lf

1932 Monroe Monarchs Roster adapted from
The Complete Book of Baseball's Negro Leagues: The Other Half of Baseball History, by John Holway[4]

The Holway book includes batting averages and/or pitching wins and losses. These are included below and can be compared with the compiled statistics from appendix 4. In the list below, the spelling and rendering of players' names and nicknames are shown as they appear in Holway's book.

Chuff Alexander	.293
Bob Saunders	.225
Leroy Morney	.313
Big Boy Dallas	.342
Zolley Wright	.289
Red Parnell	.500
Hoss Walker	.107
Bill Harris	.200
Graham Williams	10–5
Dick Matthews	7–5
Big Boy Morris	6–4
Red Parnell	5–1
Purvis	1–0
Sandy Thompson	0–1
Rube Curry	0–1
Square Moore	0–1
Bob Harvey	0–1
Yellowhore Morris	0–1
Murray Gillespie	0–2

1932 Monroe Monarchs Roster adapted from *The Biographical Encyclopedia of the Negro Baseball Leagues,* by James A. Riley[5]

In the list below, the spelling and rendering of players' names and nicknames are shown as they appear in Riley's book.

Alexander, Chuffy	of, if
Allen, Homer	p
Burnham, Willie "Bee"	p
Carter, Marlin "Mel" "Pee Wee" Theodore	3b
Curry, Homer "Blue Goose" "Rube"	p, of
Dallas, Porter "Big Boy"	3b
Else, Harry	c
English, H. D.	officer
Foster, Leland	p
Gillespie, Murray "Lefty"	p
Harris, Bill	c, of
Harris, Samuel "Sam"	of
Johnson, Frank	of, m
Liggons, James	of

Matthews, Dick	p
Moore, P. D. "Square"	c
Morney, Leroy	ss
Morris, Barney "Big Ad" "Big Boy"	p
Morris, Harold "Yellowhorse"	p
Parnell, Roy "Red"	p
Pervis	p
Saunders, Bob	2b
Sheppard, Ray	p
Smith, Hilton	p
Stovall, Fred	owner
Thompson, Samuel	p
Walker, Hoss	c
Walker, W.	lf
White, Clarence "Red"	p
Williams, Elbert	p
Williams, Graham	p
Wright, Zollie	rf

Additional Monarchs Players Listed in *The Biographical Encyclopedia of the Negro Baseball Leagues,* by James A. Riley, for Years Other Than 1932

Willard Jesse Brown	cf	1934
Lloyd "Ducky" "Bear Man" Davenport	of	1934
Otis Henry	if	1934
John Mathew "Johnny" Markham	p	date not listed
Zearlee "Jiggs" Maxwell	3b	1931
Eldridge "Chili" "Ed" Mayweather	1b	1934
B. Muse	2b, ss	1934
Thomas "Tom" "Big Train" Parker	p	1934
Willie "Bill" Simms	of	1934
Ernest Smith	position unknown	mid-1930s

APPENDIX 4
Statistical Analysis of the Available Data for the 1932 Monroe Monarchs

Team and individual totals are based on available box scores. Highlights or significant figures from games with accompanying newspaper descriptions, but lacking
box scores, will be noted following the available box score data. (Where appropriate,
however, pitching wins are included in the statistical data from newspaper reports
as well as box scores.) Exhibition games with box scores *are* included in the aggre-
gate. Since the only constant among the available box scores are "at bats," "hits," and
"runs," these are the categories used to derive player and team statistics. The players
are listed in order of appearance.

Key to Appendix 4:

AB: At Bats	PH: Pinch Hitter
BA: Batting Average	R: Runs
C: Catcher	RBI: Runs Batted In
CF: Center Fielder	RF: Right Fielder
E: Errors	SAC: Sacrifices
H: Hits	SB: Stolen Bases
HR: Home Runs	SP: Slugging Percentage
HRR: Home Run Ratio	SS: Shortstop
IP: Innings Pitched	TB: Total Bases
IsPo: Isolated Power	W: Wins
L: Losses	WP: Winning Percentage
LF: Left Fielder	1B: First Baseman
OF: Outfielder	2B: Second Baseman or Doubles
P: Pitcher	3B: Third Baseman or Triples

First-Half Statistics (through July 4, 1932)

Note: Batting average in the chart below is the only statistic in this section not physically provided by the actual box scores. Further derivative statistics follow under the section "Derivative Statistics" below.

Position Players

Player; Position	AB	H	R	E	2B	3B	HR	SB	RBI	SAC	BA
Morney, Leroy; SS	154	57	36	12	1	4	2	11	5	0	.370
Saunders, Augustus; 2B	129	31	18	5	2	0	0	4	9	2	.240
Heller, (first name unknown); 1B	24	5	5	0	1	0	1	0	0	0	.208
Wright, Zollie; RF	135	37	23	0	3	5	3	3	10	0	.274
Dallas, Porter; 3B	135	35	17	12	4	0	1	4	3	4	.259
Walker, W.; LF[1]	122	26	15	1	2	0	1	2	7	5	.213
Harris, Samuel; CF (LF, 3B, RF)	63	12	5	1	2	0	0	2	2	3	.190
Else, Harry; C	107	25	11	1	1	2	0	2	4	1	.234
Matthews, Dick; P	34	6	1	0	1	0	0	0	1	1	.176
Murray, Red; P	3	0	0	0	0	0	0	0	0	0	.000
Burnham, Willie; P	1	1	0	0	0	0	0	0	0	0	1.00
Morris, Barney; P	41	6	3	1	0	0	0	0	0	0	.146
Markham, Johnny; P	2	2	0	0	0	0	0	0	0	0	1.00
Williams, Elbert; P	32	4	4	1	1	0	0	0	2	3	.125
Sias, George; 3B	6	0	0	1	0	0	0	0	0	0	.000
Carter, Marlin; 2B	6	2	1	0	0	1	0	0	0	0	.333
Sanders, Samuel; P	1	1	0	0	0	0	0	0	0	0	1.00
Alexander, Chuffie; 1B	124	30	20	7	5	2	0	6	5	5	.242
Parnell, Roy; CF (P)	122	43	30	2	6	9	1	3	19	0	.352
Johnson, Frank; LF (CF, manager)	4	1	1	0	0	0	0	0	1	0	.250
Foster, Leland; P	0	0	0	0	0	0	0	0	0	0	.000
Sheppard, Ray; 2B (SS, PH)	11	2	1	0	1	0	0	0	0	0	.182
Walker, Hoss; C	6	3	3	0	0	0	0	0	0	0	.500

Pitchers

Note: Winning percentage is the only pitching statistic not physically provided by the actual box scores. The lack of consistent details about specific pitching performance categories makes derivative pitching statistics virtually impossible to provide. The percentage is calculated by dividing the number of wins by the number of decisions.

P	W	L	WP
Matthews, Dick	11	2	.846
Murray, Red	1	0	1.00
Morris, Barney	11	3	.769
Williams, Elbert	9	4	.692
Gillespie, Murray	1	0	1.00
Parnell, Roy	4	0	1.00
Purvis, (first name unknown)	1	0	1.00

Untallied Highlights from Games Not Recorded with a Box Score

April 19, Houston (away): 5 runs, 11 hits, 3 errors
April 22–24, Little Rock (away):

    Home runs by Parnell and Morney

    Triples by Wright, Walker, Saunders, Alexander

    April 24 doubleheader: went 8 for 8: homer, triple, 2 doubles, 4 singles; Wright hit 2 doubles

May 28, Montgomery (away):

    Home runs by Else and Wright

    Total of 16 hits for the game with 2 errors

May 29, Montgomery (away, doubleheader):

    10 hits, 4 errors in game one; 6 hits, 1 error in game two

    Home runs by Parnell, Wright, and Else

May 30, Montgomery (away):

    9 hits, 3 errors

    Home run by Parnell

Second-Half Statistics (through August 30)

Note: The number of second-half games is far less than the number of first-half games. In addition, the majority of these games are without box scores. The box score tabulation, as a result, is less substantial, and the untallied highlights more so. The World Series is treated separately below; the final exhibition games against the Crawfords, Lincoln Giants, and Little Rock Greys are not included at all (as it is postseason, and no box scores exist). The players are listed in order of appearance. Batting average in the chart below is the only statistic in this section not physically provided by the actual box scores. Further derivative statistics follow under the section "Derivative Statistics" below.

Position Players

Player; Position	AB	H	R	E	2B	3B	HR	SB	RBI	SAC	BA
Morney, Leroy; SS	62	15	12	8	7	4	0	3	0	2	.242
Sheppard, Ray; 1B (3B, SS, P)	13	6	1	0	1	0	0	0	0	0	.462
Wright, Zollie; RF	68	15	12	2	3	0	2	0	1	5	.221
Dallas, Porter; 3B	53	22	12	3	4	0	3	1	3	0	.415
Johnson, Frank; LF	10	0	0	0	0	0	0	2	0	0	.000
Harris, Samuel; CF (PH)	35	6	5	0	0	0	0	0	2	0	.171
Saunders, Augustus; 2B	63	20	4	6	4	0	0	0	4	0	.317
Else, Harry; C	53	14	8	3	5	1	0	0	3	0	.264
Morris, Barney; P	13	2	4	1	0	0	0	0	0	0	.154
Parnell, Roy; CF (P, PH, 3B)	62	20	10	3	5	0	0	4	7	2	.323
Alexander, Chuffie; FB (PH)	58	20	10	3	2	0	1	2	1	2	.345
Walker, W.; LF (PH)	42	11	4	0	1	0	0	1	2	2	.262
Walker, Hoss; C (LF)[2]	5	2	3	0	0	0	0	0	0	0	.400
Matthews, Dick; P	9	2	1	0	0	0	0	0	0	0	.222
Williams, Elbert; P (PH)	16	3	0	0	0	0	0	0	1	0	.188
Curry, Homer; LF	10	6	3	0	1	0	0	1	0	0	.600
Harvey, Bob; P	1	0	0	0	0	0	0	0	0	0	.000

Pitchers

Note: Winning percentage is the only pitching statistic not physically provided by the actual box scores. The lack of consistent details about specific pitching performance categories makes derivative pitching statistics virtually impossible to provide. The percentage is calculated by dividing the number of wins by the number of decisions.

P	W	L	WP
Morris, Barney	3	3	.500
Parnell, Roy	4	0	1.00
Matthews, Dick	3	4	.429
Williams, Elbert	3	4	.429
Thompson, Samuel	0	1	.000
Curry, Homer	0	1	.000
Murray, Red	1	0	1.00

Untallied Highlights from Games Not Recorded with a Box Score

July 24, Louisville (away; doubleheader): Morney's error in the ninth allowed the winning run to score for Louisville in the second game of the doubleheader
Game one, 10 hits; game two, 7 hits
August 11, Lincoln Giants (away): 9 hits, no errors
August 12, Lincoln Giants (away): 4 hits; Curry had a hit and a steal, and Alexander single scored him for the only run
August 13–16, Algiers (away): Porter "Sugar" Dallas "starred throughout the series" according to the *Louisiana Weekly*
August 20, Austin (away): 8 hits, no errors; "Curry led the Monroe hitting" according to the *Monroe Morning World*
August 21, Austin (away): 8 hits, 1 error
August 22, Austin (away): 9 hits

World Series Statistics (September 3–12)

Position Players

Note: Batting average in the chart below is the only statistic in this section not physically provided by the actual box scores. Further derivative statistics follow under the section "Derivative Statistics" below. The players are listed in order of appearance.

Player; Position	AB	H	R	E	2B	3B	HR	SB	RBI	SAC	BA
Alexander, Chuffie; 1B	12	2	1	0	0	0	0	0	0	0	.167
Morney, Leroy; SS	14	9	7	1	3	2	0	0	0	0	.642
Parnell, Roy; CF (3B)	14	4	0	0	2	1	0	1	4	0	.286
Dallas, Porter; 3B	8	2	0	0	1	0	0	0	0	0	.250
Wright, Zollie; 3B	15	5	0	0	1	0	0	0	1	0	.333
Saunders, Augustus; 2B	13	3	0	3	0	0	0	0	0	0	.231
Curry, Homer; LF	12	3	1	0	1	0	0	0	1	0	.250
Else, Harry; C	5	0	0	1	0	0	0	0	0	0	.000
Walker, Hoss; C	3	0	0	0	0	0	0	0	0	0	.000
Morris, Barney; P	6	0	0	1	0	0	0	0	0	0	.000
Murray, Red; P (PH)	2	1	1	0	0	0	0	0	0	0	.500
Williams, Elbert; P	0	0	0	0	0	0	0	0	0	0	.000
Smith, Hilton; P (PH)	3	0	0	0	0	0	0	0	0	0	.000
Walker, W.; CF (PH)	6	1	1	0	0	0	0	0	0	0	.167
Harvey, Bob; P	0	0	0	1	0	0	0	0	0	0	.000
Harris, Samuel; PH	1	0	0	0	0	0	0	0	0	0	.000
Johnson, Frank; PH	0	0	1	0	0	0	0	0	0	0	.000

Pitchers

Note: Winning percentage is the only pitching statistic not physically provided by the actual box scores. The lack of consistent details about specific pitching performance categories makes derivative pitching statistics virtually impossible to provide. The percentage is calculated by dividing the number of wins by the number of decisions.

P	W	L	WP
Williams, Elbert	1	0	1.00
Gillespie, Murray	0	1	.000
Harvey, Bob	0	2	.000

Untallied Highlights from Games Not Recorded with a Box Score

September 3, Pittsburgh (away): Nothing but the 3–7 score was reported

September 5, Pittsburgh (away; game one): An abbreviated box score for this game exists, but it does not include "at bats" in its list of given statistics. Inclusion, therefore, would skew the sample, as estimated numbers of at bats would be required. In the interest of keeping the absolutely known facts absolutely accurate, giving the best possible representative picture of the success and failure rates of the players, what information exists about the game is not included above, but is as follows: Morney, Parnell, Wright, and Dallas each had 1 hit; Saunders had two hits; Dallas scored a run, as did Hoss Walker, though he never recorded a hit; Alexander, Curry, Else, Harris, and Gillespie played, but neither hit nor scored.

September 5, Pittsburgh (away; game two): Parnell and Wright each had an RBI; Curry and Parnell scored the team's two runs; the team had 9 hits; Parnell had 1 double

September 10, Pittsburgh (home): Future Major League Baseball Hall of Fame inductee Hilton Smith pitched his first innings for the Monarchs: 5 ⅔ innings, 6 hits, 4 runs, 2 strikeouts in a game ended by dark as a 6 to 6 tie, leaving Smith with a no decision. Box score included above

September 12, Pittsburgh (home): Nothing but the 6–9 score was reported

Season Totals

Position Players

Note: Batting average in the chart below is the only statistic in this section not physically provided by the actual box scores. Further derivative statistics follow under the section "Derivative Statistics" below. The players are listed in descending order by number of at bats.

Player; Position	AB	H	R	E	2B	3B	HR	SB	RBI	SAC	BA
Morney, Leroy; SS	230	81	55	21	11	10	2	14	5	2	.352
Wright, Zollie; RF	218	57	35	2	7	5	5	3	12	5	.261
Saunders, Augustus; 2B	205	54	22	14	6	0	0	4	13	2	.263
Parnell, Roy; CF (PH, P, 3B)	198	67	40	5	13	10	1	8	30	2	.338
Alexander, Chuffie; 1B (PH)	194	52	31	10	7	2	1	8	6	7	.268
Dallas, Porter; 3B	196	59	29	15	9	0	4	5	6	4	.301
Walker, W.; LF (CF, PH)	170	38	20	1	3	0	1	3	9	7	.224
Else, Harry; C	165	39	19	4	6	3	0	2	7	1	.236
Harris, Samuel; CF, LF, RF, 3B, PH	99	18	10	1	2	0	0	2	4	3	.182
Morris, Barney; P	60	8	7	3	0	0	0	0	0	0	.133
Williams, Elbert; P (PH)	48	7	4	1	1	0	0	0	2	3	.146
Matthews, Dick; P	43	8	2	0	1	0	0	0	1	1	.186
Sheppard, Ray; 2B, 1B, SS, PH, P	24	8	2	0	2	0	0	0	0	0	.333
Curry, Homer; LF	22	9	4	0	2	0	0	1	1	0	.409
Heller, (first name unknown); 1B	24	5	5	0	1	0	1	0	0	0	.208
Walker, Hoss; C (LF)	14	5	6	0	0	0	0	0	0	0	.357
Johnson, Frank; LF (CF, PH, manager)	14	1	2	0	0	0	0	2	1	0	.071
Carter, Marlin; 2B	6	2	1	0	0	1	0	0	0	0	.333
Sias, George; 3B	6	0	0	1	0	0	0	0	0	0	.000
Murray, Red; P (PH)	5	1	1	0	0	0	0	0	0	0	.200
Smith, Hilton; P (PH)	3	0	0	0	0	0	0	0	0	0	.000
Markham, Johnny; P	2	2	0	0	0	0	0	0	0	0	1.00
Burnham, Willie; P	1	1	0	0	0	0	0	0	0	0	1.00
Sanders, Samuel; P	1	1	0	0	0	0	0	0	0	0	1.00
Harvey, Bob; P	1	0	0	1	0	0	0	0	0	0	.000
Foster, Leland; P	0	0	0	0	0	0	0	0	0	0	.000

Pitchers

P	W	L
Matthews, Dick	14	6
Morris, Barney	14	6
Williams, Elbert	13	8
Parnell, Roy	8	0
Murray, Red	2	0
Gillespie, Murray	1	1
Harvey, Bob	0	2
Purvis, (first name unknown)	1	0
Thompson, Samuel	0	1
Curry, Homer	0	1

Team Statistics[3]

Wins:	60
Losses:	30
Ties:	1
Winning percentage:	.659
Shutouts:	13
Shutouts against:	1
Total runs scored	
First Half:	302
Second Half:	153
World Series:	25
Season:	*480*
Total runs allowed	
First Half:	141
Second Half:	88
World Series:	50
Season:	*279*

	AB	H	R[4]	E	2B	3B	HR	SB	RBI	SAC	BA
1932 Monroe Monarchs	1,949	523	295	80	71	31	15	52	97	37	.268

Derivative Statistics

The given statistics are few, and only for offensive categories. While doubles, triples, and home runs were consistently provided in all formats (regardless of newspaper), stolen bases, RBIs, and sacrifices were not. Therefore, in the interest of consistency and accurate representation, only statistics derivative of the consistent numbers are created below. A brief description of the meaning of each statistic appears in a corresponding footnote.

Player; Position	BA[5]	SP[6]	TB[7]	IsPo[8]	HRR[9]
Morney, Leroy; SS	.352	.513	118	.161	.009
Wright, Zollie; RF	.261	.408	89	.146	.023
Saunders, Augustus; 2B	.263	.293	60	.029	.000
Parnell, Roy; CF (PH, P, 3B)	.338	.520	103	.182	.005
Alexander, Chuffie; FB (PH)	.268	.340	66	.072	.005
Dallas, Porter; 3B	.301	.408	80	.107	.020
Walker, W.; LF (CF, PH)	.224	.259	44	.035	.006
Else, Harry; C	.236	.309	51	.073	.000
Harris, Samuel; CF, LF, RF, 3B, PH	.182	.202	20	.020	.000
Morris, Barney; P	.133	.133	8	.000	.000
Williams, Elbert; P (PH)	.146	.167	8	.021	.000
Matthews, Dick; P	.186	.209	9	.023	.000
Sheppard, Ray; 2B, 1B, SS, PH, P	.333	.417	10	.083	.000
Curry, Homer; LF	.409	.500	11	.227	.000
Heller, (first name unknown); FB	.208	.375	9	.167	.042
Walker, Hoss; C (LF)	.357	.357	5	.000	.000
Johnson, Frank; LF (CF, PH, manager)	.071	.071	1	.000	.000
Carter, Marlin; 2B	.333	.667	4	.333	.000
Sias, George; 3B	.000	.000	0	.000	.000
Murray, Red; P (PH)	.200	.200	1	.000	.000
Smith, Hilton; P (PH)	.000	.000	0	.000	.000
Markham, Johnny; P	1.00	1.00	2	.000	.000
Burnham, Willie; P	1.00	1.00	1	.000	.000
Sanders, Samuel; P	1.00	1.00	1	.000	.000
Harvey, Bob; P	.000	.000	0	.000	.000
Foster, Leland; P	.000	.000	0	.000	.000

The Monarchs as a Comparative Statistical Success

When making comparisons between groups with varying numbers of games, at bats, and so on, the derivative statistics measuring percentages are understandably the only measures that offer fair evaluations of comparative statistical success. Therefore, the derivative batting statistics (minus total bases) and pitcher's winning percentage are the only categories included. While the other individuals on other teams in other leagues have far more available data, only that comparative to existing data for the 1932 Monroe Monarchs is considered below.

Statistics Produced by 1932 Monarchs' Opponents[10]

The teams are listed in alphabetical order.

Team

(Total number of games)		AB	H	R	E	2B	3B	HR	SB	RBI	SAC	BA
Algiers (New Orleans)	(3)	97	19	6	12	6	0	0	4	5	0	.196
Austin	(3)	97	17	6	4	0	0	0	2	5	2	.175
Birmingham	(3)	87	15	5	3	2	1	0	1	4	0	.172
Chicago	(5)	169	25	15	8	5	0	0	0	0	0	.148
Cleveland	(4)	127	13	5	5	1	1	0	4	2	4	.102
Houston	(2)	51	10	2	1	1	1	0	1	2	1	.196
Little Rock	(4)	131	27	7	8	4	1	0	4	7	2	.206
Memphis	(16)	500	116	54	32	13	2	1	15	7	5	.232
Montgomery	(8)	240	48	17	22	4	3	0	3	13	5	.200
Nashville	(6)	191	49	22	5	7	2	0	5	3	3	.257
Pittsburgh	(4)[11]	141	38	21	3	6	1	1	5	10	1	.270

Opponent totals

(58 games)	AB	H	R	E	2B	3B	HR	SB	RBI	SAC	BA
	1,831	377	140	103	49	12	2	44	58	23	.184

Derivative Statistics Produced by 1932 Monarchs' Opponents

The teams are listed in alphabetical order.

Team

(Total number of games)		BA	SP	TB	IsPo	HRR
Algiers (New Orleans)	(3)	.196	.258	25	.062	.000
Austin	(3)	.175	.175	17	.000	.000
Birmingham	(3)	.172	.218	19	.046	.000
Chicago	(5)	.148	.178	30	.030	.000
Cleveland	(4)	.102	.126	16	.024	.000
Houston	(2)	.196	.255	13	.059	.000
Little Rock	(4)	.206	.252	33	.046	.000
Memphis	(16)	.232	.272	136	.040	.002
Montgomery	(8)	.200	.242	58	.042	.000
Nashville	(6)	.257	.314	60	.058	.000
Pittsburgh	(4)	.270	.348	49	.078	.007
Opponent totals (58 games)		.184	.249	456	.043	.001

1932 Pittsburgh Crawfords World Series Statistics

The players are listed in order of appearance.

Position Players

Player; Position	AB	H	R	E	2B	3B	HR	SB	RBI	SAC	BA
Page, Ted; RF, CF	12	4	4	0	0	0	0	1	4	0	.333
Crutchfield, Jimmie; CF	9	1	1	0	0	0	0	1	1	0	.111
Wilson, Jud; LF, 3B[12]	13	5	2	0	0	0	0	1	2	0	.385
Gibson, Josh; C	14	4	4	0	2	0	1	0	2	0	.286
Johnson, Judy; 3B, RF	12	2	3	0	1	0	0	0	1	0	.167
Charleston, Oscar; 1B	11	5	0	0	0	1	0	0	0	0	.455
Russell, Johnny; 2B	10	3	0	1	1	0	0	0	0	1	.300
Stevens, Jake; SS	11	0	1	2	0	0	0	1	0	0	.000
Streeter, Sam; P	4	1	0	0	0	0	0	0	0	0	.250
Kincannon, Harry; P	3	0	1	0	0	0	0	1	0	0	.000
Radcliffe, Ted; P, C	5	2	1	0	1	0	0	0	0	0	.400
Paige, Satchel; P	1	0	0	0	0	0	0	0	0	0	.000
Bell, William; P	2	0	1	0	0	0	0	0	0	0	.000

Pitchers

P	W	L	WP
Streeter, Sam	0	1	.000
Bell, William	2	0	1.00
Paige, Satchel	1	0	1.00

1932 East–West League Statistics

The East–West League, the other major Negro baseball league in 1932, folded early in June of that year. The final statistical release by the league was published in the Baltimore *Afro-American,* on June 11, 1932. The statistics and derivative numbers for individual and team East–West sections come from that source.

1932 East–West League Individual Leaders

Player (Team)	BA[13]	SP	IsPo	HRR	WP
Wilson, Ernest "Jud" (Homestead)	.500				
Finley, Thomas (Baltimore)		.724			
Siki, Roque (Cuban Stars)			.307	.055	
Smith, Herb (Baltimore)					1.00[14]

1932 East–West League Team Leaders

Team	BA	SP	IsPo	HRR	WP
Homestead Grays	.315				
Cuban Stars			.451	.143	.018[15]
Baltimore Black Sox					.690[16]

1932 Cotton States League Statistics

The Cotton States League was a white minor league of teams from Louisiana, Arkansas, and Mississippi. It included, among other teams, the Monroe Twins, who played across town from the Monarchs in Forsythe Park. After it folded early in July, the final statistical release by the league was published in the *Monroe Morning World,* on July 10, 1932. The statistics and derivative numbers for individual and team Cotton States sections come from that source, as do the Monroe Twins statistics below.

1932 Cotton States League Individual Leaders

Player (Team)	BA	SP	IsPo	HRR	WP[17]
Glass, Clyde (El Dorado)	.393	.679	.286		
Baker, Bill (Monroe)					.051
Danforth, C. B.[18] (Pine Bluff)					.857

1932 Cotton States Team Leaders

Team	BA	SP	IsPo	HRR	WP
Monroe	.298				
Baton Rouge		.422		.020	.707
El Dorado			.135		

1932 Monroe Twins Individual Statistics

Player; Position	BA	SP	IsPo	HRR	WP
Bilgere, Joe; SS	.389	.545	.246	.024	
Terrier, Phil; OU	.327	.463	.136	.007	
Crouch, Bill; P	.313	.333	.021	.000	
Baker, Bill; OU	.309	.515	.206	.051	
Ezzell, Homer; FB	.297	.365	.068	.005	
West, Tommy; C	.297	.465	.159	.022	
Moses, Wallace; OU	.294	.411	.117	.013	
Smith, Red; 2B	.280	.413	.133	.028	

Continued on the next page

Player; Position	BA	SP	IsPo	HRR	WP
Hammack, Sterling; 3B	.275	.365	.090	.011	
Kitchens, Frank; C	.212	.242	.030	.000	
Perez, Elisea; P				.416	
Florrid, Dick; P				.400	
Lanning, Johnny; P				.500	
Erwin, Ben; P				.333	
Crouch, Bill; P				.214	
Bryant, Dobie; P				.000	

1932 Monroe Twins Team Statistics

BA	SP	IsPo	HRR	WP
.298	.421	.123	.015	.456

1932 Major League Baseball Statistics

1932 American League Individual Leaders[19]

Player (Team[s])	BA	SP	IsPo	HRR	WP
Alexander, Dale (Detroit, Boston)	.367				
Foxx, Jimmie (Philadelphia)		.749	.385	.099	
Allen, Johnny (New York)					.810

1932 American League Team Leaders

Team	BA	SP	IsPo	HRR	WP
Philadelphia	.290	.457		.031	
New York			.169		.643

1932 National League Individual Leaders

Player (Team)	BA	SP	IsPo	HRR	WP
O'Doul, Lefty (Brooklyn)	.368				
Klein, Chuck (Philadelphia)		.646	.298		
Ott, Mel (New York)				.067	
Warneke, Lon (Chicago)					.786

1932 National League Team Leaders

Team	BA	SP	IsPo	HRR	WP
Philadelphia	.292	.442	.151	.022	
Chicago					.558

All-Time Major League Individual Leaders[20]

Player (Year)	BA	SP	IsPo	HRR	WP
Duffy, Hugh (1894)	.440				
Bonds, Barry (2001)		.863	.536	.153	
Face, Roy (1959)					.947

Notes

Note: Authors and titles for newspaper articles are not included. Authors for such accounts were rarely listed, as most game descriptions were submitted by teams themselves. Each paper then provided different titles for similar accounts. Instead, dates and page numbers will direct anyone interested to the necessary sources.

Introduction

1. *Insurance Map of Monroe and West Monroe, Louisiana, 1932* (New York: Sanborn Map Company, 1932), Composite, 18:28–30, 19:26; and "Property of the Heirs of William Thomas; Section 76, Township 18N, R4E" (maps), Plat Book, Ouachita Parish, Book 2, page 2, 12, Ouachita Parish Clerk of Court, Ouachita, LA.

2. *New Orleans Item,* 6 May 1919, 8.

3. *Kansas City Call,* 18 March 1932, 5B; and *Atlanta World,* 11 March 1932, 7; 20 March 1932, 7.

4. "The Golden Years," Negro Leagues Baseball Museum, Kansas City, MO.

5. Michael Lomax argues in his study of nineteenth-century black baseball entrepreneurship that the Negro Leagues as a "unifying element" of a community is a common and self-evident historical conclusion. But what makes it unifying? The actual feelings one could experience on a drive through the "Booker T. Washington" district of 1932 Monroe and the true constitution of that "unifying element" are difficult to know. Lomax notes the common tendency to create uncritical, laudatory accounts of black baseball's relationship to its constituent metropolitan area—a sort of fallback position, a cheat, in which the presence of a baseball team itself (particularly one with colorful or talented stars) begins as a "unifying element." Such studies then use that a priori assumption as evidence, rather than finding evidence to prove that their original "unifying element" even existed in the first place. Black baseball histo-

rians, he argues, are putting the cart before the horse. That isn't to say that the cart doesn't belong there at all. Black baseball teams *did* serve as a "unifying element" for their communities. And the Monroe Monarchs served as a "unifying element" for theirs. The team's relationship with both the black and white press, as well as its relationship with its league, helped build its status in the community. So too did that community's desperation, its need for release and/or hope in troubled times. If hope was the thing, however, there needed to be something more than just relationships. Historian Harold Seymour has argued that twentieth-century sport gave the black population an ephemeral but powerful opportunity for success. African Americans made more permanent achievements in other fields, he notes, but athletics brought meaningful black successes to popular attention. And so, victories (however ephemeral) mattered, too. They did, in fact, drive the development of those other makers of unity. Winning led to community interest, which led to increased newspaper coverage, which helped ensure the preservation of box scores, game write-ups, and opinion pieces. It offered no guarantees. But it made contemporary and historical survival possible. Michael E. Lomax, *Black Baseball Entrepreneurs, 1860–1901: Operating by Any Means Necessary* (Syracuse, NY: Syracuse University Press, 2003), xv–xvi, xvii; and Harold Seymour, "Blacks and Sport: Depression and After," Harold and Dorothy Seymour Papers, 1830–1998, Box 31, Card 200, Collection No. 4809, Cornell University, Ithaca, NY.

Chapter 1

1. *Monroe News-Star,* 30 April 1919, 1; *Monroe News-Star,* 8 May 1919, 4; and *New Orleans Times-Picayune,* 12 May 1919, 5.

2. These numbers come from the count of the NAACP. Similar counts by Tuskegee proved even higher for 1919. The different counts stem from different definitions about the nature of lynching. The NAACP of 1919 defined lynching as a mob of three or more persons, representing the intentions of an entire community. By the end of the decade, the NAACP would no longer require community support as a necessary element of lynching. The change in definition, notes Christopher Waldrep, was not the result of an improvement in white behavior. It was the politics of the continually changing definition of "lynching." Waldrep describes the first four decades of the twentieth century as an arena in which various institutions fought to present their own definitions of the word to serve their own respective political ends. Christopher Waldrep, *The Many Faces of Judge Lynch: Extralegal Violence and Punishment in America* (New York: Palgrave Macmillan, 2002), 5–7, 127–45.

3. The reaction to the lynching came almost entirely from the press, the religious community, and random letter writers. No politician in state government recorded

an official comment on the lynching. William Ivy Hair, *The Kingfish and His Realm: The Life and Times of Huey P. Long* (Baton Rouge: Louisiana State University Press, 1991), 98.

4. *New Orleans Times-Picayune,* 12 May 1919, 5; *Monroe News-Star,* 12 March 1918, 1; *Monroe News-Star,* 23 April 1918, 1.

5. *Monroe News-Star,* 29 April 1919, 1; *Monroe News-Star,* 30 April 1919, 1.

6. *Monroe News-Star,* 29 April 1919, 1; and *Fourteenth Census of the United States,* vol. 3, *Population, 1920: Composition and Characteristics of the Population by States* (Washington, DC: U.S. Government Printing Office, 1922), 396, 399. According to the census, 26.9 percent of Monroe's black population was illiterate. 32.7 percent of Ouachita Parish's black population was illiterate. These figures, if nothing else, demonstrate that Bolden's attackers would have ample reason to doubt his authorship, even without specific information.

7. *Monroe News-Star,* 29 April 1919, 1; *Monroe News-Star,* 8 May 1919, 4; and *New Orleans Times-Picayune,* 12 May 1919, 5.

8. *Monroe News-Star,* 30 April 1919, 1; *Monroe News-Star,* 1 May 1919, 1; *Monroe News-Star,* 8 May 1919, 4.

9. *Monroe News-Star,* 30 April 1919, 1; *Monroe News-Star,* 1 May 1919, 1.

10. *Monroe News-Star,* 28 April 1919, 1; and "A Midnight Romance," American Film Institute, http://www.afi.com (accessed 23 October 2010).

11. Seventy-six of the eighty-three lynching victims in 1919 were African American. Seven of the total occurred in Louisiana. The previous year, nine of sixty-two total lynchings occurred in Louisiana. *Lynchings by States and Race, 1882–1959* (Tuskegee, AL: Department of Records and Research, Tuskegee Institute, 1959), 2; "Lynchings in 1919," *Literary Digest* 64 (17 January 1920): 20; Robert R. Moton, "The Lynching Record for 1918," *Outlook,* 22 January 1919, 159. Communist vilification, though not the focus of Red Summer, was evident in the portrayal of Bolshevism in the press. *New York Tribune,* 30 April 1919, 4; *New York Tribune,* 1 May 1919, 6; and *Washington Post,* 1 May 1919, 2; *Washington Post,* 2 May 1919, 9.

12. Margaret MacMillan, *Paris 1919: Six Months That Changed the World* (New York: Random House, 2002), 296–305; Donald L. Grant, *The Anti-Lynching Movement: 1883–1932* (San Francisco: R and E Research Associates, 1975), 121–22; Jacquelyn Dowd Hall, *Revolt against Chivalry: Jessie Daniel Ames and the Women's Campaign against Lynching* (New York: Columbia University Press, 1979), 60; "Omaha," *Nation* (11 October 1919): 491; "On the Firing-Line during the Chicago Race-Riots," *Literary Digest* (23 August 1919): 44–46; Theodore Kornweibel Jr., *"Seeing Red": Federal Campaigns against Black Militancy, 1919–1925* (Bloomington: Indiana University Press, 1998), 22–23; and Robert L. Zangrando, *The NAACP Crusade against Lynching, 1909–1950* (Philadelphia: Temple University Press, 1980), 53–54.

13. Lawrence D. Hogan, *Shades of Glory: The Negro Leagues and the Story of African-American Baseball* (Washington, DC: National Geographic, 2006), 6–9, 18–21.

14. Christopher Hauser, *The Negro Leagues Chronology: Events in Organized Black Baseball, 1920–1948* (Jefferson, NC: McFarland and Company, 2006), 1–2; Dick Clark and Larry Lester, eds., *The Negro Leagues Book* (Cleveland, OH: Society for American Baseball Research, 1994), 73–75; and Hogan, *Shades of Glory,* 104–6, 146–51.

15. "Organizing 100,000 for Negro Rights, 'To Make America Safe for Americans': National Conference in Cleveland, June 21 to 29," *Papers of the NAACP,* part 1, reel 8, *Annual Conference Proceedings, 1910–1950* (Bethesda, MD: University Publications of America, 1982); *New Orleans Item,* 6 May 1919, 4, 14; Grant, *Anti-Lynching Movement,* 67; Zangrando, *NAACP Crusade against Lynching,* 46–50; "For Release, Monday, May 5," *Papers of the NAACP,* part 7: The Anti-Lynching Campaign, 1912–1955, series A, reel 12 of 30 (Bethesda, MD: University Publications of America, 1982), 359–60 [hereafter cited as *Papers of the NAACP,* part 7, series A, reel 12]; "Minutes of the Meeting of the Board of Directors, March 10, 1919," *Papers of the NAACP,* part 1, reel 1, *Minutes of the Meetings of the Board of Directors, 1909–1950* (Bethesda, MD: University Publications of America, 1982); Greta de Jong, *A Different Day: African American Struggles for Justice in Rural Louisiana, 1900–1970* (Chapel Hill: University of North Carolina Press, 2002), 67; and Adam Fairclough, *Race and Democracy: The Civil Rights Struggle in Louisiana, 1915–1972* (Athens: University of Georgia Press, 1995), 20. Interestingly, the "address" did not specifically demand a federal anti-lynch law, but the NAACP's national conference, held the following month, proclaimed that its goal was "To Make America Safe for Americans." The NAACP's first Louisiana branch was in Shreveport in 1914. New Orleans, Alexandria, and Baton Rouge established branches by the end of the decade, with Monroe finally participating in 1925. None, however, wielded any real power. Dr. Claude Hudson, Shreveport branch president, wrote in 1923, "The NAACP is thoroughly hated in this section."

16. Hall, *Revolt against Chivalry,* 62–64, 159–75, 193–97; and Waldrep, *Many Faces of Judge Lynch,* 132–34. In the early 1930s, Jessie Daniel Ames's Association of Southern Women for the Prevention of Lynching would take a similar moral stand against mob violence that argued against federal legislation. If people just allowed southern courts to try black men for crimes considered worthy of lynching, the courts would convict. She sought to convince white southerners to change by emphasizing successful recourses to law instead of harping on southern male barbarism.

17. Herbert J. Seligmann, "Protecting Southern Womanhood," *Nation,* 14 June 1919, 938–39; "How Shall the Black Man's Burden Be Lifted?" *Current Opinion* 67 (August 1919): 111–12; "*New York Age*—May 24, 1919," *Papers of the NAACP,* part

7, series A, reel 12, 403–4; "*New Orleans Vindicator*—May 17, 1919," *Papers of the NAACP*, part 7, series A, reel 12, 401; Robert R. Moton, "The South and the Lynching Evil," *South Atlantic Quarterly* 18 (July 1919): 191–93; "The Lynching Evil from a Southern Standpoint," *Review of Reviews* 60 (November 1919): 531–32; Zangrando, *NAACP Crusade against Lynching*, 48; "The Lynching Evil," *New Republic*, 3 May 1919, 7; "The Fight in Texas against Lynching," *World's Work* 37 (April 1919): 616; and "New Phases of the Fight against Lynching," *Current Opinion* 67 (July 1919): 45. Though African American newspapers such as the *New York Age* and *New Orleans Vindicator* echoed Seligmann's sentiments, they remained far more hopeful that justice would be served. Robert Russa Moton, Booker T. Washington's successor at the Tuskegee Institute and a leading anti-lynching advocate, viewed lynching as a distinctly southern problem (and the national figures bear him out). Moton described lynching as "evil," as did the national publications *Review of Reviews, New Republic,* and *World's Work. Current Opinion* called lynching a "national disgrace." These national publications, like the speakers at the national conference on lynching, opposed the practice on moral grounds. They took their readers' opposition for granted. For more on the debates on lynching in the first decades of the twentieth century, including the definitions used to categorize the practice, see Waldrep, *Many Faces of Judge Lynch*; W. Fitzhugh Brundage, *Lynching in the New South: Georgia and Virginia, 1880–1930* (Urbana: University of Illinois Press, 1993); and Stewart E. Tolnay and E. M. Beck, *A Festival of Violence: An Analysis of Southern Lynchings, 1882–1930* (Urbana: University of Illinois Press, 1995).

18. *Monroe News-Star,* 29 April 1919, 1; *Monroe News-Star,* 30 April 1919, 1; *New Orleans Times-Picayune,* 30 April 1919, 12; *New Orleans Item,* 30 April 1919, 5; *Arkansas Gazette,* 30 April 1919, 16; *Arkansas Democrat,* 30 April 1919, 9; *Memphis Commercial Appeal,* 30 April 1919, 3.

19. *Monroe News-Star,* 1 May 1919, 1.

20. *Monroe News-Star,* 2 May 1919, 5; *Monroe News-Star,* 3 May 1919, 1, 2; *Monroe News-Star,* 5 May 1919, 1; *Monroe News-Star,* 10 May 1919, 10. Monroe's Victory Liberty Loan campaign was also a success. The city surpassed its quota and won a captured German cannon for its effort.

21. *New Orleans Item,* 6 May 1919, 8; National Association for the Advancement of Colored People, *Thirty Years of Lynching in the United States, 1889–1918* (New York: Arno Press, 1969), 71–73, 104–5; and *Papers of the NAACP,* part 7, series A, reel 12, 348–52, 354, 356, 373–80, 383, 393. The *Item* wasn't the only newspaper to notice. The *Times-Picayune* carried similar commentary, as did the *Southwestern Christian Advocate. New Orleans Times-Picayune,* 12 May 1919, 8; "The Monroe Lynching," *Southwestern Christian Advocate,* 12 June 1919, 1–2.

22. *Papers of the NAACP,* part 7, series A, reel 12, 410–13; *New Orleans Item,* 6

May 1919, 8; *Monroe News-Star,* 8 May 1919, 4; *New Orleans Times-Picayune,* 12 May 1919, 8; "1940s Front," archival photograph, St. Francis Medical Center Department of Public Relations; and *Insurance Map of Monroe and West Monroe, Louisiana, 1932,* 18:16.

23. *Monroe News-Star,* 8 May 1919, 4; *Monroe News-Star,* 9 May 1919, 4; *Monroe News-Star,* 10 May 1919, 4.

24. The League of Women Voters of Monroe, *Monroe: The New and Old* (Monroe, LA: League of Women Voters, 1960), 6; *Monroe News-Star,* 10 May 1919, 4; *Monroe News-Star,* 13 May 1919, 1, 3, 4; *New Orleans Item,* 13 May 1919, 2; and *New Orleans Times-Picayune,* 11 May 1919, B14.

25. *Monroe News-Star,* 15 May 1919, 1; *Monroe News-Star,* 19 May 1919, 1; *Monroe News-Star,* 20 May 1919, 1; *Monroe News-Star,* 21 May 1919, 1; *State of Louisiana v. R. R. McCord,* "Indictment for carrying a firearm on premises of a St. Francis Sanitarium," index no. 15248, 20 May 1919, Clerk of Court, Criminal Division, Ouachita Parish Courthouse; and *State of Louisiana v. R. R. McCord,* "Indictment for trespass on property of sanitarium," index no. 15249, 20 May 1919, Clerk of Court, Criminal Division, Ouachita Parish Courthouse.

26. *New Orleans Item,* 25 May 1919, 4; *Monroe News-Star,* 19 May 1919, 1; *Monroe News-Star,* 30 May 1919, 4; *Monroe News-Star,* 31 May 1919, 4.

27. *Shreveport Journal,* 16 May 1919, 6; *Monroe News-Star,* 2 June 1919, 4.

28. *Monroe News-Star,* 28 April 1919, 1; and "The Test of Honor," American Film Institute, http://www.afi.com (accessed 24 October 2010).

29. *New York Tribune,* 1 May 1919, 10.

Chapter 2

1. Bruce J. Evensen, *When Dempsey Fought Tunney: Heroes, Hokum, and Storytelling in the Jazz Age* (Knoxville: University of Tennessee Press, 1996), ix; Randy Roberts, *Jack Dempsey: The Manassa Mauler* (Baton Rouge: Louisiana State University Press, 1979), 67; Michael Oriard, *King Football: Sport and Spectacle in the Golden Age of Radio and Newsreels, Movies and Magazines, the Weekly and the Daily Press* (Chapel Hill: University of North Carolina Press, 2001), 7, 29, 89; and Benjamin G. Rader, *Baseball: A History of America's Game,* 2nd ed. (Urbana: University of Illinois Press, 2002), 110–11, 124–29.

2. *Ouachita Citizen,* 5 May 1932, 2.

3. *Lynchings by States and Race,* 2; and Waldrep, *Many Faces of Judge Lynch,* 134–45. Again, these numbers come from the NAACP's official tally. Though the decline would continue in various counts of lynchings each year, the counts would be

inevitably different because of the different definitions used to describe the practice. See also chapter 1, note 2.

4. Jerry Malloy, "Chicago American Giants," MFF 308, National Baseball Hall of Fame, Cooperstown, NY.

5. Leslie A. Heaphy, ed., *Black Baseball and Chicago: Essays on the Players, Teams, and Games and Games of the Negro Leagues' Most Important City* (Jefferson, NC: McFarland, 2006), 153; Neil Lanctot, *Negro League Baseball: The Rise and Ruin of a Black Institution* (Philadelphia: University of Pennsylvania Press, 2004), 9; and Malloy, "Chicago American Giants," MFF 308, National Baseball Hall of Fame.

6. Richard Bak, *Turkey Stearnes and the Detroit Stars: The Negro Leagues in Detroit, 1919–1933* (Detroit, MI: Wayne State University Press, 1994), 198.

7. Paul Debono, *The Indianapolis ABCs: History of a Premier Team in the Negro Leagues* (Jefferson, NC: McFarland, 1997), 106; *California Eagle,* 24 June 1932, 9; *Pittsburgh Courier,* 26 March 1932, 2–4; and *Afro-American,* 26 March 1932, 14.

8. Lanctot, *Negro League Baseball,* 6–8; Harold Cruse, *The Crisis of the Negro Intellectual* (New York: William Morrow, 1967), 11–111; and Carter Godwin Woodson, *The Negro Professional Man and the Community, with Special Emphasis on the Physician and the Lawyer* (Washington, DC: Association for the Study of Negro Life and History, 1934), 36–37.

9. Lanctot, *Negro League Baseball,* 7–8, 9, 13–15, 25; Harold Cruse, *Crisis of the Negro Intellectual,* 11–63; Nathan Huggins, *Harlem Renaissance* (New York: Oxford University Press, 1971), 3–12, 52–83, 137–89; and David Levering Lewis, *When Harlem Was in Vogue* (New York: Alfred A. Knopf, 1981), 156–97, 282–307.

10. *Pittsburgh Courier,* 24 December 1932, 2–5; *Kansas City Call,* 1 April 1932, 4B; and *California Eagle,* 8 April 1932, 9.

11. John Holway, *The Complete Book of Baseball's Negro Leagues: The Other Half of Baseball History* (Fern Park, FL: Hastings House Publishers, 2001), 282–84; *Kansas City Call,* 15 January 1932, 4B; *Nashville Independent,* 11 July 1931, 5; and *Birmingham Reporter,* 23 January 1932, 8.

12. J. Fair Hardin, "Don Juan Filhiol and the Founding of Fort Miro, The Modern Monroe, Louisiana," *Louisiana Historical Quarterly* 20 (April 1937): 463–64, 472–73; E. Russ Williams Jr., *Encyclopedia of Founding Families of the Ouachita Valley of Louisiana, 1785 to 1850* (Monroe, LA: Williams Genealogical and Historical Publications, 1997), 2:163–64; *Ouachita Citizen, A Pictorial History of Ouachita Parish* (Marceline, MO: D-Books Publishing, 1997), 4; and The League of Women Voters of Monroe, *Monroe: The New and Old* (Monroe: League of Women Voters, 1960), 5–6.

13. "Monroe—A Natural Gas City," *Blue Flame* 1 (September 1931): 5–6, in

Louisiana-Monroe History—Gas Fields, Gas Fields #2, Special Collections, Ouachita Parish Public Library, Monroe, LA; Berney Oakland, "Development of the Gas
Industry," *Monroyan* (1933), in Louisiana-Monroe History—Gas Fields, Gas Fields
#1, Special Collections, Ouachita Parish Public Library, Monroe, LA; and Louis Cos-
per, "The Romance of Gas," *Monroyan* (1933), in Louisiana-Monroe History—Gas
Fields, Gas Fields #1, Special Collections, Ouachita Parish Public Library, Monroe,
LA. Carbon black, a form of burned natural gas, acted as a strengthening agent for
rubber, and for automobile tires in particular.

14. Oakland, "Development of the Gas Industry"; "Monroe—A Natural Gas
City," *The Blue Flame* 1 (September 1931): 8; Ken Purcell, *A Pictorial History of
Monroe, La.* (Monroe, LA: Good Impressions, 1983), 35–40. Another gas field in the
Texas panhandle outstripped it the following year for the title of "world's largest,"
but the impact of Monroe's industry remained vast. Oakland, "Development of the
Gas Industry."

15. "Monroe—A Natural Gas City," 8–9; "Natural Gas," *Gas Industry-Monroe,
La. (V.F.) General Bulletin Handbook, Minerals Division* (January 1933), in Louisiana-
Monroe History—Gas Fields, Gas Fields #1, Special Collections, Ouachita Parish
Public Library, Monroe, LA.

16. *Pittsburgh Courier,* 9 April 1932, 2–4; and *Memphis World,* 12 April 1932, 5.

17. *Louisiana Weekly,* 25 June 1932, 8; and Norman Thomas, *Human Exploitation
in the United States* (New York: Frederick A. Stokes, 1934), 189.

18. Robert S. Lynd and Helen Merrell Lynd, *Middletown: A Study in Contemporary American Culture* (New York: Harcourt, Brace, 1929), 82; Rita Barnard, *The
Great Depression and the Culture of Abundance: Kenneth Fearing, Nathanael West,
and Mass Culture in the 1930s* (New York: Cambridge University Press, 1995), 23, 27.

19. *Louisiana Weekly,* 25 June 1932, 8.

20. Thomas, *Human Exploitation in the United States,* xiv–xv; Lanctot, *Negro
League Baseball,* 6; Hogan, *Shades of Glory,* 224–25; Kari Frederickson, *The Dixiecrat
Revolt and the End of the Solid South, 1932–1968* (Chapel Hill: University of North
Carolina Press, 2001), 13; and Harris Gaylord Warren, *Herbert Hoover and the Great
Depression* (New York: W. W. Norton, 1967), 241–42.

21. *Fifteenth Census of the United States, 1930,* vol. 3, part 1, *Alabama-Missouri*
(Washington DC: US Government Printing Office, 1932), 982, 990, 999, 1003; *Lou-
isiana's Resources and Purchasing Power* (Baton Rouge: Louisiana Department of
Commerce and Industry, 1938), 188; Betty M. Field, "Louisiana and the Great De-
pression," in *The Louisiana Purchase Bicentennial Series in Louisiana History,* vol.
3, *The Age of the Longs in Louisiana, 1928–1960,* ed. Edward F. Haas (Lafayette,
LA: Center for Louisiana Studies, 2001), 4–5; and *Houston Informer,* 7 May 1932, 3.
"The Southern states are among those at the bottom of the literacy list," said Edwin

R. Embree, president of the Julius Rosenwald Fund, at a New Orleans meeting of the American Library Association. He noted a lack of library facilities and a lack of books, adding that though southern black literacy rates were extremely low, "figures for whites alone still leaves [*sic*] the South far below all other sections."

22. William E. Leuchtenburg, *Franklin D. Roosevelt and the New Deal, 1932–1940* (New York: Harper and Row, 1963), 1; Edward Robb Ellis, *A Nation in Torment: The Great American Depression, 1929–1939* (1970; New York: Kodansha International, 1995), 189, 201–4; Robert S. McElvaine, *The Great Depression: America, 1929–1941* (New York: Times Books, 1984), 122; and T. H. Watkins, *The Hungry Years: A Narrative History of the Great Depression in America* (New York: Henry Holt, 1999), 102.

23. Donald J. Lisio, *Hoover, Blacks, and Lily-Whites: A Study of Southern Strategies* (Chapel Hill: University of North Carolina Press, 1985), 258–60.

24. Leuchtenburg, *Franklin D. Roosevelt and the New Deal,* 9–12; and Richard Oulahan, *The Man Who . . . : The Story of the 1932 Democratic National Convention* (New York: Dial Press, 1971), 15–16.

25. *Negro World,* 21 May 1932, 3; *Houston Informer,* 12 March 1932, 1; and Monroe N. Work, ed., *Negro Year Book: An Annual Encyclopedia of the Negro, 1931–1932* (Tuskegee, AL: Negro Year Book, 1931), 111–12. Louisiana's suffrage restriction amendment to its state constitution took effect in 1898.

26. Meyers qtd. in Fairclough, *Race and Democracy,* 25.

27. Edgar Eugene Robinson, *They Voted for Roosevelt: The Presidential Vote, 1932–1944* (Stanford, CA: Stanford University Press, 1947), 34, 41, 45, 51, 56–57, 103, 193; Edgar Eugene Robinson, *The Presidential Vote, 1896–1932* (Stanford, CA: Stanford University Press, 1934), 51, 221, 385; and Fairclough, *Race and Democracy,* 25. Louisiana's Democrat vote was 249,418. Its Republican vote was 18,853. All sixty-four of Louisiana's parishes would vote Democrat in the 1932 election. And both the state and local votes were far from an aberration. Beginning in 1896, Democrats in the previous nine elections garnered 80 percent of the presidential vote. In Ouachita Parish, Democrats received almost 83 percent. The national election proved just as successful for Roosevelt. The Democrats took 57.4 percent of the vote. Hoover managed to win only six states, all in the Northeast, and fifty-nine electoral votes. The country was depressed. It wanted a change. 1932 would be the last year of Republican rule until Dwight Eisenhower took the oath of office in January 1953.

28. *Atlanta Daily World,* 19 June 1932, 1, 5; and *Black Dispatch,* 18 June 1932, 1, 2.

29. David M. Anderson, "'Legal Lynching' or Justice in Transition?: The Acquittal of Jack Ross and the Nature of Jury Trials in Jim Crow–era Louisiana," paper presented at the First Annual Louisiana Studies Conference, Northwestern State University, September 2009.

30. *Houston Informer,* 23 April 1932, 3; *Boston Chronicle,* 31 December 1932, 1; *Indianapolis Recorder,* 9 July 1932, 2; and *Lynchings by States and Race, 1882–1959,* 2. In the first six months of 1932, five people in the nation were lynched, three black and two white. The lynchings were disturbing, but a vast improvement from ten years prior. The 1923 total of twenty-nine lynchings would never be duplicated. But Louisiana would buck the national trend, as the state's decline would actually reverse in the early 1930s with an increase in lynchings. The total number of 1932 lynchings was disputed by the NAACP and Tuskegee Institute, as the numbers had been in 1919 and throughout the 1920s. (See chapter 1, notes 2 and 15.) The NAACP tallied eleven lynchings in 1932, down from fourteen in 1931. Only one occurred in Louisiana. Tuskegee recognized only eight lynchings, which was five fewer than the thirteen they calculated for 1931. For elaboration on Louisiana's upsurge in lynching, see Fairclough, *Race and Democracy,* 25–28.

Chapter 3

1. *Monroe News-Star,* 10 January 1932, 1; *Monroe Morning World,* 10 January 1932, 1; and *Vicksburg Evening Post,* 23 December 1931, 1. The *Memphis Commercial Appeal* reported rises in the upper Ouachita River, as well. *Memphis Commercial Appeal,* 1 January 1932, 1, 4. The situation that residents were urged not to fear was the devastating Mississippi River flood of 1927, which also flooded the Ouachita River and much of the Monroe area.

2. *Insurance Map of Monroe and West Monroe, Louisiana, 1932,* 18:28–30, 19:26; *Monroe Morning World,* 13 January 1932, 1. The author also found great assistance in the use of photographs taken during the early days of February by a local photographer. Though not individually cited, the photos proved invaluable. See Durwood Griffin, *Flood Scenes; Monroe, Louisiana 1932,* Ouachita Parish Public Library Special Collections, Monroe, LA. Many of the photos can also be accessed through the Ouachita Digital Archive. See http://catalog.oplib.org/polaris/search.

3. *Monroe Morning World,* 8 January 1932, 10; *Monroe Morning World,* 9 January 1932, 3.

4. *Monroe Morning World,* 14 January 1932, 1; and "Proceedings, 13 January 1932: Regular Session," Minute Book 12, Ouachita Parish Police Jury, 1931–1935, 813–15, Ouachita Parish Public Library Special Collections, Monroe, LA. Police juries in Louisiana act in much the same capacity that Boards of County Commissioners act in other states. The twelve-member bodies were originally charged with "execution of whatever concerns the interior and local police and administration of the parish." Police Jury Association of Louisiana, http://www.lpgov.org (accessed 26 November 2005).

5. *Monroe Morning World,* 15 January 1932, 1.

6. *Monroe Morning World,* 11 February 1932, 1; *Monroe Morning World,* 12 February 1932, 10; *Monroe Morning World,* 13 February 1932, 3; and *Monroe News-Star,* 11 February 1932, 1.

7. *Monroe Morning World,* 31 January 1932, 3; *Monroe Morning World,* 6 February 1932, 3.

8. *Monroe Morning World,* 9 January 1932, 4.

9. *Monroe News-Star,* 10 January 1932, 1; and *Monroe Morning World,* 10 January 1932, 1, 5.

10. *Monroe Morning World,* 28 January 1932, 1; *Monroe Morning World,* 31 January 1932, 1; and *Monroe News-Star,* 31 January 1932, 1.

11. *Monroe Morning World,* 30 January 1932, 1; *Monroe Morning World,* 2 February 1932, 1; and *Monroe News-Star,* 1 February 1932, 1. Ouachita Parish Junior College was the new name for Northeast Junior College, referenced in chapter 2. The school underwent a series of name changes after its founding, a trend that would continue through its development into a university. It is now the University of Louisiana at Monroe.

12. *Insurance Map of Monroe and West Monroe, Louisiana, 1932,* 18:28–30; and *Monroe Morning World,* 3 February 1932, 1.

13. "Population: Table 13—Composition of the Population, by Parishes: 1930," *Fifteenth Census of the United States: 1930,* vol. 3, part 1, *Alabama-Missouri,* 983; "Population: Table 15—Composition of the Population, for Cities: 1930," *Fifteenth Census of the United States: 1930,* vol. 3, part 1, *Alabama-Missouri* (Washington: US GPO, 1932), 990; "Monroe, Louisiana," Works Progress Administration Writer's Project, 1937, Ouachita Digital Archive, Ouachita Parish Public Library, Monroe, LA, 3–4; *Monroe Morning World,* 2 February 1932, 5; *Monroe Morning World,* 5 February 1932, 5; and *Monroe Morning World,* 23 February 1932, 10. A 1900 population of 5,480 had risen to over 24,000 by 1930, based largely on the availability of carbon black and paper mill work. These workers, already laboring for low wages, were the most susceptible to the Depression and to the flood and constituted the bulk of levee workers. "Population: Table 13—Composition of the Population, by Parishes: 1930," *Fifteenth Census of the United States: 1930,* vol. 3, part 1, *Alabama-Missouri,* 983.

14. *Monroe News-Star,* 4 February 1932, 1; *Monroe Morning World,* 4 February 1932, 1; and *Monroe Morning World,* 13 February 1932, 1.

15. *Monroe Morning World,* 4 February 1932, 1; *Monroe Morning World,* 6 February 1932, 6; *Monroe Morning World,* 2 March 1932, 4.

16. *Monroe Morning World,* 17 February 1932, 1; *Monroe Morning World,* 22 January 1932, 1; *Monroe Morning World,* 2 March 1932, 1.

17. *Monroe Morning World,* 1 February 1932, 1; and W. David Lewis and Wesley

Phillips Newton, *Delta: The History of an Airline* (Athens: University of Georgia Press, 1979), 11–29. See also Geoff Jones, *Delta Air Lines: Seventy-five Years of Airline Excellence* (Charleston, SC: Arcadia, 2003). The young Delta Air Service specialized in crop dusting and small-range transportation. Founded in Monroe, the company would soon move its headquarters to Atlanta and become one of the largest airlines in the world.

18. *Monroe Morning World,* 7 February 1932, 1.

19. *Monroe Morning World,* 17 February 1932, 1, 7.

20. J. W. Bateman, *Annual Report of Agricultural Extension Work in Louisiana, 1935* (Baton Rouge: Louisiana State University Division of Agricultural Extension, 1935), 35, 37–38, 61; J. W. Bateman, *Annual Report of Negro Agricultural Extension Work in Louisiana, 1935* (Baton Rouge: Louisiana State University Division of Agricultural Extension, 1935), 13–15; and "An Economic Assessment of Cantaloupe: Executive Summary," USDA, http://www.rma.usda.gov/pilots/feasible/txt/cantloup.txt (accessed 24 November 2005).

21. The last frost of 1932 occurred on March 13. There were only 3.87 inches of rain in March, and only 2.53 in April. Michael R. Helfert, *Climate and Climatic Normals of Monroe, Louisiana, 1887–1977,* Northeast Louisiana University Climatic Research Center, Occasional Publication, no. 1 (Monroe, LA: Climatic Research Center, 1978), 75, 87.

22. *Louisiana Weekly,* 26 March 1932, 3.

23. "History of Zion Traveler Baptist Church," December 1993, typed document in the possession of Rev. Dr. Tracy C. DeWitt, Zion Traveler Baptist Church, Monroe, LA; and "History," no available date, revised version of "History of Zion Traveler Baptist Church" for use in church bulletin, document in the possession of Rev. Dr. Tracy C. DeWitt, Zion Traveler Baptist Church, Monroe, LA; *Monroe, Louisiana and West Monroe, Louisiana City Directory, 1930* (Springfield, MO: Interstate Directory Company, 1930), 337; and *Monroe Morning World,* 1 March 1932, 6.

24. *Monroe Morning World,* 1 March 1932, 6; *Monroe Morning World,* 2 March 1932, 2; *Monroe Morning World,* 28 April 1932, 10; and *Zion Traveler's Baptist Church v. W. W. Hill,* no. 20679, minutes of District Court, Ouachita Parish, Book N, 20 November 1930–2 November 1932, Ouachita Parish Courthouse, Civil Division, 513, 517, 521, 533, 544.

25. *Memphis World,* 25 September 1932, 5.

26. *Pittsburgh Courier,* 9 April 1932, 2–4; and *Memphis World,* 12 April 1932, 5.

27. "Fred A. Stovall," in *Eastern Louisiana: A History of the Watershed of the Ouachita River and the Florida Parishes,* Frederick William Williamson and George T. Goodman, eds. (Louisville, KY: Historical Record Association, 1939), 585–86; Lyle

Keith Williams, *The Stovall Family and Related Lines,* 2 vols. (Ft. Worth, TX: self-published, 1984), 1:108–9, 120; "Fred Stovall," *Who's Who in the Twin Cities* (West Monroe, LA: H. H. Brinsmade, 1931), 167; Judith Walker Linsley, Ellen Walker Rienstra, and Jo Ann Stiles, *Giant under the Hill: A History of the Spindletop Oil Discovery at Beaumont, Texas, in 1901* (Austin: Texas State Historical Association, 2002), 1–4, 211–12; Spencer W. Robinson, ed., *Spindletop: Where Oil Became an Industry* (Beaumont: Spindletop 50th Anniversary Commission, 1951), 7; and Paul N. Spellman, *Spindletop Boom Days* (College Station: Texas A&M University Press, 2001), 42–53.

28. "Fred A. Stovall," in *Eastern Louisiana,* Williamson and Goodman, eds., 585–86; Williams, *Stovall Family,* 1:108–9, 120; and "Fred Stovall," *Who's Who in the Twin Cities,* 167; "Article of Incorporation of Stovall Drilling Company," record 29808, 17 June 1922, Corporation Charters Record, Ouachita Parish, Book C, 85–91, Ouachita Parish Clerk of Court; "Articles of Incorporation of J.M. Supply Company, Inc.," record 41198, 30 September 1923, Corporation Charters Record, Ouachita Parish, Book C, 311–21, Ouachita Parish Clerk of Court; "Articles of Incorporation of Stovall Navigation Company, Inc.," record 57436, 6 July 1925, Corporation Charters Record, Ouachita Parish, Book C, 620–25, Ouachita Parish Clerk of Court; and "Articles of Incorporation of Bob Halle Construction Company, Inc.," record 140873, 13 June 1930, Corporation Charters Record, Ouachita Parish, Book C, 111–17, Ouachita Parish Clerk of Court.

29. *Memphis World,* 18 September 1932, 5; *Monroe Morning World,* 27 June 1930, 1; *Monroe Morning World,* 1 July 1930, 2; *Monroe Morning World,* 14 July 30, 9; *Monroe Morning World,* 10 October 1958, 5A; Steve Rock, "Former Monarchs Pitcher Hilton Smith Elected to Baseball Hall of Fame," *Kansas City Star,* 7 March 2001, D1; Joe Posnanski, "Hall of Fame Inductee Hilton Smith Often Felt Overshadowed by Paige," *Kansas City Star,* 4 August 2001, D1; Robert Peterson, *Only the Ball Was White: A History of Legendary Black Players and All-Black Professional Teams* (New York: Oxford University Press, 1970), 122; and DeMorris Smith, interview with author, 2 September 2004.

30. *Pittsburgh Courier,* 9 April 1932, 4; "The Realty Investment Co. Ltd. to J.M. Supply Co. Inc.—Mortgage Deed, Sale of Land," record 79482, 23 April 1927, Conveyance Record, Ouachita Parish, Book 157, 775–78, Ouachita Parish Clerk of Court; "J.M. Supply Co., Inc. to The Realty Investment Co., Ltd.—Mortgage Deed, Vendor's Lien," record 79482, 23 April 1927, Mortgage Record, Ouachita Parish, Book 129, 707–710, Ouachita Parish Clerk of Court; "J.M. Supply Co., Inc. to Fred Stovall—Cash Deed, Sale of Land," record 139386, 21 May 1930, Conveyance Record, Ouachita Parish, Book 20, 435–56, Ouachita Parish Clerk of Court; Philip J.

Lowry, *Green Cathedrals: The Ultimate Celebration of Major League and Negro League Ballparks* (New York: Walker and Company, 2006), 81; and "Fred Stovall," *Who's Who in the Twin Cities*, 167.

31. *Shreveport Sun,* 17 May 1930, 5; *Shreveport Sun,* 31 May 1930, 8.

32. *Monroe Morning World,* 14 July 1930, 9; and *Monroe News-Star,* 16 July 1930, 8. As of July, Frank Johnson was playing left field. Johnson would, the next season, become the team's manager and would remain in that post through the 1932 season.

33. Baseball historian Philip J. Lowry cites these dimensions as of 1940. Ten years later, the fences were extended to 360 feet in left, 450 in center, and 330 in right. Lowry, *Green Cathedrals,* 135–36. Lowry's information came from interviews conducted with Negro League veterans at a 1982 Negro League players reunion in Ashland, Kentucky. E-mail correspondence with the author, 2 November 2006.

34. *Monroe News-Star,* 1 July 1930, 2; *Monroe News-Star,* 5 July 1930, 9; *Monroe News-Star,* 16 July 1930, 8; *Monroe News-Star,* 9 October 1958, 1A; *Monroe Morning World,* 1 July 1930, 2; *Monroe Morning World,* 14 July 1930, 9; *Monroe Morning World,* 10 October 1958, 5A; and Peterson, *Only the Ball Was White,* 122. The Monarchs were able to play under the lights at Forsythe if needed, evidenced a month later in the *Morning World:* "The Monarchs will start on a three-game series with the Black Pelicans of New Orleans tonight at 8:30 at Forsythe park. The remaining games will be played Sunday and Monday at Casino Park." *Monroe Morning World,* 27 June 1930, 1.

35. Peter Finney, *The Fighting Tigers II: LSU Football, 1893–1980* (Baton Rouge: Louisiana State University Press, 1980), 98–100. According to Finney, Heard's other motive was more specific to LSU's situation. Playing night games avoided scheduling conflicts with New Orleans universities Tulane and Loyola. LSU won that first night contest 35–0 over Spring Hill.

36. "J.M. Supply Co., Inc. to Fred Stovall—Cash Deed, Sale of Land," book 200, 435–56.

37. "Article of Incorporation of Stovall Drilling Company," Book C, 85–91; "Articles of Incorporation of J.M. Supply Company, Inc.," Book C, 311–21; and Jean Stovall Lee, interview with author, 3 August 2004. Evidence exists that suggests Stovall also governed parts of the team outside the confines of either the drilling or supply companies. His parish taxes outside the city limits indicate a heavy miscellaneous tax that pushed his payment far higher than for comparable citizens. Even his drilling company property outside the city was worth less and, notably, listed separately. "Assessment Roll for the Parish of Ouachita, Henry Johnson through Recapitulation, 1932," microfilm, City, Ouachita Parish Courthouse, Tax Collection Office; "Assessment Roll for the Parish of Ouachita, Wards, West Monroe, City

of Monroe through George Johnson, 1932," microfilm, Ward 1, Ouachita Parish Courthouse, Tax Collection Office.

38. Marlin Carter qtd. in Thom Loverro, *The Encyclopedia of Negro League Baseball* (New York: Facts on File, 2003), 281; Ollie Burns, interview with Paul J. Letlow, 13 May 1992, transcript in author's possession; *Monroe Morning World,* 28 May 1932, 9; *Monroe Morning World,* 1 June 1932, 8; Paul J. Letlow, "A Team to Remember: Monarchs' Memories Linger Sixty Years Later," *Monroe News-Star,* 16 August 1992, 1C, 5C; Peterson, *Only the Ball Was White,* 122; and Lanctot, *Negro League Baseball,* 16. Saunders's explanation is the lone hint of Monarchs salaries in 1932. The $125 per month claim seems remarkable, particularly considering the lack of funding throughout black baseball. But no financial records remain to validate his salary claim.

39. *Pittsburgh Courier,* 9 April 1932, 2–4. Pitman Nedde, sports editor of the *Shreveport Sun,* had a similar evaluation of Stovall, describing him as a "good baseball owner," who "knows what it takes for his manager to keep a team going." *Shreveport Sun,* 16 April 1932, 5.

40. Qtd. in Letlow, "A Team to Remember," 1C. No publication in 1932 describes this incident. Yet Saunders's interpretation seems consistent with other interpretations of Stovall's character.

Chapter 4

1. *Kansas City Call,* 15 April 1932, 5.

2. *Afro-American,* 9 April 1932, 12.

3. *Pittsburgh Courier,* 9 April 1932, 2–4; and *Shreveport Sun,* 16 April 1932, 5.

4. *Shreveport Sun,* 2 January 1932, 5; *Shreveport Sun,* 23 January 1932, 5; *Shreveport Sun,* 16 April 1932, 5; and *Louisiana Weekly,* 9 January 1932, 5.

5. Nedde may have embellished Jones's resume, as Neil Lanctot, author of *Fair Dealing and Clean Playing: The Hilldale Club and the Development of Black Professional Baseball, 1910–1932,* the definitive work on the Hilldale club, is unaware of Jones's time with Hilldale, much less his stardom. *Shreveport Sun,* 23 January 1932, 5; *Shreveport Sun,* 30 January 1932, 5; *Shreveport Sun,* 18 February 1932, 5; *Shreveport Sun,* 20 February 1932, 5; *Shreveport Sun,* 26 March 1932, 5. See also Neil Lanctot, *Fair Dealing and Clean Playing: The Hilldale Club and the Development of Black Professional Baseball, 1910–1932* (Jefferson, NC: McFarland, 1994).

6. *Louisiana Weekly,* 9 January 1932, 5; *Louisiana Weekly,* 16 January 1932, 8; *Louisiana Weekly,* 30 January 1932, 8; *Louisiana Weekly,* 6 February 1932, 8; *Louisiana Weekly,* 30 February 1932, 8; *Kansas City Call,* 29 January 1932, 4B; *Kansas City*

Call, 5 February 1932, 5B; *Pittsburgh Courier,* 2 January 1932, 5; and *Shreveport Sun,* 2 January 1932, 5; *Shreveport Sun,* 30 January 1932, 5; *Shreveport Sun,* 20 February 1932, 5. Though the proposed amount of the 1932 Tri-State guarantee is unknown, that of 1933 is. That season, teams were required to pay a $100 deposit on a $1,000 bond, and 1932's fees can reasonably be assumed to be similar. The payment served as a membership deposit that protected players and owners in the event of forfeits, poor attendance, and games called on account of weather. The monetary guarantee was necessary for all Negro Leagues, as player pay and owner profit were based solely on gate receipts.

7. *Louisiana Weekly,* 16 January 1932, 8; *Louisiana Weekly,* 20 February 1932, 8.

8. Jules Tygiel, *Past Time: Baseball as History* (New York: Oxford University Press, 2000), 119; Larry Lester, *Black Baseball's National Showcase: The East-West All-Star Game, 1933–1953* (Lincoln: University of Nebraska Press, 2001), 21–22, 24; "The Golden Years," Negro Leagues Baseball Museum; *Louisiana Weekly,* 26 March 1932, 8. There were, of course, exceptions to this practice. Dan Burley of the New York *Amsterdam News,* Randy Dixon of the *Philadelphia Tribune,* and others did cover their cities' local teams. See also Jim Reisler, "Dan Burley: The Most Versatile Black Journalist of His Generation," in *Black Writers/Black Baseball: An Anthology of Articles from Black Sportswriters Who Covered the Negro Leagues* (Jefferson, NC: McFarland, 1994), 127–44; and Lanctot, *Fair Dealing and Clean Playing.*

9. *Louisiana Weekly,* 26 November 1932, 7.

10. *Louisiana Weekly,* 16 January 1932, 8; *Louisiana Weekly,* 20 February 1932, 8.

11. *Kansas City Call,* 5 February 1932, 5B; *Atlanta World,* 3 February 1932, 5; and *Pittsburgh Courier,* 16 January 1932, 2–6.

12. *Birmingham Reporter,* 6 February 1932, 8; *Kansas City Call,* 19 February 1932, 5B; and *Atlanta Daily World,* 3 October 1932, 4.

13. *Atlanta Daily World,* 11 March 1932, 7.

14. By March, Pittsburgh joined as an associate member. Louisville and Cleveland also joined the Negro Southern League. *Atlanta World,* 11 March 1932, 7; *Louisiana Weekly,* 5 March 1932, 8; *Shreveport Sun,* 19 March 1932, 5; *Monroe Morning World,* 20 March 1932, 12; and *Kansas City Call,* 11 March 1932, 5B.

15. *Shreveport Sun,* 14 May 1932, 5; *Shreveport Sun,* 21 May 1932, 5; *Shreveport Sun,* 13 August 1932, 5; *Shreveport Sun,* 3 September 1932, 5.

16. *Monroe Morning World,* 28 February 1932, 8; *Monroe Morning World,* 30 March 1932, 12; and *Pittsburgh Courier,* 12 March 1932, 2–4. In the white media, namely the *Monroe Morning World* and *Monroe News-Star,* from which many of these reports derive, the information given by management is recounted but never quoted. A number of reasons for this omission are possible. The Monarchs were rarely given top billing on the white sports pages of Monroe. Usually relegated to a place of less

prominence and, therefore, space, quotes may have created too long an article. The editors may have assumed (correctly, in all probability) that a white audience would find the words of the paper more authoritative than those of black baseball representatives. But most likely, the omission was the result of the subtle racism of the reporters—the same subtle, though not intentionally malicious, racism that dissuaded white reporters from noting black players' first names. Whatever the reason, the descriptions of managerial proclamations in this account will attribute unquoted statements to management; quotations will be attributed to the paper of record, unless that paper directly quotes an official.

17. *Kansas City Call,* 18 March 1932, 5B; and *Atlanta World,* 11 March 1932, 7.

18. *Kansas City Call,* 18 March 1932, 5B.

19. *Pittsburgh Courier,* 2 April 1932, 2–4.

20. Jerry Malloy, "Chicago American Giants," MFF 308, National Baseball Hall of Fame.

21. *Chicago Defender,* 16 January 1932, 9; *Chicago Defender,* 23 January 1932, 8, 9; *Chicago Defender,* 30 January 1932, 9; *Chicago Defender,* 6 February 1932, 9. Louisville, Indianapolis, and Chicago would all find spots in the Southern League.

22. *Chicago Defender,* 20 February 1932, 9; *Chicago Defender,* 27 February 1932, 8.

23. *Afro-American,* 27 February 1932, 14.

24. *Kansas City Call,* 25 March 1932, 5B; *Kansas City Call,* 15 April 1932, 5B; *Pittsburgh Courier,* 16 April 1932, 2–5; *Pittsburgh Courier,* 18 June 1932, 2–5; and *Afro-American,* 16 April 1932, 15.

25. *Atlanta Daily World,* 25 March 1932, 5. On March 14, the *Atlanta World* became a daily, making it the only African American daily. Citations of articles from the *World* after March 14, 1932, reflect the paper's new name.

26. *Chicago Defender,* 9 July 1932, 9.

27. *Pittsburgh Courier,* 26 March 1932, 2–4.

28. Bak, *Turkey Stearnes and the Detroit Stars,* 199–200; "Pre-Negro Leagues Candidate Profile," *New York Age,* 9 January 1932, 6; "Cumberland Willis 'Cum' Posey, Jr.," National Baseball Hall of Fame, http://baseballhall.org/hof/posey-cum (accessed 24 October 2010); *Afro-American,* 16 January 1932, 16; *Afro-American,* 23 January 1932, 15; *Philadelphia Tribune,* 21 January 1932, 10; *Pittsburgh Courier,* 16 January 1932, 2–6; *Pittsburgh Courier,* 23 January 1932, 2–5; and *Kansas City Call,* 18 March 1932, 5B. Finally, in late March, the Kansas City Monarchs announced that they would organize in May, beginning play at Muehlebach Field during the first week of June. They announced plans to take playing trips to Mexico and Cuba. The Monarchs' first press release noted that team owner J. L. Wilkinson had offers to move the team to Chicago, Cleveland, and Detroit, but had graciously decided to keep the team in Kansas City. Of course, business rather than grace determined

the decision to stay, and columnist Frank "Fay" Young saw through Wilkinson's immodesty. "Despite the lowd [*sic*] howling on the part of some who seemed to believe they 'were in the know,' the Monarchs will not be transferred." He described the shortened season and the barnstorming junkets to Mexico and Cuba. "So much for baseball." As of early June, the team had yet to organize, and Wilkinson openly speculated on the possibility of abandoning 1932 play altogether. After returning from a trip to the East Coast and seeing the low attendance at East–West League games, Wilkinson worried about the prospects for his own squad. The Depression, he noted, had drained any expendable income—baseball money—from the average Negro Leagues baseball fan. He speculated that he might reform the team in July. "Then again," reported the *Call*, "he might not." *Kansas City Call*, 3 June 1932, 4B.

29. *Shreveport Sun*, 13 February 1932, 5; *Philadelphia Tribune*, 28 January 1932, 10; *Philadelphia Tribune*, 4 February 1932, 10, 11; and *Afro-American*, 6 February 1932, 15.

30. *Pittsburgh Courier*, 30 January 1932, 2–5.

31. *Atlanta World*, 19 February 1932, 7; *Afro-American*, 5 March 1932, 14; *Afro-American*, 12 March 1932, 15; *New York Age*, 27 February 1932, 6; *New York Age*, 12 March 1932, 6; *Philadelphia Tribune*, 18 February 1932, 11; *Boston Chronicle*, 30 January 1932, 7; New York *Amsterdam News*, 20 January 1932, 12, 13; *Shreveport Sun*, 11 January 1932, 5; and *Afro-American*, 9 January 1932, 15.

32. Lanctot, *Fair Dealing and Clean Playing*, 214; and *New York Age*, 19 March 1932, 6.

33. Two years later, Wilson would become the commissioner of Negro League baseball, governing the decisions of the Negro National League and other associated leagues. He became, according to syndicated columnist Randy Dixon, "the 'Judge Landis' of colored baseball." *Nashville Globe and Independent*, 16 March 1932, 4.

34. Alan J. Pollock, *Barnstorming to Heaven: Syd Pollock and His Great Black Teams*, ed. James A. Riley (Tuscaloosa: University of Alabama Press, 2006), 71–73, 77–78; *Pittsburgh Courier*, 6 February 1932, 4; and *Pittsburgh Courier*, 7 May 1932, 2–4.

35. *Pittsburgh Courier*, 13 February 1932, 2–5; *Philadelphia Tribune*, 25 February 1932, 11; and *Atlanta World*, 28 January 1932, 5.

36. James Bankes, *The Pittsburgh Crawfords: The Lives and Times of Black Baseball's Most Exciting Team* (Dubuque, IA: William C. Brown Publishers, 1991), 23–34. See also Lanctot, *Negro League Baseball*, 9–10. Bankes claims that Greenlee learned his craft from Harlem's Alex Pompez, a notorious bootlegger and owner of New York's Cuban Stars. By 1925, Bankes argues, Greenlee established himself as Pompez's Pittsburgh counterpart, only with a more polished reputation. He does not, however, produce evidence to demonstrate this connection.

37. Bankes, *Pittsburgh Crawfords*, 24–25; and *New York Age*, 3 September 1932, 6.

38. *Atlanta World,* 27 December 1931, 5, 6; *Atlanta World,* 2 March 1932, 5; *Memphis World,* 29 December 1931, 5, 6; *Shreveport Sun,* 2 January 1932, 5; and *Shreveport Sun,* 12 March 1932, 5.

39. *Pittsburgh Courier,* 12 March 1932, 2–5; and *Afro-American,* 12 March 1932, 14.

40. *Pittsburgh Courier,* 20 February 1932, 2–5; *Pittsburgh Courier,* 5 March 1932, 2–5; *Pittsburgh Courier,* 12 March 1932, 2–4; *Pittsburgh Courier,* 30 April 1932, 2–5; *Afro-American,* 5 March 1932, 14; *Afro-American,* 12 March 1932, 14; and *California Eagle,* 6 May 1932, 9. J. Munro Elias was elected league statistician for the East–West League. He would become the East–West counterpart of Monroe's H. D. English. In late April, the schedule finally appeared, with official games getting under way on May 7.

41. *Louisiana Weekly,* 27 February 1932, 8; *Negro World,* 20 February 1932, 4; *Philadelphia Tribune,* 18 February 1932, 10; and New York *Amsterdam News,* 17 February 1932, 13; *Pittsburgh Courier,* 6 February 1932, 2–4; *Atlanta World,* 10 February 1932, 5; *Afro-American,* 6 February 1932, 15; and *California Eagle,* 12 February 1932, 9.

42. *Pittsburgh Courier,* 16 January 1932, 2–5.

43. *Pittsburgh Courier,* 20 February 1932, 2–4; *Pittsburgh Courier,* 26 March 1932, 2–4.

44. *Afro-American,* 2 April 1932, 14.

45. *New York Age,* 23 April 1932, 6; and *Pittsburgh Courier,* 23 April 1932, 2–4.

46. *New York Age,* 23 April 1932, 6; and *Pittsburgh Courier,* 23 April 1932, 2–4.

Chapter 5

1. *Shreveport Sun,* 24 September 1932, 5.

2. *Kansas City Call,* 11 March 1932, 5B; *Atlanta World,* 2 March 1932, 5; *Atlanta Daily World,* 27 March 1932, 5; *Monroe Morning World,* 24 March 1932, 6; and *Monroe News-Star,* 24 March 1932, 6.

3. *Monroe Morning World,* 28 February 1932, 8; *Monroe Morning World,* 20 March 1932, 12; *Monroe Morning World,* 24 March 1932, 6; *Monroe Morning World,* 8 April 1932, 8; *Monroe News-Star,* 24 March 1932, 6; *Pittsburgh Courier,* 12 March 1932, 4; *Pittsburgh Courier,* 19 March 1932, 4; *Negro World,* 7 May 1932, 4; *New York Age,* 5 March 1932, 6; *New York Age,* 26 March 1932, 6; James A. Riley, *The Biographical Encyclopedia of the Negro Baseball Leagues* (New York: Carroll and Graf Publishers, 1994), 848; and Leslie A. Heaphy, *The Negro Leagues, 1869–1960* (Jefferson, NC: McFarland, 2003), 143–45.

4. *Monroe Morning World,* 25 March 1932, 6; and *Birmingham Reporter,* 2 April 1932, 3.

5. *Atlanta World,* 22 January 1932, 5; *Louisiana Weekly,* 19 December 1931, 5; *Louisiana Weekly,* 23 January 1932, 8; *Pittsburgh Courier,* 16 January 1932, 2–5; *Philadelphia Tribune,* 17 December 1931, 10; *Birmingham Reporter,* 30 January 1932, 3; and *Afro-American,* 9 January 1932, 15.

6. *Kansas City Call,* 29 January 1932, 5; *California Eagle,* 5 February 1932, 5; New York *Amsterdam News,* 3 February 1932, 13; Bob Wirz, "Oscar Charleston, Longtime Star of Negro Leagues, Elected to Hall of Fame; Exciting Performer Was Considered One of Most Popular Players of His Time," in "Player File: Charleston, Oscar McKinley," BHOF Vertical Files, National Baseball Hall of Fame, Cooperstown, NY; "Josh Gibson," in "Player File: Gibson, Joshua," Ashland Collection, National Baseball Hall of Fame, Cooperstown, NY; *Shreveport Sun,* 19 March 1932, 5; *Shreveport Sun,* 26 March 1932, 5; *Atlanta Daily World,* 15 September 1932, 5; and *Afro-American,* 12 March 1932, 14. As Greenlee bought players, he also bought transportation. A new bus would provide the Crawfords with deluxe transportation throughout the season. It cost $6,800. It seated seventeen, had seventy-nine horsepower, and could reach sixty miles an hour. Greenlee's bus was the envy of the black baseball world. *Pittsburgh Courier,* 6 February 1932, 2–5.

7. *Louisiana Weekly,* 20 February 1932, 8; and *Pittsburgh Courier,* 13 February 1932, 2–5.

8. *Pittsburgh Courier,* 23 April 1932, 2–5; and *Atlanta Daily World,* 30 March 1932, 5.

9. *Shreveport Sun,* 2 April 1932, 5; *Atlanta Daily World,* 30 March 1932, 5; and *Afro-American,* 26 March 1932, 15.

10. *Monroe Morning World,* 26 March 1932, 9; *Monroe News-Star,* 26 March 1932, 9; *Shreveport Sun,* 16 April 1932, 5; *Boston Chronicle,* 9 April 1932, 7; and *Afro-American,* 9 April 1932, 15.

11. *Monroe Morning World,* 27 March 1932, 11; and *Afro-American,* 9 April 1932, 15.

12. *Monroe Morning World,* 27 March 1932, 11; *Monroe Morning World,* 28 March 1932, 6; *Monroe News-Star,* 28 March 1932, 6; *Boston Chronicle,* 9 April 1932, 7; and *Chicago Defender,* 2 April 1932, 8.

13. *Birmingham Age-Herald,* 1 February 1932, 5.

14. Alan J. Pollock, *Barnstorming to Heaven,* 30, 83, 147, 383–84; Ben Green, *Spinning the Globe: The Rise, Fall, and Return to Greatness of the Harlem Globetrotters* (New York: Amistad, 2005), 32–71; James A. Riley, *Biographical Encyclopedia of the Negro Baseball Leagues,* 697; *Monroe Morning World,* 3 April 1932, 8; *Monroe News-Star,* 1 April 1932, 10; and *Chicago Defender,* 9 January 1932, 9; *Chicago Defender,* 20 February 1932, 8; *Chicago Defender,* 27 February 1932, 8; *Chicago Defender,* 7 May 1932, 8.

15. *Monroe Morning World,* 4 April 1932, 5; *Monroe News-Star,* 4 April 1932, 6; *Chicago Defender,* 9 April 1932, 9; and Riley, *Biographical Encyclopedia of the Negro Baseball Leagues,* 884.

16. *Monroe Morning World,* 5 April 1932, 6; and *Monroe News-Star,* 5 April 1932, 7.

17. A Southern League press release listed Pittsburgh as opening Southern League play against Nashville, then traveling to Birmingham for an April 25–26 series, but these contests seem not to have occurred. *Kansas City Call,* 15 April 1932, 4B.

18. *Pittsburgh Courier,* 13 February 1932, 2–5; *Pittsburgh Courier,* 20 February 1932, 2–4; *Pittsburgh Courier,* 9 April 1932, 2–4; *Pittsburgh Courier,* 23 April 1932, 2–5; *Pittsburgh Courier,* 9 July 1932, 2–5; *Louisiana Weekly,* 9 July 1932, 8; and *Philadelphia Tribune,* 7 April 1932, 11.

19. *Pittsburgh Courier,* 30 April 1932, 2–4; *Pittsburgh Courier,* 7 May 1932, 2–5.

20. *Monroe Morning World,* 8 April 1932, 5; and Riley, *Biographical Encyclopedia of the Negro Baseball Leagues,* 848.

21. *Indianapolis Recorder,* 14 May 1932, 3; *New York Age,* 14 May 1932, 6; *New York Age,* 21 May 1932, 6; *New York Age,* 4 June 1932, 6; and *Kansas City Call,* 13 May 1932, 4B. In late August, following his Olympic victory, Eddie Tolan refused an invitation to attend a Chicago ceremony of the Amateur Athletic Union, precisely because of the public stand the AAU took in April. J. Lyman Bingham, assistant to the president of the AAU, commented on the refusal: "Why, man alive, I talked to him like I was almost as black as he is and still he said no." *Indianapolis Recorder,* 3 September 1932, 2.

22. *Kansas City Call,* 25 March 1932, 5B; *Monroe Morning World,* 8 April 1932, 8; *Monroe News-Star,* 8 April 1932, 12; and Riley, *Biographical Encyclopedia of the Negro Baseball Leagues,* 605.

23. *Monroe Morning World,* 9 April 1932, 8; *Monroe Morning World,* 10 April 1932, 10; *Monroe Morning World,* 11 April 1932, 5; *Monroe News-Star,* 9 April 1932, 6; *Monroe Morning World,* 11 April 1932, 7; and *Louisiana Weekly,* 16 April 1932, 8.

24. *Monroe Morning World,* 11 April 1932, 5; *Monroe Morning World,* 12 April 1932, 6; and *Monroe News-Star,* 12 April 1932, 7.

25. *Kansas City Call,* 1 April 1932, 5B; *Kansas City Call,* 22 April 1932, 5B; *Chicago Defender,* 23 April 1932, 8; and *Houston Informer,* 23 April 1932, 8.

26. *Monroe Morning World,* 21 April 1932, 6; and *Monroe News-Star,* 21 April 1932, 9.

Chapter 6

1. *Kansas City Call,* 15 April 1932, 4B; and *Louisiana Weekly,* 16 April 1932, 8.

2. *Monroe Morning World,* 24 April 1932, 12; *Monroe Morning World,* 27 April

1932, 12; *Arkansas Democrat,* 23 April 1932, 6; *Arkansas Gazette,* 24 April 1932, 15; *Louisiana Weekly,* 30 April 1932, 8; and *Shreveport Sun,* 30 April 1932, 5.

3. *Atlanta Daily World,* 28 April 1932, 5; *Atlanta Daily World,* 6 May 1932, 7; *Memphis Commercial Appeal,* 1 May 1932, 18; *Memphis Commercial Appeal,* 2 May 1932, 9; *Memphis Commercial Appeal,* 3 May 1932, 11; *Monroe Morning World,* 4 May 1932, 6; *Monroe Morning World,* 7 May 1932, 8; *Monroe Morning World,* 8 May 1932, 10; *Monroe Morning World,* 4 August 1932, 7; *Monroe News-Star,* 29 April 1932, 11; *Monroe News-Star,* 4 May 1932, 6; *Monroe News-Star,* 7 May 1932, 6; and *Louisiana Weekly,* 14 May 1932, 8.

4. Though Monroe's attendance figures remain unknown, the Monarchs did not win the opening-day attendance prize. The Indianapolis ABCs drew 2,600 on opening day. Memphis came in second with 2,100 patrons. Both were awarded silver trophies at the close of the season. *Kansas City Call,* 19 August 1932, 1B.

5. The M.M. Club (presumably, the "Monroe Monarchs" Club) is not described, but more than likely served as a local booster organization for the team.

6. *Kansas City Call,* 1 April 1932, 5B; *Kansas City Call,* 29 April 1932, 5B; *Monroe Morning World,* 27 April 1932, 6; *Monroe Morning World,* 29 April 1932, 6; *Monroe Morning World,* 6 May 1932, 6; *Monroe Morning World,* 7 May 1932, 8; *Monroe Morning World,* 8 May 1932, 10; and *Monroe News-Star,* 6 May 1932, 10.

7. *Monroe Morning World,* 4 May 1932, 6; *Monroe Morning World,* 7 May 1932, 8; *Monroe Morning World,* 8 May 1932, 10; *Monroe Morning World,* 4 August 1932, 7; *Monroe News-Star,* 7 May 1932, 6; *Louisiana Weekly,* 14 May 1932, 8; and *Chicago Defender,* 14 July 1932, 9.

8. *Monroe Morning World,* 8 May 1932, 10; *Monroe Morning World,* 9 May 1932, 6; *Kansas City Call,* 13 May 1932, 5B; *Monroe News-Star,* 9 May 1932, 6; *Louisiana Weekly,* 14 May 1932, 8; *Chicago Defender,* 14 May 1932, 9; *Cleveland Gazette,* 21 May 1932, 2; *Shreveport Sun,* 28 May 1932, 5; and Riley, *Biographical Encyclopedia of the Negro Baseball Leagues,* 209.

9. *Shreveport Sun,* 7 May 1932, 5.

10. *Chicago Defender,* 30 April 1932, 8; and Riley, *Biographical Encyclopedia of the Negro Baseball Leagues,* 479. Memphis had run afoul of the law in its own league, as well. The Red Sox signed Birmingham's Clarence Lewis for the 1932 season. Lewis claimed that his lack of Birmingham paychecks made him a free agent. Meanwhile, Thomas Wilson claimed that his own stake in Birmingham's team gave him the right to sign Lewis for the Nashville Elite Giants. Memphis, however, kept Lewis in 1932 and 1933.

11. Prior to the 1923 season, Foster's Chicago American Giants were the favorites, but after the player raids, Kansas City took the National League crown. Hogan, *Shades of Glory,* 165–67.

12. *Pittsburgh Courier,* 7 May 1932, 2–4.

13. *Pittsburgh Courier,* 14 May 1932, 2–5; and *Chicago Defender,* 16 July 1932, 9.

14. For more on that level of competition in the northeast Louisiana area, including coverage of Fred Stovall's industrial team, the Monroe Black Drillers, see chapter 6.

15. *Monroe Morning World,* 12 May 1932, 6; *Monroe Morning World,* 13 May 1932, 9; *Monroe News-Star,* 12 May 1932, 8; and *Monroe News-Star,* 13 May 1932, 8.

16. *Monroe Morning World,* 16 May 1932, 1; *Monroe Morning World,* 17 May 1932, 10; *Monroe Morning World,* 20 May 1932, 10; *Monroe Morning World,* 26 May 1932, 9; *State of Louisiana v. Ellen Kennedy,* case no. 20-784, State of Louisiana, Parish of Ouachita, Fourth Judicial District Court, Ouachita Parish Clerk of Court; *State of Louisiana v. Ellen Kennedy,* case no. 20-784, 25 May 1932, minutes, 620, Clerk of Court, Criminal Division, Ouachita Parish Courthouse; and *State of Louisiana v. Clara Burns,* case no. 20-780, 18 May 1932, minutes, 614, Clerk of Court, Criminal Division, Ouachita Parish Courthouse.

17. *Atlanta Daily World,* 13 April 1932, 5; *Atlanta Daily World,* 27 April 1932, 5; *Atlanta Daily World,* 1 May 1932, 5; *Atlanta Daily World,* 15 May 1932, 15; *Atlanta Daily World,* 18 May 1932, 5; *Afro-American,* 14 May 1932, 15; *Kansas City Call,* 13 May 1932, 5B; *Kansas City Call,* 29 May 1932, 4B; *Pittsburgh Courier,* 14 May 1932, 2–4; *Chicago Defender,* 28 May 1932, 8; *Chicago Defender,* 16 July 1932, 9; *Indianapolis Recorder,* 14 May 1932, 2; *Louisiana Weekly,* 28 May 1932, 8; *Monroe Morning World,* 19 May 1932, 6; *Monroe Morning World,* 20 May 1932, 6; *Monroe Morning World,* 21 May 1932, 8; *Monroe Morning World,* 22 May 1932, 8; *Monroe News-Star,* 19 May 1932, 6; *Monroe News-Star,* 20 May 1932, 11; and *Monroe News-Star,* 21 May 1932, 6. Though a jazz band and solid play were promised for the Friday opener, rain reduced a four-game set to three.

18. *Monroe Morning World,* 23 May 1932, 1. For more on the relationship of Prohibition, homemade whiskey, and southern sports, see Neal Thompson, *Driving with the Devil: Southern Moonshine, Detroit Wheels, and the Birth of NASCAR* (New York: Crown Publishers, 2006).

19. *Chicago Defender,* 4 June 1932, 9; *Atlanta Daily World,* 3 June 1932, 5; and *Pittsburgh Courier,* 4 June 1932, 2–5.

20. *Monroe Morning World,* 27 May 1932, 11; and *Monroe News-Star,* 27 May 1932, 13.

21. *Monroe Morning World,* 28 May 1932, 9; *Monroe Morning World,* 29 May 1932, 8; *Monroe News-Star,* 28 May 1932, 6; *Atlanta Daily World,* 13 May 1932, 5; *Atlanta Daily World,* 6 June 1932, 5; Richard Ian Kimball, "Beyond the 'Great Experiment': Integrated Baseball Comes to Indianapolis," *Journal of Sport History* 26 (Spring 1999): 153; and Lanctot, *Negro League Baseball,* 107–110. See also Bill Heward and Dimitri

V. Gat, *Some Are Called Clowns* (New York: Thomas Y. Crowell, 1973). Clowning was part of mainstream major black baseball, as well, though generally frowned upon in the early 1930s. Clowning in Negro League baseball came under criticism from the black press, but owners and park operators saw in it a way to bring in significant crowds. A resurgence in clown baseball would occur later in the decade, with the rise of the Ethiopian Clowns. Lanctot, *Negro League Baseball,* 107–110; and Heward and Gat, *Some Are Called Clowns.*

22. *Monroe Morning World,* 30 May 1932, 5; *Monroe Morning World,* 1 June 1932, 8; *Monroe Morning World,* 3 June 1932, 6; *Monroe Morning World,* 5 June 1932, 8; *Monroe Morning World,* 6 June 1932, 6; *Monroe News-Star,* 1 June 1932, 7; *Monroe News-Star,* 6 June 1932, 6; *Monroe News-Star,* 8 June 1932, 6; and *Chicago Defender,* 28 May 1932, 8.

23. *Monroe, Louisiana and West Monroe, Louisiana City Directory, 1933–1934* (Springfield, MO: Interstate Directory Company, 1934), 336; and *Monroe Morning World,* 1 June 1932, 8; *Monroe Morning World,* 5 June 1932, 8; *Monroe Morning World,* 8 June 1932, 6.

24. *Louisiana Weekly,* 2 July 1932, 8.

25. *Chicago Defender,* 4 June 1932, 9; *Kansas City Call,* 3 June 1932, 4B; *Louisiana Weekly,* 4 June 1932, 8; *Pittsburgh Courier,* 4 June 1932, 2–5; *Atlanta Daily World,* 5 June 1932, 5; and *Monroe Morning World,* 10 June 1932, 9.

26. *Birmingham Age-Herald,* 21 May 1932, 10; *Birmingham Age-Herald,* 4 June 1932, 14.

27. Paul J. Letlow, "A Team to Remember: Monarchs' Memories Linger Sixty Years Later," Monroe *News-Star,* 16 August 1992, 1C, 5C; and Peterson, *Only the Ball Was White,* 122. There are no gate receipts or financial statements to prove the existence of these large biracial crowds. Players such as Augustus Saunders and Marlin Carter described them. Advertisements in Monroe's white dailies noted that up to half of the grandstand would be reserved for white patrons. What numbers do exist have often proved problematic. But player descriptions, continued coverage in white dailies, and continued reservations of half the grandstand for white patrons, even with the growth in black interest throughout the successful season, seem to make the claim reasonable. The circumstantial evidence is unfortunately the best evidence still existing.

28. *Chicago Defender,* 11 June 1932, 8; *Monroe Morning World,* 19 June 1932, 8; *Monroe Morning World,* 20 June 1932, 9; *Pittsburgh Courier,* 18 June 1932, 2–9; and *Atlanta Daily World,* 14 June 1932, 5.

29. Though there probably were five games in this series, it is possible that there were only four. The Red Sox either defeated the American Giants twice in this series, or once here and once later in the month. Either way, the Red Sox won two

games from the American Giants in the season's first half. As of June 11, the *Chicago Defender* has the American Giants winning five from Indianapolis, three from Birmingham, five from Louisville, and four from Nashville, and losing three to Indianapolis and one to Nashville. Throughout most of June, as his team fought for the pennant, Robert A. Cole vacationed in Hot Springs. *Indianapolis Recorder,* 11 June 1932, 2; *Indianapolis Recorder,* 25 June 1932, 2; *Kansas City Call,* 17 June 1932, 4B; *Pittsburgh Courier,* 18 June 1932, 2–5; *Chicago Defender,* 11 June 1932, 8; *Chicago Defender,* 18 June 1932, 8; and *Afro-American,* 18 June 1932, 15.

30. *Monroe Morning World,* 10 June 1932, 9; *Monroe Morning World,* 11 June 1932, 10; *Monroe Morning World,* 12 June 1932, 9; *Monroe Morning World,* 13 June 1932, 6; *Monroe Morning World,* 14 June 1932, 6; *Monroe News-Star,* 13 June 1932, 6; *Monroe News-Star,* 14 June 1932, 6; *Louisiana Weekly,* 18 June 1932, 8; *Chicago Defender,* 18 June 1932, 8; and *Kansas City Call,* 17 June 1932, 4B.

31. *Monroe Morning World,* 11 May 1932, 9; *Monroe Morning World,* 15 May 1932, 14; *Monroe Morning World,* 24 May 1932, 11; and *Zion Traveler's Baptist Church v. W. W. Hill,* no. 20679, minutes of District Court, Ouachita Parish, Book N, 20 November 1930–2 November 1932, Ouachita Parish Courthouse, Civil Division, 586, 604, 616, 617.

32. *Monroe Morning World,* 26 May 1932, 14; and *Zion Traveler's Baptist Church v. W. W. Hill,* no. 20679, minutes of District Court, 617.

33. *Monroe Morning World,* 16 June 1932, 6; *Monroe Morning World,* 1 September 1932, 5.

34. *Kansas City Call,* 1 April 1932, 5B; and *Pittsburgh Courier,* 2 April 1932, 2–5; 16 April 1932, 2–5.

35. *Memphis World,* 18 September 1931, 5; *Galveston Daily News,* 21 May 1931, 8; *Monroe Morning World,* 16 June 1932, 8; *Monroe Morning World,* 19 June 1932, 8; *Monroe News-Star,* 16 June 1932, 8; and Holway, *Complete Book of Baseball's Negro Leagues,* 282–84.

36. William H. Wiggins Jr., "Juneteenth: A Red Spot Day on the Texas Calendar," in *Juneteenth Texas: Essays in African-American Folklore,* ed. Francis Edward Abernethy (Denton: University of North Texas Press, 1996), 237–39; *Monroe Morning World,* 16 June 1932, 8; *Monroe Morning World,* 17 June 1932, 6; and *Monroe News-Star,* 17 June 1932, 17.

37. *Monroe Morning World,* 19 June 1932, 8; and *Pittsburgh Courier,* 25 June 1932, 2–5.

38. *Monroe Morning World,* 17 June 1932, 6; *Monroe Morning World,* 19 June 1932, 8; *Monroe Morning World,* 20 June 1932, 6; *Monroe News-Star,* 20 June 1932, 9; and *Louisiana Weekly,* 25 June 1932, 8.

39. *Monroe Morning World,* 20 June 1932, 6.

40. Heaphy, *Negro Leagues*, 144–45.

41. *Monroe Morning World*, 21 June 1932, 7; *Monroe Morning World*, 24 June 1932, 9; *Kansas City Call*, 24 June 1932, 4B; *Monroe News-Star*, 21 June 1932, 6; and *Louisiana Weekly*, 25 June 1932, 8.

42. *Monroe Morning World*, 21 June 1932, 1; *Monroe Morning World*, 22 June 1932, 6. Sharkey would win in a controversial decision. Ringside experts, along with the 72,000 fans behind them, all thought Schmelling victorious, but the judges shocked the crowd by handing the fifteen-round bout to Sharkey.

43. *Philadelphia Tribune*, 26 May 1932, 11; *Pittsburgh Courier*, 11 June 1932, 2–4; and *Afro-American*, 11 June 1932, 15.

44. *Pittsburgh Courier*, 25 June 1932, 2–4; *Philadelphia Tribune*, 9 June 1932, 11; and *Afro-American*, 25 June 1932, 15.

45. *Chicago Defender*, 2 July 1932, 82; and *Atlanta Daily World*, 30 June 1932, 5.

46. *Chicago Defender*, 11 June 1932, 8.

47. *Chicago Defender*, 18 June 1932, 8.

48. *Atlanta Daily World*, 20 June 1932, 5.

49. *Chicago Defender*, 2 July 1932, 8.

50. *Chicago Defender*, 2 July 1932, 8; *Kansas City Call*, 24 June 1932, 4B; *Louisiana Weekly*, 2 July 1932, 8; *Indianapolis Recorder*, 2 July 1932, 2; and *Pittsburgh Courier*, 2 July 1932, 2–5; *Pittsburgh Courier*, 9 July 1932, 2–4. The year prior, in 1931, Satchel Paige jumped to the Crawfords after playing with another incarnation of the Cleveland Cubs owned by Wilson. This, too, could have been an opportunity for an early meeting.

51. *Afro-American*, 4 June 1932, 14.

52. *Pittsburgh Courier*, 2 July 1932, 2–4; *Philadelphia Tribune*, 30 June 1932, 10; and *Atlanta Daily World*, 14 July 1932, 5.

53. *Pittsburgh Courier*, 2 July 1932, 2–5; *Atlanta Daily World*, 14 July 1932, 5; *Kansas City Call*, 8 July 1932, 4B; and *Afro-American*, 2 July 1932, 15.

54. *Kansas City Call*, 1 July 1932, 4B; and *Chicago Defender*, 2 July 1932, 8.

55. *Pittsburgh Courier*, 2 July 1932, 2–4.

56. For similar criticisms, see *Philadelphia Tribune*, 20 June 1932, 11; and New York *Amsterdam News*, 29 June 1932, 12.

57. *Pittsburgh Courier*, 16 July 1932, 2–4.

58. *Afro-American*, 9 July 1932, 15.

59. *Pittsburgh Courier*, 21 May 1932, 2–4; and *Indianapolis Recorder*, 28 May 1932, 2.

60. *Shreveport Sun*, 18 June 1932, 5.

61. *Monroe Morning World*, 2 July 1932, 9.

62. *Monroe Morning World*, 2 July 1932, 9; *Monroe Morning World*, 3 July 1932, 8; and *Monroe Morning World*, 4 July 1932, 6.

63. *Monroe Morning World,* 4 July 1932, 6; and *Chicago Defender,* 9 July 1932, 9.

64. *Monroe Morning World,* 4 July 1932, 1; *Monroe Morning World,* 5 July 1932, 6; *Monroe News-Star,* 5 July 1932, 6; and *Louisiana Weekly,* 9 July 1932, 8.

65. *Chicago Defender,* 9 July 1932, 9.

66. *Kansas City Call,* 1 July 1932, 5B; *Atlanta Daily World,* 28 June 1932, 5; *Shreveport Sun,* 9 July 1932, 5; *Afro-American,* 9 July 1932, 14; *Philadelphia Tribune,* 30 June 1932, 10; and *Indianapolis Recorder,* 2 July 1932, 2. Pollock's article was widely reprinted.

Table 1

1. This table's representations about baseball newspaper reporting in 1932 are based on a sample set of nineteen black newspapers, and the sample is largely the result of availability. Extant copies of the newspapers listed in table 1 provide either complete or near-complete coverage for the 1932 calendar year. There are, of course, other unincluded publications that would immensely benefit such a study. Nashville, Tennessee, and Monroe, Louisiana, for example, play significant roles in the 1932 season, and yet the black newspapers for those towns (the *Nashville Globe and Independent* and the *Southern Broadcast,* respectively) no longer survive. The absence of the *Southern Broadcast,* in fact, is perhaps the most overwhelming reason why the Monarchs' 1932 season has largely been ignored in Negro Leagues historiography. But coverage in Monroe's white dailies and the black weeklies in the sample set, along with articles in the scattered issues of rarer black newspapers like the *Nashville Globe and Independent* do provide a full account of the team's season. (There are, for example, four 1932 issues of the *Nashville Globe and Independent* surviving, and available for viewing in the Tennessee State Library and Archives. The scarcity of issues, however, omitted the paper from the sample. The *Southern Broadcast* is available for the years 1936 and 1937 at the Schomburg Center at the New York Public Library. Arkansas and Mississippi also had black weeklies in 1932, but no issues of those newspapers survive.)

Sports coverage naturally varied. The *Oklahoma City Black Dispatch,* for example, exists in its entirety for the 1932 calendar year, but rarely covers sports. It is thus not part of the sample set. (A December 1931 edition carried an article about boxer Kid Chocolate, and the paper did carry some July and August coverage of Eddie Tolan and Ralph Metcalfe's Olympic triumphs, but other than those instances, the *Black Dispatch* carried no 1932 national sports news at all.) Only the Negro Southern League completed league play for a full season. The East–West folded before the close of the season's first half. As a consequence, the statistical analysis treats coverage only of the Southern League. Categorizations and calculations throughout this and remaining tables all stem from this original core list of nineteen. All articles covering the Southern League have been tabulated. With the exception of the *Atlanta Daily World,* only the sports pages are included in the sample.

Chapter 7

1. *Atlanta Daily World,* 20 March 1932, 5; *Atlanta Daily World,* 22 March 1932, 5; *Pittsburgh Courier,* 19 March 1932, 5; *Birmingham Reporter,* 12 March 1932, 3; *Birmingham Reporter,* 26 March 1932, 2; and *Birmingham Reporter,* 2 April 1932, 3. Monroe is 153 miles from Little Rock, 215 miles from Memphis, 315 miles from Birmingham, 339 miles from Montgomery, 394 miles from Nashville, 452 miles from Atlanta, 532 miles from Louisville, 601 miles from Indianapolis, and 687 miles from Chicago.

2. *Shreveport Sun,* 16 April 1932, 5.

3. Certificate of Marriage, Reuben B. Jackson and Bertha L. Allen, 16 June 1926, Marriages, Davidson County, vol. 45, 1925–1926, roll 509, 459; *Marshall-Bruce-Polk Co.'s Nashville (Tennessee) City Directory, 1928* (Nashville: Marshall-Bruce-Polk Company, 1928), 704; *Polk's Nashville (Davidson County, Tenn.) City Directory, 1935* (St. Louis: R. L. Polk and Company, 1935), 1272; *Polk's Nashville (Davidson County, Tenn.) City Directory, 1938* (St. Louis: R. L. Polk and Company, 1938), 483; *Polk's Nashville (Davidson County, Tenn.) City Directory, 1941* (St. Louis: R. L. Polk and Company, 1941), 1234; *Polk's Nashville (Davidson County, Tenn.) City Directory, 1942* (St. Louis: R. L. Polk and Company, 1942), 430; *Polk's Nashville (Davidson County, Tenn.) City Directory, 1957* (St. Louis: R. L. Polk and Company, 1957), 493; Trustee Tax Books, Davidson County, A–K State, County, School, Etc., 1933, roll 1764, Tennessee State Library and Archives, 571; Trustee Tax Books, Davidson County, Inside E–K, 1948, roll 1779, Tennessee State Library and Archives, 497; *Nashville Globe,* 4 March 1932, 8; *Nashville Globe,* 4 February 1946, 1, 4; and *Nashville Globe and Independent,* 16 March 1934, 8. (With thanks to Sheila Lewis in the Registrar's Office and Ty Blackburn in the Alumni Affairs Office of Morris Brown College; and Barbara Grissom in the Registrar's Office and Benetta Waller in the Alumni Center of Meharry Medical College.)

4. *Nashville Globe and Independent,* 16 March 1934, 4; *Atlanta Daily World,* 16 September 1932, 4; *Atlanta Daily World,* 2 October 1932, 7; *Atlanta Daily World,* 21 October 1932, 5; Phil Dixon and Patrick J. Hannigan, *The Negro Baseball Leagues, 1867–1955: A Photographic History* (Mattituck, NY: Amereon House, 1992), 150; and Heaphy, *Negro Leagues.* Wilson eventually moved his team to Baltimore and became president of the much stronger Negro National League. In 1934, his team's last year in Nashville, Wilson negotiated with his current National League to al-

low teams from Jackson's Southern League to buy, sell, and trade interleague. In 1945, when Jackson again served another incarnation of the Negro Southern League, Wilson also played a complementary role.

5. *Atlanta Daily World,* 20 March 1932, 5.

6. *Atlanta World,* 27 December 1931, 5, 6; *Atlanta World,* 28 February 1932, 5; *Pittsburgh Courier,* 23 January 1932, 5; and *Pittsburgh Courier,* 6 February 1932, 4.

7. Riley, *Biographical Encyclopedia of the Negro Baseball Leagues,* 415; *Pittsburgh Courier,* 14 May 1932, 4; *Chicago Defender,* 30 April 1932, 8; *Chicago Defender,* 7 May 1932, 8; and *Chicago Defender,* 14 May 1932, 9.

8. *Memphis World,* 3 May 1932, 5; *Memphis World,* 13 May 1932, 5; *Pittsburgh Courier,* 4 June 1932, 5; and *Pittsburgh Courier,* 9 July 1932, 5. Some accounts have Monroe's initial victory count at twenty-nine. For more on the historiographical discrepancy in league win-loss totals, see notes 26 and 27.

9. *Chicago Defender,* 4 June 1932, 9; *Chicago Defender,* 25 June 1932, 8; *Atlanta Daily World,* 26 June 1932, 5; and *California Eagle,* 1 July 1932, 13.

10. *Memphis World,* 4 May 1932, 5; and *Afro-American,* 26 March 1932, 15. At the same time, Monarch Murray Gillespie was suspended for the season's second half. Gillespie played for the New York Black Yankees in 1931, but had been afflicted with an unidentified illness throughout the winter. The Black Yankees largely ignored their pitcher during his illness, and in response, he signed with Memphis. But New York called for him in March when spring training began. From Memphis, Gillespie came to Monroe. He would rejoin the team after serving his second-half suspension. *Atlanta Daily World,* 4 July 1932, 5.

11. *Pittsburgh Courier,* 9 July 1932, 2–5; *Pittsburgh Courier,* 16 July 1932, 2–5; and *Chicago Defender,* 9 July 1932, 9. Atlanta's franchise was transferred to Columbus, Ohio; Birmingham's to Lexington, Kentucky; and Little Rock's to Kansas City. Associate membership was then granted to both Knoxville and Alcoa, Tennessee. Though Jackson listed Kansas City as the recipient of Little Rock's franchise, the Monarchs clearly had a specific barnstorming agenda that included the NSL only peripherally. *Atlanta Daily World,* 8 July 1932, 5.

12. Riley, *Biographical Encyclopedia of the Negro Baseball Leagues,* 550; *Pittsburgh Courier,* 9 July 1932, 2–5; *Pittsburgh Courier,* 16 July 1932, 2–5; *Chicago Defender,* 9 July 1932, 9; *Atlanta Daily World,* 8 July 1932, 5; and *Birmingham Reporter,* 9 July 1932, 8. The Birmingham Black Barons had been a staple of the Southern League prior to 1932, and they would be the league's most recognizable (and one of its most successful) in the years following 1932, but in that pivotal Depression year, the group was, like so many other black baseball teams throughout the country, unable to maintain its stability.

13. *Louisiana Weekly,* 9 July 1932, 8.

14. *Chicago Defender,* 9 July 1932, 9. The *Monroe Morning World*'s account of the first-half standings was significantly different: Monroe, thirty-three wins, seven losses; Chicago, twenty-eight wins, nine losses. *Monroe Morning World,* 6 July 1932, 7 (reprinted in *Monroe News-Star,* 6 July 1932, 6). My own count, including only four games in the final series with Memphis, gives the Monarchs thirty-five first-half victories. See appendix 1.

15. *Chicago Defender,* 9 July 1932, 9.

16. *Chicago Defender,* 9 July 1932, 9.

17. *Louisiana Weekly,* 9 July 1932, 8; *Atlanta Daily World,* 8 July 1932, 5; and *Atlanta Daily World,* 12 July 1932, 5.

18. *Atlanta Daily World,* 22 July 1932, 5.

19. Lanctot, *Negro League Baseball,* 14, 22–23; Lester, *Black Baseball's National Showcase,* 15; *Atlanta Daily World,* 16 September 1932, 4; and *Atlanta Daily World,* 7 October 1932, 5. Greenlee and Wilson could have developed a relationship in 1931, when Satchel Paige jumped to the Crawfords from the Cleveland Cubs. See chapter 6, note 50.

20. *Chicago Defender,* 11 June 1932, 9; *Chicago Defender,* 18 June 1932, 8; *Chicago Defender,* 25 June 1932, 8; *Chicago Defender,* 9 July 1932, 9; *Monroe Morning World,* 4 May 1932, 6; *Monroe Morning World,* 2 July 1932, 9; *Memphis Commercial Appeal,* 30 April 1932, 13; *Memphis Commercial Appeal,* 1 May 1932, 18; *Memphis Commercial Appeal,* 2 May 1932, 9; and *Memphis Commercial Appeal,* 3 May 1932, 11.

21. *Monroe Morning World,* 3 July 1932, 8; and *Monroe Morning World,* 6 July 1932, 7.

22. Issues cited are examples of this lack in early September, when the Monarchs would be participating in the Negro World Series, though the coverage lapse extended throughout the season: *Caldwell Watchman,* 9 September and 16 September 1932; *Farmerville Gazette,* 7 September and 14 September 1932, 1; *Franklin Sun,* 1 September and 8 September 1932, 1; *Morehouse Enterprise,* 1 September, 8 September, and 15 September 1932, 6; *Ruston Daily Leader,* 6 September; *Tensas Gazette,* 2 September and 9 September 1932. The one paper that included the Zion Traveler controversy was the *Madison Journal,* 9 September 1932, 1. These papers can be found—can only be found—in the Louisiana and Lower Mississippi Valley Collection, Hill Memorial Special Collections Library, Louisiana State University, Baton Rouge, LA.

23. See *Louisville Courier-Journal,* 24 July 1932, 4-1; *Louisville Courier-Journal,* 25 July 1932, 7; *Arkansas Gazette,* 23 April 1932, 15; *Arkansas Gazette,* 24 April 1932, 15; *Arkansas Democrat,* 22 April 1932, 17; *Arkansas Democrat,* 23 April 1932, 6; *New Orleans Times-Picayune,* 13 August 1932, 8; *New Orleans Times-Picayune,* 14 August 1932, 4-2; *Chicago Tribune,* 18 July 1932, 17; *Chicago Tribune,* 19 July 1932,

19; *Chicago Tribune,* 20 July 1932, 18; *Austin Statesman,* 18 August 1932, 9; *Austin Statesman,* 20 August 1932, 5; *Austin Statesman,* 21 August 1932, 4; *Austin Statesman,* 22 August 1932, 6; *Austin American,* 18 August 1932, 9; *Austin American,* 20 August 1932, 7; and *Austin American,* 21 August 1932, 4; *Austin American,* 22 August 1932, 6. Coverage of non-mainstream sporting events in the *New York Times* and *New York Herald Tribune* can be found throughout the year's sports coverage.

24. *Monroe, Louisiana and West Monroe, Louisiana City Directory, 1930,* 193; *Monroe, Louisiana and West Monroe, Louisiana City Directory, 1949–1950* (Springfield, MO: Interstate Directory Company, 1949), 320; and *Monroe, Louisiana and West Monroe, Louisiana City Directory, 1952* (Springfield, MO: Interstate Directory Company, 1952), 217.

25. *Chicago Defender,* 23 July 1932, 8; *Chicago Defender,* 30 July 1932, 9.

26. This is the formula generally repeated in historical accounts. Robert Peterson's *Only the Ball Was White* sets the standings as follows: Cole's American Giants, 34–7, 0.829 winning percentage; Monroe Monarchs, 33–7, 0.825 winning percentage. The account of Dick Clark and Larry Lester is the same for the two front-running teams. John Holway's *The Complete Book of Baseball's Negro Leagues* offers a season total for the Southern League teams, and wrongly notes that "Nashville was awarded the first half, Chicago the second": Chicago American Giants, 52–31, 0.627 winning percentage; Monroe Monarchs, 26–22, 0.542 winning percentage. *Chicago Defender,* 23 July 1932, 8; Peterson, *Only the Ball Was White,* Clark and Lester, eds., *Negro Leagues Book,* 164; and Holway, *Complete Book of Baseball's Negro Leagues,* 288, 292–93.

27. According to the *Morning World,* the first-half standings looked like this: Monroe, 33–7, 0.825 winning percentage; Chicago, 28–9, 0.756 winning percentage. The *Pittsburgh Courier*'s first-half standings as of July 3 tallied *eight* losses for Chicago: Monroe, 31–7, 0.816 winning percentage; Chicago, 31–8, 0.795 winning percentage. In contrast to Holway's account of twenty-six wins and twenty-two losses for the season, the *Courier* tallied Monroe's total as *sixty* wins and twenty-two losses. *Monroe Morning World,* 6 July 1932, 7; *Pittsburgh Courier,* 9 July 1932, 4; and *Pittsburgh Courier,* 3 September 1932, 5.

28. *Monroe Morning World,* 28 July 1932, 6; *Pittsburgh Courier,* 16 July 1932, 5; *Chicago Defender,* 9 July 1932, 9; and *Chicago Defender,* 13 August 1932, 9.

29. New York *Amsterdam News,* 14 September 1932, 9. The *Amsterdam News*'s endorsement, in fact, was a reprint of a West Penn Service wire story.

30. A few representative examples follow: Robert Peterson's *Only the Ball Was White* sets the standings as Cole's American Giants, thirty-four wins, seven losses; Monroe Monarchs, thirty-three wins, seven losses. The account of Dick Clark and Larry Lester also places the total as Chicago, 34–7, Monroe, 33–7, as does the *2005*

ESPN Baseball Encyclopedia. John Holway's *The Complete Book of Baseball's Negro Leagues* offers only a season total for the Southern League teams, citing the American Giants as 52–31, and the Monarchs as 26–22. See Peterson, *Only the Ball Was White,* 269; Clark and Lester, eds., *Negro Leagues Book,* 164; *The 2005 ESPN Baseball Encyclopedia* (New York: Sterling Publishing Company, 2005), 1624; and Holway, *Complete Book of Baseball's Negro Leagues,* 288, 292–93.

31. *Kansas City Call,* 8 July 1932, 4B.

32. *Shreveport Sun,* 27 August 1930, 5; *Shreveport Sun,* 30 August 1930, 8; *Shreveport Sun,* 6 September 1930, 5; *Shreveport Sun,* 27 September 1930, 7; and Marshall D. Wright, *The Southern Association in Baseball, 1885–1961* (Jefferson, NC: McFarland and Company, 2002), 1–4, 289–90.

33. Lanctot, *Negro League Baseball,* 35–38, 43–44; and Malloy, "Chicago American Giants," MFF 308, National Baseball Hall of Fame.

34. Lanctot, *Negro League Baseball,* 46, 51, 53, 72.

35. Lanctot, *Negro League Baseball,* 89, 283; and Dixon and Hannigan, *Negro Baseball Leagues,* 197–98.

Chapter 8

1. Among those who printed a second-half schedule were the *Chicago Defender, Atlanta Daily World, Kansas City Call,* and *Pittsburgh Courier. Chicago Defender,* 9 July 1932, 9; *Atlanta Daily World,* 8 July 1932, 5; and *Pittsburgh Courier,* 16 July 1932, 2–5.

2. *Afro-American,* 23 July 1932, 14; and *Pittsburgh Courier,* 30 April 1932, 2–4.

3. *Kansas City Call,* 5 August 1932, 2B; *Kansas City Call,* 12 August 1932, 1B. Three of the *Kansas City Call*'s six August articles describe the American Giants–Kansas City Monarchs series.

4. *Chicago Defender,* 13 August 1932, 8.

5. *Official Report: The Games of the Xth Olympiad, Los Angeles, 1932* (Los Angeles: Xth Olympiade Committee, 1933), 409, 779; Mark Dyreson, "Marketing National Identity: The Olympic Games of 1932 and American Culture," *OLYMPIKA, The International Journal of Olympic Studies* 4 (1995): 39; *Philadelphia Tribune,* 7 July 1932, 11; *Philadelphia Tribune,* 18 August 1932, 10; *Boston Chronicle,* 23 July 1932, 7; *New York Times,* 12 June 1932, 3-1, 3-3; and *Afro-American,* 13 August 1932, 1, 2, 14, 15. While the *Afro-American*'s coverage was particularly informative, the Tolan/ Metcalfe success at the Olympics was reported on the front news page of all of the black weeklies, and is subsequently recounted in various works on the history of the Olympics. Edward Gordon, another African American athlete, won gold in the long jump. *Official Report: The Games of the Xth Olympiad,* 409, 779.

6. Mark Dyreson, "American Ideas about Race and Olympic Races from the 1890s to the 1950s: Shattering Myths or Reinforcing Scientific Racism?" *Journal of Sport History* 28 (Summer 2001): 187; David B. Welky, "Viking Girls, Mermaids, and Little Brown Men: U.S. Journalism and the 1932 Olympics," *Journal of Sport History* 24 (Spring 1997): 36; Allen Guttmann, *The Olympics: A History of the Modern Games,* 2nd ed. (Urbana: University of Illinois Press, 2002), 60; *Kansas City Call,* 12 August 1932, 1B; and *Atlanta Daily World,* 10 August 1932, 5.

7. *Louisiana Weekly,* 20 August 1932, 8. Metcalfe was a Georgia native, but segregated stadiums and universities drove him north to star at Marquette. In September 1932, white Atlanta mayor James Lee Key declared September 23 "Ralph Metcalfe Day." Michigan, home state of the other track hero, also declared an "Eddie Tolan Day."

8. *Chicago Defender,* 9 July 1932, 9.

9. *Birmingham Age-Herald,* 5 July 1932, 10; *Birmingham Age-Herald,* 6 July 1932, 8; *Birmingham Age-Herald,* 11 July 1932, 9; *Birmingham Age-Herald,* 13 July 1932, 9; *Nashville Banner,* 11 July 1932, 7; and *Monroe Morning World,* 4 July 1932, 5; *Monroe Morning World,* 5 July 1932, 5; *Monroe Morning World,* 6 July 1932, 6; *Monroe Morning World,* 7 July 1932, 8; *Monroe Morning World,* 8 July 1932, 8; *Monroe Morning World,* 9 July 1932, 5; *Monroe Morning World,* 10 July 1932, 7; *Monroe Morning World,* 11 July 1932, 5, 6; *Monroe Morning World,* 12 July 1932, 5; and *Monroe Morning World,* 13 July 1932, 6.

10. *Birmingham Age-Herald,* 15 July 1932, 11.

11. *Memphis Commercial Appeal,* 8 July 1932, 17; *Memphis Commercial Appeal,* 9 July 1932, 9; *Memphis Commercial Appeal,* 10 July 1932, 19; *Memphis Commercial Appeal,* 11 July 1932, 7; *Memphis Commercial Appeal,* 12 July 1932, 10; *Louisville Leader,* 23 July 1932, 8; *Memphis World,* 12 August 1932, 5; *Chicago Defender,* 16 July 1932, 8; and *Afro-American,* 23 July 1932, 16. Many sources also list Curry's nickname as "Blue Goose."

12. *Chicago Defender,* 23 July 1932, 8; and *Atlanta Daily World,* 22 July 1932, 5.

13. *Chicago Defender,* 23 July 1932, 8; *Atlanta Daily World,* 20 July 1932, 5; and *Afro-American,* 23 July 1932, 15.

14. *Chicago Defender,* 23 July 1932, 8; and *Chicago Tribune,* 18 July 1932, 17.

15. *Chicago Defender,* 23 July 1932, 8; and *Chicago Tribune,* 19 July 1932, 19.

16. *Atlanta Daily World,* 1 August 1932, 5.

17. *Pittsburgh Courier,* 16 July 1932, 2–4; *Afro-American,* 16 July 1932, 15; *Louisiana Weekly,* 16 July 1932, 8; and Lanctot, *Fair Dealing and Clean Playing,* 221. The Crawfords would remain $16,000 in the red for the season, and this price cut demonstrates the team's inability to draw a requisite number of fans. Notably, the small-market Monroe Monarchs never reduced prices all season, maintaining healthy

crowds throughout. (For discussion on the tenuousness of the evidence of attendance "health," see chapter 6, note 27.)

18. *Pittsburgh Courier,* 23 July 1932, 2–4; *Pittsburgh Courier,* 13 August 1932, 2–4; and *Afro-American,* 6 August 1932, 15.

19. *Pittsburgh Courier,* 23 July 1932, 2–4; *Pittsburgh Courier,* 27 August 1932, 2–4.

20. *Pittsburgh Courier,* 9 July 1932, 2–4; *Louisville Courier-Journal,* 24 July 1932, 4-1; *Louisville Courier-Journal,* 25 July 1932, 7; and *Chicago Defender,* 30 July 1932, 8.

21. *Monroe Morning World,* 1 August 1932, 5; *Monroe Morning World,* 2 August 1932, 6; *Monroe News-Star,* 29 July 1932, 17; *Monroe News-Star,* 30 July 1932, 6; *Monroe News-Star,* 1 August 1932, 6; *Monroe News-Star,* 2 August 1932, 7; and *Chicago Defender,* 6 August 1932, 9.

22. *Chicago Defender,* 30 July 1932, 8; *Chicago Defender,* 20 August 1932, 8. See chapter 9 for competing conceptions of what constituted the country's legitimate black championship.

23. *Monroe Morning World,* 4 August 1932, 7.

24. *Monroe Morning World,* 4 August 1932, 7; *Monroe Morning World,* 6 August 1932, 10; *Monroe News-Star,* 4 August 1932, 6; and *Monroe News-Star,* 6 August 1932, 7.

25. *Louisiana Weekly,* 2 April 1932, 8; *Louisiana Weekly,* 9 April 1932, 8; *Louisiana Weekly,* 16 April 1932, 8; *Louisiana Weekly,* 23 April 1932, 8; *Louisiana Weekly,* 21 May 1932, 8; *Louisiana Weekly,* 28 May 1932, 8; *Louisiana Weekly,* 4 June 1932, 8; *Louisiana Weekly,* 11 June 1932, 8; *Louisiana Weekly,* 18 June 1932, 8; *Louisiana Weekly,* 25 June 1932, 8; *Louisiana Weekly,* 2 July 1932, 8; *Louisiana Weekly,* 23 July 1932, 8; and *Monroe Morning World,* 8 August 1932, 6.

26. *Louisiana Weekly,* 13 August 1932, 8.

27. *Louisiana Weekly,* 13 August 1932, 8. For instances of Algiers engaging in various minor league contests, see *Louisiana Weekly,* 30 April 1932, 8; *Louisiana Weekly,* 7 May 1932, 8; *Louisiana Weekly,* 14 May 1932, 8; *Louisiana Weekly,* 21 May 1932, 8; *Louisiana Weekly,* 11 June 1932, 8; *Louisiana Weekly,* 18 June 1932, 8; *Louisiana Weekly,* 25 June 1932, 8; *Louisiana Weekly,* 2 July 1932, 9; *Louisiana Weekly,* 9 July 1932, 8; *Louisiana Weekly,* 16 July 1932, 8; *Louisiana Weekly,* 23 July 1932, 8; and *Atlanta Daily World,* 28 July 1932, 5.

28. *Monroe Morning World,* 8 August 1932, 6; *Monroe Morning World,* 9 August 1932, 7; *Monroe News-Star,* 9 August 1932, 7; and *Louisiana Weekly,* 13 August 1932, 8.

29. *Monroe Morning World,* 11 August 1932, 7; and *Monroe News-Star,* 11 August 1932, 8.

30. *Chicago Defender,* 13 August 1932, 8.

31. *Kansas City Call,* 19 August 1932, 1B; *Pittsburgh Courier,* 20 August 1932, 2–4; *Afro-American,* 27 August 1932, 17; *Chicago Defender,* 13 August 1932, 8; and *Atlanta Daily World,* 22 August 1932, 5.

32. *Chicago Defender,* 13 August 1932, 8.

33. *Louisiana Weekly,* 6 August 1932, 8; *Louisiana Weekly,* 13 August 1932, 8; *Louisiana Weekly,* 3 September 1932, 8; *Pittsburgh Courier,* 3 September 1932, 2–4; *Afro-American,* 3 September 1932, 14; *Shreveport Sun,* 20 August 1932, 5; *Monroe Morning World,* 27 August 1932, 8; and Riley, *Biographical Encyclopedia of the Negro Baseball Leagues,* 571.

34. *Louisiana Weekly,* 20 August 1932, 8; *Atlanta Daily World,* 18 August 1932, 5; and *Shreveport Sun,* 20 August 1932, 5.

35. *Louisiana Weekly,* 3 September 1932, 8.

36. *Louisiana Weekly,* 20 August 1932, 8; *Louisiana Weekly,* 27 August 1932, 8; *New Orleans Times-Picayune,* 14 August 1932, 4-2; *Monroe Morning World,* 19 August 1932, 6; and *Monroe News-Star,* 19 August 1932, 11.

37. *Monroe Morning World,* 21 August 1932, 9; *Monroe Morning World,* 22 August 1932, 5; *Monroe Morning World,* 23 August 1932, 6; *Monroe Morning World,* 26 August 1932, 6; *Monroe News-Star,* 22 August 1932, 6; *Monroe News-Star,* 23 August 1932, 7; *Austin Statesman,* 18 August 1932, 9; *Austin Statesman,* 20 August 1932, 5; *Austin Statesman,* 22 August 1932, 6; Austin *Sunday American-Statesman,* 21 August 1932, 4; and *Austin American,* 22 August 1932, 6.

38. *Monroe Morning World,* 23 August 1932, 6; *Monroe Morning World,* 26 August 1932, 6; *Monroe Morning World,* 27 August 1932, 8; *Monroe Morning World,* 28 August 1932, 8; *Monroe News-Star,* 26 August 1932, 11; and *Monroe News-Star,* 27 August 1932, 6.

39. *Monroe Morning World,* 26 August 1932, 6; *Monroe Morning World,* 27 August 1932, 8; *Monroe Morning World,* 28 August 1932, 8; *Monroe Morning World,* 29 August 1932, 5; and *Monroe News-Star,* 29 August 1932, 6.

40. *Monroe Morning World,* 30 August 1932, 4; *Monroe Morning World,* 31 August 1932, 6; *Monroe News-Star,* 30 August 1932, 9; and *Monroe News-Star,* 31 August 1932, 7.

41. *News-Star,* "About Us," http://www.thenewsstar.com/apps/pbcs.dll/article?AID=/99999999/CUSTOMERSERVICE02/41202001 (accessed 12 January 2007).

42. This data is based on the author's examination of each issue of the 1932 *Monroe Morning World.* Naturally, some stories dragged on for days. Each day, each mention was logged, even if repetitive. Civic and church meetings often had newspaper notices days prior to the events, and each of those mentions was also logged.

43. See note 42.

44. See introduction, note 5. Lomax, *Black Baseball Entrepreneurs,* xvii; James P. Danky, ed., *African American Newspapers and Periodicals: A National Bibliography* (Cambridge, MA: Harvard University Press Reference Library, 1993), record 3888; and *Chicago Defender,* 13 August 1932, 9.

45. Briscoe was born December 15, 1908, in Brunswick, Mississippi. In 1931, he graduated from Southern University in Baton Rouge before moving to Monroe

to serve as math, chemistry, and general science teacher at Monroe Colored High School. He also coached the football team. But Briscoe considered himself a journalist, and a year after his arrival in Monroe he founded the *Broadcast.* He would maintain the paper until 1939, when he took a job as the national news editor of the *Chicago Defender.* In 1941, he became a press officer for the U.S. Department of Agriculture, where he stayed for almost thirty years before becoming executive director of the National Newspaper Publishers Association. He and his sports editor, Haywood Jackson, launched their first issue in the throes of the Monarchs' season and almost certainly covered the team exhaustively, but though the paper thrived until the late 1930s, extant copies from the 1932 season have not survived. Jessie Parkhurst Guzman, ed., *1952 Negro Year Book: A Review of Events Affecting Negro Life* (New York: William H. Wise and Company, 1952), v; and *Who's Who among Black Americans, 1977–1978,* 2nd ed., 2 vols. (Northbrook, IL: Who's Who among Black Americans Publishing Company, 1978), 1:98; *Southern Broadcast,* 11 July 1936; and *Southern Broadcast,* 6 February 1937.

46. Ollie Burns, interview.

47. *Shreveport Sun,* 30 January 1932, 5; *Shreveport Sun,* 2 April 1932, 3, 5.

48. *Monroe News-Star,* 18 August 1927, 2; *Monroe News-Star,* 28 August 1928, 8; *Monroe News-Star,* 29 August 1928, 8; *Monroe News-Star,* 30 August 1928, 8; *Monroe News-Star,* 31 August 1928, 10; *Monroe News-Star,* 7 September 1928, 8; *Monroe News-Star,* 11 January 1929, 11; *Monroe News-Star,* 11 February 1929, 9; *Monroe News-Star,* 5 July 1930, 9; *Monroe News-Star,* 16 July 1930, 8; and *Monroe Morning World,* 14 July 1930, 9.

49. Of the 147 such articles in the white *Morning World,* 52 covered local stories (35.4 percent), 60 covered national stories (40.8 percent), 26 covered state stories (17.9 percent), and a few scattered articles covered regional and international news. A similar perusal of the 153 such articles in the *Daily World* demonstrates that 79 covered local stories (51.6 percent), 54 covered national stories (35.3 percent), and a small handful covered state, regional, and international news.

Of the total, 56.5 percent of the *Morning World*'s articles covered politics. Of that number, 8.4 percent covered the Democratic presidential campaign, 13.3 percent covered Prohibition legislation, and 22.9 percent covered tax and budget concerns. The *Daily World* devoted only 19 percent of its coverage to politics. None of that number concerned the Democratic campaign or tax and budget issues. Only one article covered Prohibition. Two of its articles, however, offered in-depth analyses of the convicted rapists in Scottsboro, Alabama. Not surprisingly, the white *Morning World* made no mention of the Scottsboro boys.

In another editorial difference, the *Morning World* devoted 27.9 percent of its top-line stories to violence and crime. Of the *Daily World*'s May sample, 43.8 percent dealt with crime. Of course, May 1932 was notorious as the month when the body of the kidnapped child of flyer Charles Lindbergh was discovered. 29.3 percent of the *Morning World*'s coverage of violence dealt with the Lindbergh baby (8.7 percent of the total). The *Daily World* also covered the kidnapping, but to a lesser degree. 11.9 percent of its violence coverage involved the Lindberghs (5.2 percent of the total).

Finally, 15.7 percent of the *Daily World*'s coverage was church-related, ranging from guest speakers coming to local churches to blanket coverage of the national African Methodist Episcopal church conference. None of the *Morning World*'s May coverage pandered to such religious interests. These papers catered to what their subscribers wanted to read. See *Atlanta Daily World,* May 1932; and *Monroe Morning World,* May 1932.

50. *California Eagle,* 12 February 1932, 9.

51. *Chicago Defender,* 20 August 1932, 8.

52. *Kansas City Call,* 19 August 1932, 2B.

53. *Kansas City Call,* 19 August 1932, 2B; and *Pittsburgh Courier,* 20 August 1932, 2–4.

Chapter 9

1. *Chicago Defender,* 20 August 1932, 8.

2. *Chicago Defender,* 20 August 1932, 8.

3. *Kansas City Call,* 26 August 1932, 2B; *Pittsburgh Courier,* 27 August 1932, 2–4; *Chicago Defender,* 27 August 1932, 8; *Atlanta Daily World,* 31 August 1932, 5; and *Indianapolis Recorder,* 10 September 1932, 2. The radio broadcasts, if they occurred, were not national. Monroe's NBC and CBS stations did not announce the games in their published schedules, printed daily on page 4 of the *Monroe Morning World.*

4. *Pittsburgh Courier,* 27 August 1932, 4B; and *Atlanta Daily World,* 31 August 1932, 5.

5. *Louisiana Weekly,* 20 August 1932, 8; and *Afro-American,* 27 August 1932, 17.

6. *California Eagle,* 16 September 1932, 9; and *Kansas City Call,* 2 September 1932, 1B.

7. *Pittsburgh Courier,* 3 September 1932, 2–4. The *Courier* listed Monroe team batting averages at the time of the World Series—including only Southern League games: Leroy Morney, 0.363; Roy Parnell, 0.358; Zollie Wright, 0.336; Porter Dallas, 0.330; Augustus Saunders, 0.314; Chuffie Alexander, 0.312; W. C. Walker, 0.306 (left field); Harry Else, 0.306; and Sam Harris, 0.300.

8. *Pittsburgh Courier,* 20 August 1932, 2–4; *Pittsburgh Courier,* 27 August 1932, 2–4; *Pittsburgh Courier,* 31 December 1932, 2–5; *Monroe Morning World,* 13 September 1932, 6; New York *Amsterdam News,* 24 August 1932, 9; New York *Amster-*

dam News, 14 September 1932, 9; *California Eagle,* 16 September 1932, 9; *Louisville Leader,* 17 September 1932, 8; and *Memphis World,* 16 September 1932, 5.

9. *Monroe Morning World,* 31 August 1932, 6.

10. *Pittsburgh Courier,* 10 September 1932; *Monroe Morning World,* 5 September 1932, 6; *Monroe Morning World,* 9 September 1932, 10; *Indianapolis Recorder,* 3 September 1932, 2; *Louisville Leader,* 3 September 1932, 7; and *Louisville Leader,* 10 September 1932, 8. The series had been scheduled as a nine-game series, but evolved into a best-of-seven.

11. *Monroe Morning World,* 5 September 1932, 6; *Monroe News-Star,* 5 September 1932, 7; *Pittsburgh Courier,* 10 September 1932, 2–4; *Afro-American,* 10 September 1932, 16; *Indianapolis Recorder,* 17 September 1932, 2; and *Louisville Leader,* 17 September 1932, 8.

12. *Pittsburgh Courier,* 10 September 1932, 2–4.

13. "Great Negro Athlete Pitches Bismarck to Title," *Bismarck Tribune,* 28 August 1935, in "Player File: Paige, Leroy Robert," BHOF Vertical Files, Ashland Collection, National Baseball Hall of Fame, Cooperstown, NY.

14. "LeRoy (Satchel) Paige," BHOF Vertical Files, Ashland Collection, National Baseball Hall of Fame, Cooperstown, NY. See also Mark Ribowsky, *Don't Look Back: Satchel Paige in the Shadows of Baseball* (New York: Simon and Schuster, 1994).

15. *Pittsburgh Courier,* 10 September 1932, 2–4.

16. *Pittsburgh Courier,* 10 September 1932, 2–4; *Monroe News-Star,* 6 September 1932, 6; and *Afro-American,* 10 September 1932, 16.

17. *Kansas City Call,* 2 September 1932, 2B; *Afro-American,* 10 September 1932, 16; *Afro-American,* 17 September 1932, 16; *Chicago Defender,* 10 September 1932, 8; *Atlanta Daily World,* 8 September 1932, 5; and *Atlanta Daily World,* 12 September 1932, 5.

18. *Chicago Defender,* 17 September 1932, 9; *Chicago Defender,* 24 September 1932, 8; *Chicago Defender,* 1 October 1932, 8; *Chicago Defender,* 8 October 1932, 8; and *Atlanta Daily World,* 23 September 1932, 5.

19. *Shreveport Sun,* 10 September 1932, 5.

20. *Monroe Morning World,* 9 September 1932, 10; *Monroe News-Star,* 9 September 1932, 15; and *Shreveport Sun,* 10 September 1932, 5.

21. *Monroe Morning World,* 10 September 1932, 10; *Monroe News-Star,* 10 September 1932, 6; and Hilton Smith, "My Greatest Thrill: Hilton Smith Tells of Thrills He Got against Big Leaguers," in "Player File: Smith, Hilton," BHOF Vertical Files, National Baseball Hall of Fame, Cooperstown, NY.

22. *Louisiana Weekly,* 3 September 1932, 8; *Atlanta Daily World,* 1 September 1932, 5; and *Shreveport Sun,* 3 September 1932, 5.

23. *Shreveport Sun,* 10 September 1932, 5; *Shreveport Sun,* 24 September 1932, 5; and *Pittsburgh Courier,* 3 September 1932, 2–4.

24. *Monroe Morning World,* 10 September 1932, 10; *Monroe Morning World,* 11 September 1932, 9; and *Monroe News-Star,* 16 August 1992, 1C.

25. *Pittsburgh Courier,* 17 September 1932, 2–4; *Monroe Morning World,* 12 September 1932, 6; and *Monroe News-Star,* 12 September 1932, 7. The *Pittsburgh Courier* lists the Monarchs as losing 11–2, with no runs in the ninth.

26. *Monroe Morning World,* 12 September 1932, 6; *Monroe Morning World,* 13 September 1932, 6; *Kansas City Call,* 23 September 1932, 2B; *Monroe News-Star,* 13 September 1932, 6; and *Pittsburgh Courier,* 17 September 1932, 2–4.

27. *Kansas City Call,* 23 September 1932, 2B.

28. *Louisiana Weekly,* 27 August 1932, 8; *Louisiana Weekly,* 17 September 1932, 8; *Monroe Morning World,* 13 September 1932, 6; and *Memphis World,* 16 September 1932, 5. The teams' original plans were to travel to Jackson, Mississippi, after the series. Neither the *Morning World* nor the *Louisiana Weekly* explained why the plans changed.

29. *Kansas City Call,* 2 September 1932, 1B; *Pittsburgh Courier,* 27 August 1932, 2–4; *Pittsburgh Courier,* 3 September 1932, 2–4; *Pittsburgh Courier,* 17 September 1932, 2–4; *Chicago Defender,* 27 August 1932, 8; and *Chicago Defender,* 17 September 1932, 8. Pittsburgh planned an extensive barnstorming tour after the series, throughout the Northeast and throughout the country.

30. *Pittsburgh Courier,* 10 September 1932, 2–4; *Pittsburgh Courier,* 17 September 1932, 2–4; *Pittsburgh Courier,* 24 September 1932, 2–5; and *Chicago Defender,* 24 September 1932, 8.

31. *Atlanta Daily World,* 10 October 1932, 5; *Afro-American,* 8 October 1932, 17; and *Houston Informer,* 8 October 1932, 8.

32. *Atlanta Daily World,* 10 October 1932, 5; and John J. Lane, "The Immortal 'Babe' Ruth," in "Collection of Articles by John J. Lane: manuscript, typescript, [1932–1974?]," Archive BA EPH 1/2, National Baseball Hall of Fame, Cooperstown, NY.

33. *Chicago Defender,* 24 September 1932, 8.

34. *Atlanta Daily World,* 22 September 1932, 5; *Shreveport Sun,* 17 September 1932, 5; *Shreveport Sun,* 24 September 1932, 5; *Shreveport Sun,* 1 October 1932, 5; *Louisiana Weekly,* 24 September 1932, 8; *Louisiana Weekly,* 1 October 1932, 8; and *Louisiana Weekly,* 5 November 1932, 8. Dick Matthews, for example, returned to New Orleans to finish the season with Peter Robertson's Crescent City Stars.

35. *Monroe Morning World,* 6 October 1932, 6; *Monroe Morning World,* 7 October 1932, 6; *Monroe Morning World,* 9 October 1932, 10; *Louisiana Weekly,* 1 October

1932, 8; *Monroe News-Star,* 6 October 1932, 6; *Monroe News-Star,* 7 October 1932, 6; and *Monroe News-Star,* 9 October 1932, 10.

Chapter 10

1. *Houston Informer,* 17 September 1932, 3.

2. *Monroe Morning World,* 1 September 1932, 5; *Monroe Morning World,* 5 September 1932, 2.

3. *Monroe Morning World,* 5 September 1932, 2; *Baton Rouge State-Times Advocate,* 5 September 1932, 12; *Houston Informer,* 10 September 1932, 3; and *Louisiana Weekly,* 10 September 1932, 1.

4. *Monroe Morning World,* 5 September 1932, 2; *Baton Rouge State-Times Advocate,* 5 September 1932, 12; *Houston Informer,* 10 September 1932, 3; *Madison Journal,* 9 September 1932, 1; and *Louisiana Weekly,* 10 September 1932, 1.

5. *Monroe Morning World,* 8 September 1932, 2.

6. *Monroe Morning World,* 12 September 1932, 8; and *Office Criminal Docket G,* Fourth District Court, Clerk of Court, Criminal Division, Ouachita Parish Courthouse, Ouachita, LA, 301–6.

7. *Monroe Morning World,* 5 September 1932, 2.

8. Vivian Hester, interview with author, 16 June 2005; Margaret Newman, interview with author, 15 June 2005; Clara Poe, interview with author, 15 June 2005; and Carolyn Kennedy, interview with author, 14 June 2005.

9. *Pittsburgh Courier,* 3 September 1932, 2–5; *Afro-American,* 10 September 1932, 16; *Philadelphia Tribune,* 4 August 1932, 10; *Philadelphia Tribune,* 13 October 1932, 9; and *Indianapolis Recorder,* 6 August 1932, 2. Griffith's Senators remained in the cellar of the American League, watching as the New York Yankees finished in first place and earned the right to play in the World Series against the National League champion Chicago Cubs. The Yankees would win the series four games to none.

10. Lanctot, *Negro League Baseball,* 18–19; *Pittsburgh Courier,* 24 December 1932, 2–4; *Indianapolis Recorder,* 10 December 1932, 2; and *Indianapolis Recorder,* 17 December 1932, 2.

11. Debono, *Indianapolis ABCs,* 111–12; and Bak, *Turkey Stearnes and the Detroit Stars,* 202. In 1934, with Cole's stadium booking problems resolved, he moved the team back to Chicago.

12. *Atlanta Daily World,* 6 October 1932, 5C; *Kansas City Call,* 7 October 1932, 2B; *Chicago Defender,* 8 October 1932, 8; *Philadelphia Tribune,* 3 November 1932, 9; and *Pittsburgh Courier,* 8 October 1932, 2–5.

13. *Kansas City Call,* 14 October 1932, 2B; *Pittsburgh Courier,* 15 October 1932, 2–4; *Shreveport Sun,* 15 October 1932, 5; and *Louisiana Weekly,* 22 October 1932, 7.

14. *Kansas City Call,* 28 October 1932, 2B; *Kansas City Call,* 11 November 1932, 2B; *Atlanta Daily World,* 27 October 1932, 5; *Atlanta Daily World,* 7 November 1932, 5; *Atlanta Daily World,* 11 November 1932, 5; *Chicago Defender,* 29 October 1932, 9; and *Afro-American,* 12 November 1932, 17.

15. *Louisiana Weekly,* 8 October 1932, 7; *Louisiana Weekly,* 22 October 1932, 7; *Louisiana Weekly,* 14 January 1933, 7; *Louisiana Weekly,* 21 January 1933, 7; *Louisiana Weekly,* 28 January 1933, 7; *Louisiana Weekly,* 4 February 1932, 7; *Louisiana Weekly,* 11 February 1933, 7; *Atlanta Daily World,* 6 October 1932, 5C; *Atlanta Daily World,* 27 October 1932, 5C; *Atlanta Daily World,* 7 November 1932, 5C; *Atlanta Daily World,* 11 November 1932, 5C; *Atlanta Daily World,* 12 November 1932, 17; *Chicago Defender,* 8 October 1932, 8; *Chicago Defender,* 29 October 1932, 9; *Pittsburgh Courier,* 8 October 1932, S2, 5; *Pittsburgh Courier,* 15 October 1932, S2, 4; *Shreveport Sun,* 15 October 1932, 5; *Shreveport Sun,* 22 October 1932, 5; *Shreveport Sun,* 11 February 1933, 3; and *Shreveport Sun,* 18 February 1933, 5.

16. *Louisiana Weekly,* 25 February 1932, 7; *Louisiana Weekly,* 4 March 1933, 7; *Louisiana Weekly,* 25 March 1933, 7; *Louisiana Weekly,* 15 April 1937, 7; *Louisiana Weekly,* 29 April 1933, 7; *Louisiana Weekly,* 6 May 1932, 6; *Indianapolis Recorder,* 10 December 1932, 2; *Indianapolis Recorder,* 11 March 1933, 5; *Shreveport Sun,* 18 February 1933, 5; and *Shreveport Sun,* 11 March 1932, 5.

17. *Louisiana Weekly,* 29 April 1933, 7.

18. *Louisiana Weekly,* 13 May 1933, 5.

19. *Louisiana Weekly,* 25 February 1932, 7; *Louisiana Weekly,* 4 March 1933, 7; *Louisiana Weekly,* 25 March 1933, 7; *Louisiana Weekly,* 15 April 1937, 7; *Louisiana Weekly,* 29 April 1933, 7; *Louisiana Weekly,* 6 May 1932, 6; *Indianapolis Recorder,* 10 December 1932, 2; *Indianapolis Recorder,* 11 March 1933, 5; *Shreveport Sun,* 18 February 1933, 5; and *Shreveport Sun,* 11 March 1932, 5. After the league's breakup, English left Monroe to work as the press agent for Sam Mangino and his Crescent City Stars.

20. *Louisiana Weekly,* 13 May 1933, 5; *Louisiana Weekly,* 20 May 1933, 5; *Louisiana Weekly,* 3 June 1933, 5; *Louisiana Weekly,* 1 July 1933, 5; *Louisiana Weekly,* 29 July 1933, 5.

21. *Nashville Globe,* 2 October 1931, 8; *Atlanta Daily World,* 16 September 1932, 4; 2 October 1932, 7; 7 October 1932, 5; 14 October 1932, 5; 21 October 1932, 5; 23 October 1932, 7; 24 October 1932, 5; 28 October 1932, 5; and *Kansas City Call,* 16 December 1932, 2. The Louisville Tigers would join the league as the season progressed.

22. Grambling State Alumni Foundation, *Grambling: Cradle of the Pros* (Baton Rouge: Moran Publishing, 1981), 1; and Southern University and A&M College, "History of Southern University," http://www.subr.edu/historysubr.html (accessed 2 February 2007). See also http://www.gram.edu/about/history.

23. *Louisiana Weekly,* 26 March 1932, 3.

24. *Monroe Morning World,* 15 October 1932, 1, 8; and *Monroe Morning World,* 16 October 1932, 1, 8.

25. "Football Record, 1932," Southern University of Baton Rouge Athletic Department; *Shreveport Sun,* 22 October 1932, 5; and *Shreveport Sun,* 29 October 1932, 1, 8. The game was the first in what would become the Bayou Classic, the nation's most significant historically black football rivalry, between Southern (which would change its nickname to "Jaguars") and Normal (which would undergo a series of name changes until it became known in the 1970s as Grambling State University). *See* Thomas Aiello, *Bayou Classic: The Grambling-Southern Football Rivalry* (Baton Rouge: LSU Press, 2010).

26. Qtd. in Pollock, *Barnstorming to Heaven,* 79–81.

27. Lanctot, *Fair Dealing and Clean Playing,* 221; Lester, *Black Baseball's National Showcase,* 14; and Bankes, *Pittsburgh Crawfords,* 131–32.

28. *Louisiana Weekly,* 23 October 1933, 5; *Louisiana Weekly,* 30 October 1933, 1; and Malloy, "Chicago American Giants," MFF 308, National Baseball Hall of Fame.

29. *Pittsburgh Courier,* 19 November 1932, 2-4, 2-5.

30. Heaphy, *Negro Leagues,* 145–46.

31. *Monroe News-Star,* 12 July 1936, 10; *Bismarck Tribune,* 9 July 1935, 6; *Lincoln Star,* 30 July 1934, 6; *Southern Broadcast,* 8 August 1936, 7; *Southern Broadcast,* 15 August 1936, 7; *Southern Broadcast,* 22 August 1936, 7; *Southern Broadcast,* 29 August 1932, 7, 8; and *Southern Broadcast,* 17 October 1936, 7.

32. *Atlanta World,* 20 March 1932, 5. In 1932, Dubisson served as an administrator for the Little Rock Greys.

33. *Chicago Defender,* 25 June 1932, 8; *Shreveport Sun,* 22 August 1936, 5; *Shreveport Sun,* 10 October 1936, 5; *Louisiana Weekly,* 11 April 1936, 8; *Louisiana Weekly,* 18 April 1936, 8; *Louisiana Weekly,* 25 April 1936, 8; *Arkansas Democrat-Gazette,* 4 July 2002, 1C, 8C; and *Swingin' Timber: The Story of the Claybrook Tigers,* videocassette, produced and directed by David D. Dawson, Lemke Department of Journalism, University of Arkansas, Fayetteville, AR, 2001. Radcliffe was a Pittsburgh Crawford in 1932 and 1933.

34. *Monroe News-Star,* 19 July 1936, 9; *Monroe News-Star,* 23 July 1936, 6; *Monroe News-Star,* 24 July 1936, 8; *Monroe News-Star,* 26 July 1936, 9; *Monroe News-Star,* 27 July 1936, 5; *Monroe News-Star,* 12 August 1936, 6; *Monroe News-Star,* 23 August 1936, 8; *Monroe News-Star,* 25 August 1936, 5; *Monroe News-Star,* 26 August 1936, 6; *Monroe News-Star,* 28 August 1936, 7; *Monroe News-Star,* 31 August 1936, 6; *Monroe News-Star,* 1 September 1936, 5; *Monroe News-Star,* 2 September 1936, 6; *Monroe News-Star,* 4 September 1936, 17; *Monroe News-Star,* 7 September 1936, 5; *Monroe News-Star,* 8 September 1936, 6; *Monroe News-Star,* 9 October 1936, 10; *Mon-*

roe *News-Star,* 16 October 1936, 10; *Monroe News-Star,* 6 November 1936, 12; *Monroe News-Star,* 25 November 1936, 7; *Monroe News-Star,* 23 December 1936, 9.

35. *Monroe News-Star,* 21 December 1936, 11; *Monroe News-Star,* 5 January 1937, 5; *Monroe News-Star,* 31 January 1937, 7; *Monroe News-Star,* 21 February 1937, 8; *Monroe News-Star,* 28 February 1937, 9; *Monroe News-Star,* 2 March 1937, 6; *Monroe News-Star,* 4 March 1937, 8; *Monroe News-Star,* 5 March 1937, 10; *Monroe News-Star,* 7 March 1937, 9; *Monroe News-Star,* 9 March 1937, 7; *Monroe News-Star,* 11 March 1937, 11; "Fred Stovall to Monroe Baseball Club, Inc.—Lease of Park," record 258871, 4 March 1938, Mortgage Record, Ouachita Parish, Book 213, 341–43, Ouachita Parish Clerk of Court; "Fred Stovall to Monroe Baseball Club, Inc.—Lease," record 273921, 7 May 1940, Mortgage Record, Ouachita Parish, Book 223, 169–71, Ouachita Parish Clerk of Court; "Fred Stovall to Twin City Baseball Association, Inc.—Lease," record 236603, 7 January 1937, Mortgage Record, Ouachita Parish, Book 207, 188–91, Ouachita Parish Clerk of Court; "Fred Stovall to White Sox Baseball Club, Inc.—Lease," record 278260, 10 March 1941, Mortgage Record, Ouachita Parish, Book 226, 142–44, Ouachita Parish Clerk of Court; and *Monroe Morning World,* 4 September 1938, 5.

36. Riley, *Biographical Encyclopedia of the Negro Baseball Leagues,* 206–7, 209, 266–67, 568, 569–70, 605, 723–25, 781–82, 884–85; *Tri-State Defender,* 13 April 1974; *Nashville Globe and Independent,* 30 March 1932, 8; "Pre-Negro Leagues Candidate Profile: Roy A. 'Red' Parnell," National Baseball Hall of Fame, http://baseballhall .org (accessed 21 February 2006); and "Pre-Negro Leagues Candidate Profile: Willard Jessie 'Home Run' Brown," National Baseball Hall of Fame, http://baseballhall.org/ hof/brown-willard (accessed 24 October 2010). Parnell was ultimately not included in the final group of enshrined players.

37. Hilton Smith, "My Greatest Thrill"; Steve Rock, "Former Monarchs Pitcher Hilton Smith Elected to Baseball Hall of Fame," *Kansas City Star,* 7 March 2001; and *Bismarck Tribune,* 9 July 1935, 6. Willard Brown, who joined the Monarchs in 1934, would be the second and only other Monarch to enter the Hall of Fame. He was inducted in 2006. "Player File: Brown, Willard Jesse," Ashland Collection, National Baseball Hall of Fame, Cooperstown, NY.

38. *Southern Broadcast,* 14 November 1936, 1, 7, 8.

39. Letlow, "A Team to Remember," 5C; "Monroe Monarchs," photograph, 1932, Ouachita Digital Archive, Ouachita Parish Public Library, Ouachita, LA; Jean Stovall Lee, interview with author, 3 August 2004; and *Louisiana Weekly,* 3 September 1932, 8. Other mentions refer to the Crawfords as Eastern League champions or more broadly as "champions of the East."

40. Letlow, "A Team to Remember," 1C, 5C.

41. Roosevelt Wright, interview with author, 17 June 2005; and Roosevelt Wright

Jr., *The Game: A Black Heritage Drama in Two Acts* (Monroe, LA: Free Press Publishers, 1996).

Conclusion

1. *Pittsburgh Courier,* 24 December 1932, 2–5.

2. *Pittsburgh Courier,* 31 December 1932, 2–4.

3. *Afro-American,* 1 October 1932, 16.

4. Qtd. in Letlow, "A Team to Remember," 5C. For more on the tenuousness of the evidence of those capacity crowds, see chapter 6, note 27.

5. Again, without financial records, the evidence for profit is circumstantial. But that circumstantial evidence makes a strong case.

6. *Kansas City Call,* 11 November 1932, 2B.

7. Ollie Burns, interview.

8. *Shreveport Sun,* 10 September 1932, 1.

Appendix 1

1. The exhibitions were against the Rube Foster Memorial Giants, often confused— even in contemporary press reports—as the Chicago American Giants. A series of articles in the *Kansas City Call* in early April reports on both teams and makes their differences clear. *Kansas City Call,* 8 April 1932, 1.

2. The first-half game total by this count is forty-two (minus the exhibitions), with thirty-five wins and six losses. This differs from any other account, contemporary or historical, of the season's first half. I stand by this count. The selective presentation by newspapers and the overall confused state of Negro League baseball in 1932 both argue for the necessity of a new count. The contemporary and historical controversy over the first-half standings, if nothing else, discredits any consistency in former counts. See below for a catalog of other tallies and for the Monarchs' original schedule as announced by the Negro Southern League in March 1932.

3. Available box scores come from the following sources: *Monroe Morning World,* 28 March 1932, 6; *Monroe Morning World,* 4 April 1932, 5; *Monroe Morning World,* 5 April 1932, 6; *Monroe Morning World,* 11 April 1932, 5; *Monroe Morning World,* 12 April 1932, 6; *Monroe Morning World,* 7 May 1932, 8; *Monroe Morning World,* 8 May 1932, 10; *Monroe Morning World,* 9 May 1932, 6; *Monroe Morning World,* 15 May 1932, 10; *Monroe Morning World,* 22 May 1932, 8; *Monroe Morning World,* 12 June 1932, 10; *Monroe Morning World,* 13 June 1932, 6; *Monroe Morning World,* 14 June 1932, 6; *Monroe Morning World,* 19 June 1932, 8; *Monroe Morning World,* 20 June 1932, 6; *Monroe Morning World,* 21 June 1932, 6; *Monroe Morning World,* 3 July 1932,

8; *Monroe Morning World,* 4 July 1932, 6; *Monroe Morning World,* 5 July 1932, 6; *Monroe Morning World,* 1 August 1932, 5; *Monroe Morning World,* 2 August 1932, 6; *Monroe Morning World,* 8 August 1932, 6; *Monroe Morning World,* 9 August 1932, 7; *Monroe Morning World,* 29 August 1932, 5; *Monroe Morning World,* 30 August 1932, 4; *Monroe Morning World,* 31 August 1932, 6; *Monroe Morning World,* 5 September 1932, 6; *Monroe Morning World,* 11 September 1932, 9; *Monroe Morning World,* 12 September 1932, 6; *Monroe News-Star,* 16 May 1932, 6; *Monroe News-Star,* 17 May 1932, 7; *Monroe News-Star,* 23 May 1932, 8; *Memphis Commercial Appeal,* 1 May 1932, 18; *Memphis Commercial Appeal,* 2 May 1932, 9; *Memphis Commercial Appeal,* 3 May 1932, 11; *Memphis Commercial Appeal,* 10 July 1932, 19; *Memphis Commercial Appeal,* 11 July 1932, 7; *Memphis Commercial Appeal,* 12 July 1932, 10; *Pittsburgh Courier,* 10 September 1932, 2-5; *Kansas City Call,* 22 April 1932, 4B; *Chicago Defender,* 11 June 1932, 8; *Chicago Defender,* 2 July 1932, 9; *Chicago Defender,* 16 July 1932, 9; *Chicago Defender,* 23 July 1932, 8; *Atlanta Daily World,* 30 June 1932, 5; *Afro-American,* 23 July 1932, 5; and *Louisiana Weekly,* 17 September 1932, 7.

4. The four final games with the Lincoln Giants of Alexandria, Louisiana, are considered exhibition games, as were the final games against Little Rock, as they took place after the close of the World Series.

5. *Pittsburgh Courier,* 19 March 1932; and *Atlanta Daily World,* 22 March 1932.

6. *Pittsburgh Courier,* 16 July 1932; and *Chicago Defender,* 9 July 1932.

7. Peterson, *Only the Ball Was White,* 269; and Clark and Lester, eds., *Negro Leagues Book,* 164.

8. Holway, *Complete Book of Baseball's Negro Leagues,* 288, 292–93.

9. *Monroe Morning World,* 6 July 1932, 6.

10. *Pittsburgh Courier,* 9 July 1932, 4; *Pittsburgh Courier,* 3 September 1932, 2-5.

11. *Pittsburgh Courier,* 3 September 1932, 2-5.

Appendix 2

1. *Louisiana Weekly,* 5 March 1932, 8; and *Shreveport Sun,* 19 March 1932, 4.

2. Murray never played for the Monarchs in the first half of the season. He somehow made his way to Memphis, before returning to the Monarchs in late August. (See August 20–22 acquisition listing for Murray in appendix 2.) *Monroe News-Star,* 24 March 1932, 5.

3. In some accounts of Monarchs players, this pitcher's name appears as "Mathews."

4. *Chicago Defender,* 2 April 1932, 8.

5. *Monroe Morning World,* 8 April 1932, 8.

6. *Monroe Morning World,* 9 April 1932, 8.

7. *Monroe Morning World,* 21 April 1932, 6.

8. *Louisiana Weekly,* 21 May 1932, 5; and *Monroe Morning World,* 27 May 1932, 11.

9. Thompson, described by the *Chicago Defender* as the "former Indianapolis twirler," was the losing pitcher during the Monarchs' Tuesday, July 19, 1932, loss to Chicago. *Chicago Defender,* 23 July 1932, 8.

10. These acquisitions were announced in the *Monroe Morning World* on August 26, 1932. But the players appeared in games versus the Lincoln Giants beginning on August 11.

11. Murray's first appearance with the Monarchs came at Austin on August 22, 1932. *Monroe Morning World,* 26 August 1932, 8.

12. *Monroe Morning World,* 10 September 1932, 5.

Appendix 3

1. See appendix 4, note 2, for explanation of a discrepancy involving two possible players named "Walker."

2. Gillespie was suspended by the Southern League for the second half of the season. See *Pittsburgh Courier,* 7 September 1932, 5, for his return.

3. Clark and Lester, eds., *Negro Leagues Book,* 109.

4. Holway, *Complete Book of Baseball's Negro Leagues,* 292–93.

5. Riley, *Biographical Encyclopedia of the Negro Baseball Leagues,* 28, 30–31, 136, 157–58, 206–7, 209, 266, 267, 292, 319, 358–59, 363, 432, 482, 520, 565, 568–69, 569–70, 605, 621, 698, 711, 723–25, 746, 781–82, 809, 811, 835, 848, 850, 884–85.

Appendix 4

1. On June 12, the Monarchs played a doubleheader with the Montgomery Grey Sox, and the box score for the first game lists the left fielder as Maher—a name never mentioned before or after. The number of incorrect spellings and misinterpretations of player names in printed materials then and more recently leads the observer to conclude that the handwritten box score submission that probably included Walker appeared to be "Maher" to the *Monroe Morning World*'s typesetter. Walker (Maher) was one for four with no runs. These statistics are included as part of Walker's total.

2. There here exists a discrepancy that must be acknowledged. James Riley's *The Biographical Encyclopedia of the Negro Baseball Leagues* lists two Walkers as players for the 1932 Monarchs. Neither are very well known. W. Walker is listed as a left fielder. H. Walker is listed as a catcher. In a game against the Chicago American Giants, the box score of which appears in the *Chicago Defender,* 23 July 1932, "Walker" is listed as playing left field and catcher in the Saturday box score. The dearth of information available about these players (even accurate first names for

them) leaves open at least a slight possibility that these two players are the same, particularly with the prevalence of box score typographical errors. Box scores generally list "Walker" and a position, so absolute accuracy is impossible. For the sake of the best possible sample, however, I have separated the catching Walker from the left fielding Walker. One newspaper account, however, describes W. Walker as "W. C. Walker," "former Campbell College star." Another account in the *Kansas City Call* refers to him as "Shorty." This information doesn't discount the possibility that H. Walker and W. Walker were different players, but it seems to suggest that there was one known Walker on the team, making more than plausible the possibility that W. C. Walker was the only member of the 1932 Monarchs. *Atlanta Daily World,* 15 September 1932, 5; *Kansas City Call,* 29 April 1932, 5B; and Riley, *Biographical Encyclopedia of the Negro Baseball Leagues,* 809, 811.

3. All totals are derived from the available data. Wins, losses, and scores are totals from appendix 1: 1932 Monroe Monarchs Schedule and Results. Statistical performance numbers are totals from the "Season Totals" section above, in appendix 4. As in the first- and second-half statistical breakdowns, exhibition games with available scores (with the exception of those taking place after the close of the World Series) are included in the total runs scored and allowed.

4. The run totals for this section of the team statistics are derived from available box scores, and thus from fewer games than are the run totals based solely on the reported wins and losses. Addition of runs not included in the box scores cannot be included in this section, as they would skew the representative sample the box score statistical analysis is supposed to provide.

5. Batting average is simply the batter's number of hits divided by his number of at bats (AB above).

6. Slugging percentage follows this formula: [singles + (2 × doubles) + (3 × triples) + (4 × home runs)] divided by at bats.

7. The total bases statistic follows this formula: singles + (2 × doubles) + (3 × triples) + (4 × home runs).

8. The isolated power statistic follows this formula: total bases minus hits divided by at bats. The original formula calculated the "total bases" by awarding a 0 for singles, 1 for doubles, 2 for triples, and 3 for home runs. Here, total bases is calculated as described in note 7 above.

9. Home run ratio is calculated by dividing the number of a batter's home runs by his number of at bats.

10. Note, as mentioned above, that hits, runs, errors, and at bats are the most consistently noted statistics. In this section, for example, though Chicago has scored 15 runs, they have no listed RBIs. The box scores for games with Chicago did not include RBI as a statistic, and so that statistic is not there. While the first four num-

bers are clearly the most complete, the numbers to the left of the RBI column are reasonably accurate. The same derivatives generated above are generated below the hard numbers section. The given numbers are for the games noted in appendix 1, as having an available box score. The total number of games used to derive each team's statistics against the Monarchs follows the team name in parentheses.

11. The Pittsburgh statistics presented here include the three World Series games with available box scores and the early exhibition game. Pittsburgh's individual and team World Series statistics are also included.

12. This Jud Wilson, one in a litany of future Hall of Fame inductees from the 1932 Crawfords, is the same Jud Wilson who led the 1932 East–West League in batting average for 1932. Wilson moved to the Crawfords after the East–West collapse.

13. Minimum of fifty at bats, for batting average and the rest of the East–West League statistical leaders.

14. Smith was 4 and 0 in six games, with thirty innings pitched.

15. The Cuban Stars' home run ratio just edges Baltimore's .017.

16. This statistic comes from the Baltimore *Afro-American,* 25 June 1932. Soon after this standings release, the league folded.

17. A minimum of fifty innings pitched has been imposed by the author.

18. This Pine Bluff rookie came from Dallas, and though the local paper used first names in its reports on the Pine Bluff Judges, Danforth was always called C. B., often with the nickname "Tarzan" added. *Pine Bluff Daily Graphic,* 22 April 1932, 5; *Pine Bluff Daily Graphic,* 24 April 1932, 4; *Pine Bluff Daily Graphic,* 26 April 1932, 4; *Pine Bluff Daily Graphic,* 1 May 1932, 4; *Pine Bluff Daily Graphic,* 15 May 1932, 5; *Pine Bluff Daily Graphic,* 27 May 1932, 5.

19. All 1932 Major League batting average, slugging percentage, and winning percentage statistics are taken from www.baseball-reference.com (accessed 20 June 2005), which exacts a minimum requirement of 3.1 plate appearances per game, 1 inning pitched per game, or 0.1 decision per game for single-season leader eligibility. Isolated power and home run ratio were derived by the author from individual player (and, where appropriate, team) statistics found at www.baseball-reference.com (accessed 20 June 2005). This citation applies to the following four segments detailing the 1932 Major League season.

20. Batting average, slugging percentage, and winning percentage statistics are taken from www.baseball-reference.com (accessed 20 June 2005), which exacts a minimum requirement of 3.1 plate appearances per game, 1 inning pitched per game, or 0.1 decision per game for single-season leader eligibility. Isolated power and home run ratio were derived by the author from individual player statistics found at www .baseball-reference.com (accessed 20 June 2005).

Bibliographic Essay

Though there is a vast literature—surprisingly vast, considering the relative dearth of salvaged records—on the Negro Leagues, the Monroe Monarchs have been almost universally excluded. The broader world of southern black baseball has also received short shrift. The principal source of information for this study, then, is the surviving newspaper record from the nation's black press (and white press) in 1932. That record is often ignored by historians of black baseball because southern newspapers are far less likely to have survived, far less likely to have been saved and collected within the stifling environment of Jim Crow. Many of those southern black newspapers that do exist in either complete or partial form are in severely dilapidated shape, and for that reason they are often—even the microfilms—scattered throughout special collections departments all over the South. Such realities have left the papers largely ignored as black baseball source material. With scholars focusing on northern urban newspapers to piece together Negro Leagues seasons, the role of the South is diminished by default. The black papers used in this study are:

Arkansas Survey
Atlanta World / Daily World
Baltimore *Afro-American*
Birmingham Reporter
Boston Chronicle
California Eagle
Chicago Defender
Cleveland Gazette
Hot Springs Echo
Houston Informer

Indianapolis Recorder
Kansas City Call
Louisiana Weekly
Louisville Leader
Memphis World
Nashville Globe
Nashville Globe and Independent
Nashville Independent
Negro Voice
Negro World
New Orleans Vindicator
New York Age
New York *Amsterdam News*
Oklahoma City Black Dispatch
Philadelphia Tribune
Pittsburgh Courier
Shreveport Sun
Southern Broadcast
Tri-State Defender

Of course, the other benefit of relying on such sources is that each provides a unique insight into the racism that pervaded the Depression-era South. But they were not alone. White southern newspapers had a firsthand knowledge of both black baseball and the racism and race violence endemic to the region, and thus many white newspapers proved inordinately valuable, as well:

Arkansas Democrat
Arkansas Democrat-Gazette
Arkansas Gazette
Austin American
Austin Statesman
Austin Sunday American-Statesman
Baton Rouge State-Times Advocate
Birmingham Age-Herald
Bismarck Tribune
Caldwell Watchman
Chicago Tribune
Farmerville Gazette

Franklin Sun
Galveston Daily News
Kansas City Star
Lincoln Star
Louisville Courier-Journal
Madison Journal
Memphis Commercial Appeal
Monroe Morning World
Monroe News-Star
Monroe News Star-World
Morehouse Enterprise
Nashville Banner
New Orleans Item
New Orleans Times-Picayune
New York Herald-Tribune
New York Journal American
New York News
New York Times
New York Tribune
New York World Telegram
Osceola Times
Ouachita Citizen
Pine Bluff Daily Graphic
Pittsburgh Post-Gazette
Ruston Daily Leader
Shreveport Journal
Tensas Gazette
Vicksburg Evening Post
Washington News
Washington Post

Another core factor hindering analysis of the Monroe Monarchs and the Negro Southern League (NSL) is that the high point of both occurred in 1932. The statement mentioned in the introduction is true. The permanent exhibition at the Negro Leagues Baseball Museum in Kansas City includes a massive and incredibly informative timeline of black participation in baseball. Its first section ends in 1931, and its second begins in 1933. So the one season in which southern black baseball became a major league is the one that time forgot. There are two possible reasons for this. Either the confusion of baseball's troubled times in 1932 has kept scholars away, and because of that, the Southern League's one season in the sun has been lost in the clutter; or the reverse is true: since the bulk of organizational success in 1932 was in the South, and the aforementioned hindrances to studying southern black baseball are so palpable, what was actually a surprisingly successful season for the Negro Southern League in its one "major" season hasn't seemed so to those who rely on northern black newspapers as their dominant source material. In the end, a combination of the two probably comes closest to telling the tale, but the second reason surely dominates the synthesis. Though certainly the preceding text acknowledges a significant contemporary confusion that pervaded the season, it also demonstrates the relative success of the NSL in 1932. Either way, with a vacuum of secondary materials detailing the season—and the Monarchs in particular—this study relies heavily on primary source material.

Archival and primary sources on the black baseball season itself are available in bits and pieces from several places. The A. Bartlett Giamatti Research Center at the National Baseball Hall of Fame in Cooperstown, New York, carries player files for many of the former Pittsburgh Crawfords (being that so many of them made the Hall of Fame) and on Hilton Smith and Willard Brown, the two former Monarchs to be inducted. Its collection of articles by John Lane also proved helpful. The Harold and Dorothy Seymour Papers at the Division of Rare and Manuscript Collections at Cornell University's Koch Library provided broader analysis for the entire baseball season. The Memphis/Shelby County Public Library Special Collections materials on the Memphis Red Sox provided a strong source base on the team, for both 1932 and other years of its existence, as did the Kenneth Spencer Research Library at the University of Kansas for the Kansas City Monarchs. Its collection of the papers of Thomas Baird, co-owner of the Kansas City Monarchs, provides information on his team, but also on its interaction with the rest of black baseball.

Perhaps the biggest hindrance to studying the 1932 Southern League season was the enigmatic Reuben B. Jackson, who played such a large role in league machinations but was obscured to the point of disappearing by both contemporary newspaper accounts and the secondary historical record. The Tennessee State Library and Archives proved inordinately helpful on this count. Jackson's marriage and tax records, combined with a series of annual city directories from the 1920s to the 1950s, aided local black newspaper searches outside of the sports section and provided a portrait of the Southern League president. Often when dealing with obscure actors in a historical narrative, this kind of genealogical approach can best fill in the biographical gaps left by contemporary tellers of the tale.

The Monarchs and their city, however, are also obscured by the secondary source record. The Special Collections of the Ouachita Parish Public Library provided information on and photographs of the 1932 winter flood that so dominated the first months of the year, as did the William F. and Catherine D. Norrell Collection at the University of Arkansas. Documents from the Federal Emergency Management Agency, the U.S. Department of Agriculture, and the Red Cross—all of whom played a role in Monroe's recovery—provided additional information. The Fourteenth and Fifteenth national censuses proved vital for reconstructing the evolving condition of Monroe in the Great Depression. So, too, did Louisiana State University's Division of Agricultural Extension Annual Reports and the Louisiana Department of Commerce and Industry's reports on the state's resources and purchasing power. The Works Progress Administration's Writer's Project sent agents to Monroe, and their descriptions provided insightful assessments of the town, its economic climate, and its racial situation.

That racial situation was dire, but suitably hushed by Monroe itself. The study then relies on contemporary accounts and editorials from outside the city to contextualize its problem with racial violence. Articles from *World's Work, Current Opinion, New Republic, Review of Reviews, Literary Digest, Southwestern Christian Advocate, Outlook, South Atlantic Quarterly,* and *Nation* all aided the effort. The Papers of the NAACP and Tuskegee's *Negro Year Book* for 1932 did so, as well. In recounting specific incidents such as the Bolden lynching, I benefited from the St. Francis Medical Center Department of Public Relations, as well as the indictments of R. R. McCord from the Ouachita Parish Clerk of Court. The Zion Traveler murders that dominated the headlines concurrently with the Monarchs' season come from minutes of the district court of Ouachita Parish, histories of the event from church records, and interviews with Reverend Tracy C. DeWitt and congregants Vivian Hester, Carolyn Kennedy, Margaret Newman, and Clara Poe.

The Monarchs themselves, their park, and their owner also lacked any truly substantial secondary-source treatment. Proof of the former location of Casino Park and Stovall's various and convoluted attempts to secure it come from Sanborn Fire Insurance Maps, along with myriad conveyance records, mortgage deeds, plat books, police jury minutes, vendor's liens, cash purchase records, articles of incorporation, and civil suit case records, all housed in the bowels of the Ouachita Parish Courthouse. But for me to fully understand those sources, Stovall himself had to appear in fuller form. The courthouse carries assessment rolls from the Ouachita Parish Tax Collection Office, the articles of incorporation for his various companies, and those same civil court documents, all of which helped produce his portrait. Additionally, Special Collections at the Ouachita Parish Public Library holds histories of Monroe's gas fields and the University of Louisiana at Monroe houses a collection of Stovall family photographs. City directories again aided the search, as they allow historians to track the movement of people over time. The Monroe city directories aided the finding of both Stovall and other team officials, as did 1931's *Who's Who in the Twin Cities* (West Monroe, LA: H. H. Brinsmade, 1931). An understanding of the team's relationship to its town was aided by interviews with publisher Roosevelt Wright; DeMorris Smith, son of Hilton Smith; Jean Stovall Lee, granddaughter of Fred Stovall; and Ollie Burns.

But though primary materials were crucial to reconstructing the stories of Monroe, the Monarchs, and the 1932 Negro Southern League season, a litany of secondary sources provided factual and contextual material integral to the narrative. A self-published genealogical volume by Lyle Keith Williams titled *The Stovall Family and Related Lines,* 2 vols. (Ft. Worth, TX: self-published, 1984), for example, helped find the team's owner, as did studies of the Spindletop oil phenomenon of the early century. Judith Walker Linsley, Ellen Walker Rienstra, and Jo Ann Stiles's *Giant under the Hill: A History of the Spindletop Oil Discovery at Beaumont, Texas, in 1901* (Austin: Texas State Historical Association, 2002) and Paul N. Spellman's *Spindletop Boom Days* (College Station: Texas A&M University Press, 2001), along with Spencer W. Robinson's edited collection, *Spindletop: Where Oil Became an Industry* (Beaumont: Spindletop 50th Anniversary Commission, 1951) all provide apt treatments of both the boom and the people who benefited from it.

Following Stovall's success in Texas, however, he came to Monroe. J. Fair Hardin's "Don Juan Filhiol and the Founding of Fort Miro, The Modern Monroe, Louisiana" (*Louisiana Historical Quarterly* 20 [April 1937]: 463–75) provides detail on Monroe's inception, as does E. Russ Williams Jr.'s *Encyclopedia of Founding Families of the Ouachita Valley of Louisiana, 1785 to 1850,* 2 vols. (Monroe, LA: Williams Genealogical and Historical Publications, 1997). Ken Purcell's *A Pictorial History of Monroe, La.* (Monroe, LA: Good Impressions, 1983) and *Tales along the Ouachita: Stories and Folklore of Monroe, West Monroe, LA* (West Monroe: self-published, 2003) give accurate retellings of the town's evolution from Fort Miro, as do the League of Women Voters of Monroe's *Monroe: The New and Old* (Monroe, LA: League of Women Voters, 1960) and the *Ouachita Citizen's A Pictorial History of Ouachita Parish* (Marceline, MO: D-Books Publishing, 1997). The problem with such local histories, however, is that most tread lightly (or do not tread at all) over ground that might shed a negative light on their subject. That being the case, Ouachita Parish's history of racial violence is given short shrift in these accounts.

The two most prominent, helpful analyses of Louisiana's struggles with race and civil rights are Adam Fairclough's *Race and Democracy: The Civil Rights Struggle in Louisiana, 1915–1972* (Athens: University of Georgia Press, 1995) and Greta de Jong's *A Different Day: African American Struggles for Justice in Rural Louisiana, 1900–1970* (Chapel Hill: University of North Carolina Press, 2002). Both of these books, however—like most books treating the history of Louisiana—provide comparatively less material on northeast Louisiana, choosing instead to focus the bulk of their attention on other, more well-known sections of the state. Additionally, the broad swath of time they cover leaves little room for an intensive focus on lynching. The Bolden story, in fact, is mentioned in neither. Instead, it appears in William Ivy Hair's *The Kingfish and His Realm: The Life and Times of Huey P. Long* (Baton Rouge: Louisiana State University Press, 1991). Luckily, however, the historiography of lynching is vast. Many such sources are used in this study, some of which include Tuskegee Institute's *Lynchings by States and Race, 1882–1959* (Tuskegee, AL: Department of Records and Research, Tuskegee Institute, 1959); the NAACP's *Thirty Years of Lynching in the United States, 1889–1918* (New York: Arno Press, 1969); Robert L. Zangrando's *The NAACP Crusade against Lynching, 1909–1950* (Philadelphia: Temple University Press, 1980); Christopher Waldrep's *The Many Faces of Judge Lynch: Extralegal Violence and Punishment in America* (New York: Palgrave Macmillan, 2002); and Stewart E. Tolnay and E. M. Beck's *A Festival of Violence: An Analysis of Southern Lynchings, 1882–1930* (Urbana: University of Illinois Press, 1995). In addition, tangential studies by W. Fitzhugh Brundage, Richard A. Buckelew, Donald L. Grant, Jacquelyn Dowd Hall, Theodore Kornweibel Jr., and Patricia A. Schechter also proved vital.

To contextualize that violence and the Monarchs' success within it, broad studies of the Great Depression were necessary. Chief among them was Betty M. Field's "Louisiana and the Great Depression," reprinted in *The Louisiana Purchase Bicentennial Series in Louisiana History*, vol. 3, *The Age of the Longs in Louisiana, 1928–1960*, ed. Edward F. Haas (Lafayette, LA: Center for Louisiana Studies, 2001). Rita Barnard's *The Great Depression and the Culture of Abundance: Kenneth Fearing, Nathanael West, and Mass Culture in the 1930s* (New York: Cambridge University Press, 1995), Donald J. Lisio's *Hoover, Blacks, and Lily-Whites: A Study of Southern Strategies* (Chapel Hill: University of North Carolina Press, 1985), and Edward Robb Ellis's *A Nation in Torment: The Great American Depression, 1929–1939* (1970; New York: Kodansha International, 1995) all give solid syntheses of the Depression and its relationship to the southern economy. In addition to these studies, works by William E. Leuchtenburg, Robert S. McElvaine, Studs Terkel, Harris Gaylord Warren, T. H. Watkins, and Elliot A. Rosen, among others, provided valuable information, quotes, and statistics about the lived realities of the economic collapse in the early 1930s.

Though much has already been said about the larger historiographical ignorance of 1932's black baseball season, this study could not have happened without the careful work of a vast panoply of Negro League historians. Most immediately, localized histories of other teams lent significant information on Monarchs opponents and proved to be valuable case studies of how to go about constructing the history of a baseball club. James Bankes's *The Pittsburgh Crawfords: The Lives and Times of Black Baseball's Most Exciting Team* (Dubuque, IA: William C. Brown Publishers, 1991), Neil Lanctot's *Fair Dealing and Clean Playing: The Hilldale Club and the Development of Black Professional Baseball, 1910–1932* (Jefferson, NC: McFarland, 1994), Paul Debono's *The Indianapolis ABCs: History of a Premier Team in the Negro Leagues* (Jefferson, NC: McFarland, 1997), Richard Bak's *Turkey Stearnes and the Detroit Stars: The Negro Leagues in Detroit, 1919–1933* (Detroit, MI: Wayne State University Press, 1994), Alan J. Pollock's *Barnstorming to Heaven: Syd Pollock and His Great Black Teams,* edited by James A. Riley (Tuscaloosa: University of Alabama Press, 2006), and Jerry Malloy's "Chicago American Giants," which is available at the A. Bartlett Giamatti Research Center at the National Baseball Hall of Fame, all evaluate the histories of teams with far more seasons in the sun than the Monroe Monarchs. In addition, Ben Green's *Spinning the Globe: The Rise, Fall, and Return to Greatness of the Harlem Globetrotters* (New York: Amistad, 2005) included vital information on Abraham Saperstein and his barnstorming black baseball clubs, and Leslie Heaphy's edited collection *Black Baseball and Chicago: Essays on the Players, Teams, and Games of the Negro Leagues' Most Important City* (Jefferson, NC: McFarland, 2006) is an inordinately valuable collection of research on the Chicago American Giants, Rube Foster, and the other black baseball teams, owners, and personalities in Chicago throughout the lifespan of the Negro Leagues. Larry Lester's *Black Baseball's National Showcase: The East-West All-Star Game, 1933–*

1953 (Lincoln: University of Nebraska Press, 2001) is similarly reductionist, focusing on the annual all-star game that was created following the 1932 season.

Still, those localized studies would mean nothing without the context provided by larger, more comprehensive works on the Negro Leagues. The two newest works in this vein are Neil Lanctot's *Negro League Baseball: The Rise and Ruin of a Black Institution* (Philadelphia: University of Pennsylvania Press, 2004), which is the definitive study of the business of black baseball, and Lawrence D. Hogan's *Shades of Glory: The Negro Leagues and the Story of African-American Baseball* (Washington, DC: National Geographic, 2006), commissioned by the National Baseball Hall of Fame in conjunction with its election of new Negro League players to Cooperstown. Those works are descendants of others such as Robert Peterson's *Only the Ball Was White: A History of Legendary Black Players and All-Black Professional Teams* (New York: Oxford University Press, 1970) and Leslie A. Heaphy's *The Negro Leagues, 1869–1960* (Jefferson, NC: McFarland, 2003). Accompanying such narrative evaluations are encyclopedic, biographical, and statistical accounts such as Dick Clark and Larry Lester's *The Negro Leagues Book* (Cleveland, OH: Society for American Baseball Research, 1994), John Holway's *The Complete Book of Baseball's Negro Leagues: The Other Half of Baseball History* (Fern Park, FL: Hastings House Publishers, 2001), Thom Loverro's *The Encyclopedia of Negro League Baseball* (New York: Facts On File, 2003), and James A. Riley's *The Biographical Encyclopedia of the Negro Baseball Leagues* (New York: Carroll and Graf Publishers, 1994). Other work by Jules Tygiel, Philip J. Lowry, Phil Dixon, Patrick J. Hannigan, Bruce Chadwick, Bruce Adelson, Christopher Hauser, and Sol White, the original historian of black baseball, was essential to reconstructing the story surrounding the Monarchs.

As valuable as such studies are, they served as an accompaniment to the contemporary black press, which was both a fount of information and a subject of the study itself. The grounding documents of any analysis of the black press are the *N. W. Ayer and Son's Directory of Newspapers and Periodicals* annual editions, published in Philadelphia. Additionally, James P. Danky's *African American Newspapers and Periodicals: A National Bibliography* (Cambridge, MA: Harvard University Press Reference Library, 1998), Charles A. Simmons's *The African American Press: A History of News Coverage during National Crises, with Special Reference to Four Black Newspapers, 1827–1965* (Jefferson, NC: McFarland, 1998), and Roland E. Wolseley's *The Black Press, USA* (Ames: Iowa State University Press, 1971) provide extensive context on the development of the black press, as does Jim Reisler's collection, *Black Writers/Black Baseball: An Anthology of Articles from Black Sportswriters Who Covered the Negro Leagues* (Jefferson,

NC: McFarland, 1994), which deals specifically with the sports coverage of those papers. Other studies by Julius Eric Thompson, Amanda Saar, David B. Welky, and Todd Vogel also helped.

Of course, the monographs and authors mentioned above are neither comprehensive to their individual fields nor to this book. They do, however, provide the connective tissue that joins the Great Depression, the Negro Southern League, the Monroe Monarchs, and the racial tension in northeast Louisiana in 1932. For specific and additional references used in this study, see the notes.

Index

95, 98–99, 110, 127–28, 150, 153, 154, 155, 158, 171

Birmingham Reporter, 50, 81, 82, 84, 85, 87, 88, 94, 95, 99, 106

Bismarck Cubs, 141, 143

Bismarck Tribune, 127, 226

Black Ball News, 34

Black Bayou (Monroe), 26

black press, 2–3, 5, 23, 49, 76, 77–78, 81–89, 93–94, 99–100, 106–7, 109, 111–12, 118, 122–23, 126, 131–32, 137–38, 178n5, 200n21, 225–26

Bolden, George, 4, 7–11, 13–15, 16, 17, 19, 23, 61, 135, 179n6, 229, 231

Bonds, Barry, 175

Bowen, Charles Isaac, 126

Briscoe, Sherman, 121, 141, 211–12n45

Brown, Jim, 63, 155

Brown Stadium (Monroe), 139

Brown, Willard, 144, 161, 228

Bryant, Dobie, 174

Buck Weaver's All-Stars, 117, 132

Burke, Clifford, 21

Burnett, R. W., 142

Burnham, Willie, 158, 159, 160, 163, 168, 170

Burns, Clara, 69

Burns, Ollie, 121, 143, 147

Burrell, Clarence, 135

B. W. Willis Dairy, 16–17

Calderone, Sam, 115

Caldwell Parish, Louisiana, 8

California Eagle, 18, 81, 82, 84, 86, 88, 94, 122, 126, 225

Capital City League (Nashville), 74

Carlyle, Thomas, 21

Carmichael, Luther, 113, 114

Carter, Marlin, 34, 158, 159, 160, 163, 168, 170

Casino Park, 1, 36, 37, 59, 62, 65, 66, 69, 70, 71, 73, 79, 114, 117, 119, 121, 133, 147; biracial crowds, 4, 71, 145–46;

building, 32–33, 229; current state of, *46,* 144; as home to white minor league teams, *45,* 142; hosting football, 37, 139, 142; hosting World Series, 130–31; violence at, 68–69. *See also* Monroe Monarchs; Negro World Series (1932)

Chapman, "Pork Chop," 70

Charleston, Oscar, *45,* 59, 60, 61, 127, 172

Chattanooga Black Lookouts, 19, 127

Chattanooga Lookouts, 107

Chattanooga Wolverines, 139

Cheniere, Louisiana, 7, 8, 10, 11

Chicago American Giants, 2–3, 10, 17, 42, 47, 48, 50, 51–53, 57, 58, 63, 67–68, 71, 72, 73, 75–76, 79–80, 83, 95–96, 97–104, 105–8, 110, 111, 112–13, 115, 117, 123, 124–26, 128–29, 131, 136, 137, 140, 141, 143, 151, 153, 154, 155, 171, 232. *See also* Cole, Robert

Chicago Black Sox (1919), 16, 17

Chicago Cubs, 132, 174

Chicago Defender, 18, 52, 53, 67, 68, 75, 76, 77, 80, 81, 82, 84, 85, 86, 88, 94, 98, 99–100, 103, 105, 106, 110, 117, 123, 128, 132, 225

Chicago Tribune, 104, 226

Christian Street YMCA (Philadelphia), 57

Clark, John L., 20, 31, 34, 47, 55, 56, 60–61, 75, 77, 80, 126, 135–36, 145, 149–50, 153, 154, 155, 171

Clark, Joseph Samuel, 30, 139

Claybrook, John C., 141–42

Claybrook Tigers, 141–42

Cleveland Cubs, 2, 52, 53, 63, 66, 128, 202, 206

Cleveland Indians, 62

Coates, Allen, 28

Cobb, L. S. N., 51

Cole Field (Chicago), 53, 112

Cole, Robert, vi, 2, 6, *42,* 43, 50, 51, 52, 53, 68, 72, 97, 98, 100, 101, 103–4, 107, 108, 123, 124, 128, 132, 136, 140,